CURRICULUM DEVELOPMENT & DESIGN

IN CAREER & TECHNICAL EDUCATION

CURRICULUM DEVELOPMENT & DESIGN

IN CAREER & TECHNICAL EDUCATION

Dr. Michelle L. Conrad

Dr. Kevin Elliott

Dr. Edward C. Fletcher Jr.

Dr. Howard R.D. Gordon

Dr. Alisha Hyslop

Dr. Kemaly Parr

Dr. Mark Threeton

Dr. Larae Watkins

Foreword by Dr. Gary Moore
Edited by Dr. Michelle L. Conrad and Dr. Larae Watkins

TABLE OF CONTENTS

FOREWORD

by Dr. Gary Moore

If you were going to build a house what are some of the factors that should be considered? Even though there are hundreds of details to consider in building a house, I would first focus on three important considerations—the blueprint/building plan, the foundation for the house, and the builder.

Professionals who design and teach classes in Career and Technical Education (CTE) should have a comparable set of concerns. This book is designed to help in the course building process in Career and Technical Education.

The blueprint/building plan for a house will answer many questions. How big will the house be? What rooms will be in the house? How fancy or plain will it be? What will it look like inside and outside? You get the idea.

The curriculum planned for a class is similar. It will identify the content to be taught along with the scope and sequence of the content to be taught. It will identify the intended outcomes of the class. It will take into consideration the available resources. It will also take into consideration the characteristics of the students. But the question is "How is this curriculum created.?" The answer is found in this book.

Most of the courses we teach in Career and Technical Education are designed to prepare people for careers. However, there may be times when our courses are designed to promote basic technical literacy such as teaching basic computing skills or bookkeeping skills. Then some course may be avocational or of personal interest such as floral arrangement or graphic design. Thus, the outcome (the end) of the class must be in forefront of our curriculum planning.

Stephen Covey in his book *The 7 Habits of Highly Effective People* identifies "Begin With the End in Mind" as one of the seven habits. This is certainly true in curriculum development. What are we trying to accomplish in our classes? What is the end goal?

In building a house the foundation is critical. We must have a solid foundation. If the foundation is defective or weak, problems will likely occur. There will be cracks in the walls and windows and doors may not open or close properly. Or even worse, the house could fall down.

Likewise, the curriculum serves as the foundation for our teaching. Quality teaching must have a solid foundation, and that foundation is the curriculum. Teaching methods are important, but they must be rooted in a quality curriculum.

There is a parable about two builders. One built a house on solid rock and the other built a house on sand. When the wind and rains came the house built on sand fell. In Career and Technical Education a well-planned curriculum is like building your house on a rock.

After providing a historical perspective to provide context for this book in Chapter 1, the authors build the required solid foundation for the book in Chapter 2. They describe the ACTE Quality CTE Program of Study Framework project in which twelve elements of a quality CTE program are discussed. The chapters that follow then build on that framework, just like one would in building a house.

In Chapter 3 the authors provide an overview of several different curriculum design frameworks. In building a house there are different approaches to construction based on the climate, building materials, soil conditions, zoning regulations, and such. There are several different approaches to creating a curriculum framework and these are described. The reader can then embrace the curriculum design framework that is most applicable for the given situation.

One way to begin with the "end in mind" as Covey advocates is to involve professionals from the fields for which we are preparing students to help identify what should be taught. Various approaches for accomplishing this are discussed in Chapter 4.

In building a house there are typically building inspectors who inspect the foundation, the electrical wiring, the plumbing, and other critical components that go into a house. The house has to meet specific standards. Likewise, in Career and Technical Education there are standards and certifications that have to be met. In Chapter 5 the authors discuss how educators can design the curriculum to ensure that technical standards and certifications are met.

There is more to educating a CTE student than teaching technical skills. In the 1700s craftsman who took on apprentices had to agree to teach basic literacy skills in addition to the trade. The same holds true today. In many states the academic standards (Common Core State Standards) required of all students have been identified and incorporated into the CTE curriculum. Often the best way to teach academic content is to show how that information is used in the real world. In Chapter 6 the authors delve into the integration of academics into the CTE curriculum

The ability to communicate clearly and work as a team is important for all students in the 21st Century. Technical expertise and mastery of academics will get one only so far in the global economy in which we live. Our students need to have employability skills. The curriculum should address this. That is to focus of Chapter 7.

How do students learn best? That is a question educators have pondering over time. Should one take a subject matter approach to teaching or a student-centered approach to teaching? How do Career and Technical Student Organizations (CTSOs) enter into the curriculum framework? Those questions are addressed in Chapter 8.

Building a curriculum framework is half of the job in teaching. After the content of the curriculum is identified, it then must be taught to the students. In Chapter 9 various approaches to teaching the content are examined.

All students can benefit from Career and Technical Education. It is for everyone. This point is addressed in Chapters 10 and 11. Diversity in CTE and working with students with special needs is the focus of these two chapters.

Have you heard the saying "Where the Rubber Hits the Road?" This saying means a theory or idea, or in this case, the curriculum needs to be implemented. The final three chapters in the book are where the rubber meets the road. In Chapter 12 we learn how to convert the curriculum content into measurable learning objectives for our students and how to assess their learning. The process of determining the scope and sequence of the course content and planning units of instruction including lesson plans is described in Chapter 13. Finally, in Chapter 14, the authors address methods of assessing the curriculum and using the information obtained for program improvement.

In the first paragraph of the this Forward it was mentioned that the quality and reputation of the house builder was a third important factor to consider in building a house. The same can be said of the authors of this book. As a past president of both the Association for Career and Technical Education and the American Vocational Education Research Association (now the Association for Career and Technical Education Research) I know the authors and have worked with several of them. They know what they are talking about. This book is an important update and contribution to the body of knowledge regarding curriculum development in Career and Technical Education.

EDITOR ACKNOWLEDGEMENTS

There are a number of people to thank in the development of this text.

- Dr. Howard R. D. Gordon whose encouragement to even embark on this writing adventure was the "push" needed to pursue and complete the writing of a book. His mentorship and reminders of the importance of this text to the field are truly valued and appreciated.
- Our author colleagues, Kevin, Eddie, Howard, Alisha, Kemaly, and Mark, thank you for lending your expertise to the chapters in this text and your patience with random emails, rearranging chapters, and requests to do just one more thing! We could not have done this without you!
- Special thanks to the "Voices from the Field" contributors who were willing to write those personal perspectives and stories (please see the Voices from the Field Contributor list).
- The Association for Career & Technical Education, specifically Alisha Hyslop and Michael Connet, for walking us through the process of publishing a book.
- Dr. Gary Moore for contributing the Forward for this text. We appreciate his historical perspective of CTE and how this text fits into the fabric of career and technical education.

VOICES FROM THE FIELD CONTRIBUTORS

CTE curriculum is just a document with words on paper until it gets into the hand of a talented CTE educator. We would like to thank the following talented CTE professionals for sharing their thoughts, experiences and perspectives on a wide range of curriculum topics in CTE. Your "voices" put the real world spin on the CTE curriculum content.

- Amanda Bastoni, Former Photo/Video Teacher ConVal Regional High School, Former CTE Director Nashua Technology Center, CAST Research Scientist, Peterborough, NH
- Kirstin Bullington, Next Energy Engineering Instructor, Richland Two Institute of Innovation, Columbia, SC
- Abraham Ewing Woodshop & Manufacturing Teacher, ConVal Regional High School, Peterborough, NH
- Jeff Green, Assistant Director, Northland Career Center, Platte County, MO
- Martin P. Hanley, Director, Pike-Lincoln Technical Center, Eolia, MO
- Andrea Heisner, Health Science Teacher McCracken County High School, Paducah, Kentucky
- Leone Herring, Missouri ProStart Coordinator, National Restaurant Association; Former Director, Family Consumer Science and Human Services, Missouri Department of Elementary & Secondary Education
- Benjamin Leskovansky, Insight Pennsylvania Cyber Charter School, Exton, PA
- Bill Lieb, Automotive Technology Instructor, Skills USA Advisor, The Career & Technology Center at Fort Osage, Independence, MO
- Rachael Mann, Keynote Speaker, Author, Consultant Phoenix, AZ
- Chelsea McCreary, Audio, Video, Technology, and Film, Teacher Ola High School, McDonough, Georgia
- Terry Miller, Franklin County Career and Technology Center in Pennsylvania, Chambersburg, PA

- J.T. Payne, Agriculture Teacher and FFA Advisor Henderson County High School, Henderson, Kentucky
- Karen Pitts, Interactive Creative Educational Videos (iCEV) Curriculum Consultant, Clarksville, TN
- Matt Pratt, Machine Tool Instructor/WCHS Girls Soccer, Webster County Area Technology Center, Kentucky
- Melissa Scott, former Assistant Director of Career and Technical Education, Nevada Department of Education
- Mindi Tobias, Central Pennsylvania Institute of Science and Technology, Pleasant Gap, PA
- Vincent Villella, Northwest Area Health Education Center Director, Nome, AK
- Barton Washer, Assistant Commissioner, Office of College and Career Readiness, Missouri Department of Elementary and Secondary Education
- David M. Yost, Associate Professor, CTE Teacher Educator, Marshall University, WV

CONTRIBUTING AUTHORS

Dr. Michelle L. Conrad is an Associate Professor and Graduate Programs Coordinator for Career and Technical Education at the University of Central Missouri. She teaches courses for new CTE teachers from industry, as well as advanced coursework in curriculum development theory and research. She earned her PhD from the University of Kansas (KU) in Higher Education Administration, an MS in Counseling Psychology also from KU, an MA in Student Affairs Administration in Higher Education from Ball State University, and a BA in English from the University of Akron. Michelle has worked with the Asia Society and Longview Foundation developing global competency resources and trainings for CTE. She has also worked with ACTE on content for CTE Learn courses, including academic integration and administrator trainings. Michelle serves as a consultant for the Missouri Department of Elementary & Secondary Education's new CTE teacher induction programs and on statewide CTE curriculum development and revision.

Dr. Kevin Elliott has been in the classroom for 28 years. The first 20 years of his career were at the secondary level teaching woodworking and construction courses. In 2014, he completed doctoral studies at the University of Missouri and transitioned to a role in post-secondary education. At Pittsburg State University (KS), he is involved in teacher education courses and the Kansas Center for Career and Technical Education. Dr. Elliott's areas of research interest include teacher retention, training of substitute teachers, and safety. Teaching emphases include safety, project-based learning, classroom management, and facility design. Additionally, he has taught courses in teaching techniques, work-based learning, leadership, assessment, student organizations, and mentoring. His favorite aspect of teaching is helping students have success in their own classrooms and labs.

Dr. Edward C. Fletcher Jr. is a Distinguished Associate Professor and Chair in the Workforce Development and Education program at The Ohio State University, and a Faculty Associate in the Center for Education and Training for Employment. He is also a Co-Editor for the Journal of Career and Technical Education. His research agenda focuses on the role and impact of career and technical education contexts (e.g., career academies) on students' schooling experiences and long-term outcomes related to postsecondary education and the labor market, particularly for ethnically and racially diverse as well as students who come from economically disadvantaged backgrounds. His research agenda has garnered over $3.5 million of federal funding from the National Science Foundation.

Dr. Howard R.D. Gordon is a Professor in the Department of Teaching and Learning at the University of Nevada, Las Vegas. A native of Jamaica, West Indies, Dr. Gordon has made numerous contributions to the discipline through research, presentations, and publications. Gordon's background includes a B.S. in Animal & Poultry Sciences, and a M.S. in Agricultural Education from Tuskegee University. His doctorate is in Agricultural Education from Virginia Tech. He is the author of the textbook, "*The History and Growth of Career and Technical Education in America*" (2020, 5th edition). Gordon served as editor (2009-2010) of the *Career and Technical Education Research* journal. In 2009, Gordon served as Interim Chair of the Educational Leadership Department at UNLV. His areas of interest include teaching effectiveness, career and technical education, servant leadership, quantitative research design and methodology, and injury epidemiology. He is the founder of the *Journal of Research in Technical Careers*. https://digitalscholarship.unlv.edu/jrtc/

Dr. Alisha Hyslop has spent over 20 years working with CTE and is currently the Senior Director of Public Policy at the Association for Career and Technical Education (ACTE). At ACTE, Alisha leads the organization's legislative, advocacy, research, and policy implementation efforts that cover both secondary and postsecondary policy issues, and is particularly involved in efforts related to the Carl D. Perkins CTE Act and ACTE's High-quality CTE Initiative. Previously she worked with the Florida House of Representatives and with career and technical student organizations on a local, state and national level. Alisha received her Bachelor's in Public Relations and Family and Consumer Sciences Education from Florida State University, her Master's in Career and Technical Education from Virginia Tech University, and her Ph.D. in Career and Workforce Education from the University of South Florida, where she developed specific expertise in program evaluation and has also served as an adjunct instructor.

Dr. Kemaly Parr is an Associate Professor and the Director of Career and Technical Education in the Murray State University (MSU) College of Education and Human Services (COEHS) Department of Adolescent, Career, and Special Education. She holds a Doctor of Philosophy degree in Adult Education from Auburn University and a Master's of Science in Dental Hygiene from the University of Tennessee. She is a member of the Association for Career and Technical Education (ACTE), the Kentucky Association for CTE (KACTE), the Association for Career Tech Ed Research (ACTER), and the American Dental Hygienists Association (ADHA) serving as a trustee for the Kentucky Dental Hygienists Association (KYDHA). Dr. Parr was recognized as the 2020 KACTE Postsecondary Teacher of the Year and the 2021 ACTE Region II Postsecondary Teacher of the Year. She received the MSU COEHS Outstanding Collegiate Researcher Faculty Award in 2020 and the MSU COEHS Outstanding Faculty Research and Creativity Award in 2019. Email: kparr@murraystate.edu

Dr. Mark Threeton is an Associate Professor of Learning and Performance Systems and Coordinator of career and technical teacher education within the Workforce Education and Development program at Pennsylvania State University. He consults, teaches, and conducts research in the areas of training and development, facilities management, occupational safety, and experiential learning to promote enhanced learning and skill development. His research has been published widely in scholarly research journals and books. He holds a B.S. in Technical Education from Pittsburg State University, a M.S. in Higher Education Personnel Administration from Kansas State University, and a Ph.D. from Pennsylvania State University in Workforce Education and Development. Prior to joining the Pennsylvania State University faculty, he was a career and technical educator and professional in the field of automotive technology.

Dr. Larae Watkins currently serves as an Assistant Professor of Career & Technology Education at the University of Central Missouri. She holds a PhD in Comprehensive Vocational and Technical Education, a MS in Agriculture Education, and BS degrees in Agriculture Education and Horticulture, all from The Ohio State University. In addition to teaching courses online, Dr. Watkins worked extensively with CTE teachers on curriculum development and revision and academic integration, as well as online CTE administrator trainings. Part of her time is devoted to developing and trying out initiatives that have the potential for helping CTE teachers connect with each other and with innovative programs. Dr. Watkins works with ACTE on CTE Learn content, the Asia Society and Longview Foundation on global competencies in CTE programs, and UCM's efforts to update CTE teacher education programs, for both the traditional and nontraditional certification routes.

PART I

■

CTE CURRICULUM PAST AND PRESENT

 CHAPTER 1: HISTORICAL AND PHILOSOPHICAL PERSPECTIVES OF CTE CURRICULUM DEVELOPMENT

Chapter 1 examines the historical contributions to CTE curriculum development in America. The chapter is subdivided into two major sections. The first section provides an in-depth overview of the historical and philosophical contexts of apprenticeships and manual training and the views of selected scholars' contributions to early CTE curriculum development, including Booker T. Washington, John Dewey, and Charles Prosser. The second portion of the chapter explores significant federal legislation and its impact on CTE curriculum development. Utilizing this chapter as a resource, readers will have a greater understanding of curricular changes that have influenced the growth of today's CTE programs.

 CHAPTER 2: CAREER & COLLEGE READINESS

Chapter 2 highlights that in today's knowledge-based global economy, it is critical that high school graduates earn some type of postsecondary credential, be it a certificate, academic degree, or a combination of both. This chapter explores the paradigm shift in the US around secondary education preparing students to be college and career ready, while there appears to be little consensus of what this commitment actually entails. Therefore, the chapter outlines the three current paradigms of this phenomenon and explains ACTE's Quality Program of Study Framework and how it can be utilized to promote high-quality CTE programs and curriculum. This framework sets a foundation for quality CTE programming, which will be examined in context within the remaining chapters of this text.

 ## CHAPTER 3: CURRICULUM DESIGNS

Chapter 3 outlines the relationship between curriculum and instructional design and also explores competency-based education (CBE) and essential elements, which promote quality. Curriculum design frameworks are then explored, including Backwards Design, ADDIE, Systematic Curriculum Instructional Development (SCID), Successive Approximation Model (SAM), and Universal Design for Learning (UDL). Utilizing this chapter as a resource, readers will have a greater understanding of curriculum design frameworks and how these can be applied to enhance the quality of learning and skill development.

Chapter 1

■

HISTORICAL AND PHILOSOPHICAL PERSPECTIVES OF CTE CURRICULUM DEVELOPMENT

Howard R. D. Gordon—University of Nevada, Las Vegas, National Institute for Automotive Service Excellence

Introduction

Rapid changes in the workplace, including progress in areas of science, technology, engineering, and mathematics, make the contribution of career and technical education (CTE), formerly "vocational education," more significant than ever. As the importance of CTE has grown, it has also come under significant scrutiny, and there has been a growing need to ensure that programs are truly aligned to the needs of students, communities, and employers. Thus, curriculum development in CTE has evolved as trends in demographics of American schools, cultural diversity, labor market data, industry standards, and instruction have changed.

This chapter is organized into two major sections. The first is the historical context of apprenticeship and views of selected scholars' contributions to early CTE curriculum development. The second section presents an overview of federal legislation's impact on CTE curriculum development.

Historical Context

Overview of Apprenticeship

Apprenticeship programs, where employers provide training to an individual in exchange for work, are the oldest method and type of CTE instruction in America. American apprenticeships originated in the early colonial period and were based on a modification of the English apprenticeship system. During the period of colonization and settlement, apprenticeship was regarded as the most dominant educational agency or institution (Hawkins et al., 1951; Roberts, 1957; Venn, 1964). Gray and Herr (1994) reported that:

> Although not exactly a government-sponsored system, in colonial times the apprenticeship was a written, formalized agreement, regulated by the government and enforced by the legal system. It was also perhaps the first time that the importance or relationship between academic skills (reading, math) and occupational education skills were institutionalized. (p. 7)

In 1642, the Massachusetts General Court established compulsory apprenticeships for towns with 50 or more household members, requiring these towns to hire instructors to provide instruction in reading and writing for apprentices and children. Other colonies adapted this practice and required that their apprentices attend private institutions that offered evening and night school curricula in reading, writing, and ciphering.

During the colonial era, apprenticeship was also used as a means of pursuing selected professions, such as law and medicine (Roberts, 1957; Scott, 2014; Thompson, 1973). According to Roberts (1957), "the records indicate that apprenticeship in Colonial America was not a scheme for the exploitation of children but a means for providing elementary education and trade training for the younger citizens of the colonies" (p. 58).

Today's high-quality CTE programs offer various work-based learning pedagogies as part of the curriculum, including formal apprenticeships known as *registered apprenticeships* that are governed by the Office of Apprenticeship in the U.S. Department of Labor. The typical contract of registered apprenticeships is based on a structured occupational program with specific wage levels that progress as the apprentice gains occupational skills. Sponsorship of most apprenticeships is done by employers in business and industry or labor unions (Gordon & Schultz, 2020; Lerman & Rauner, 2012; Stone & Lewis, 2012).

Evolution of Manual/Practical Training

Another historical development that informed today's CTE was known as manual training. Manual training was designed to help improve students' skills in areas such as perception, dexterity, practical judgment, and visual accuracy, and focused on doing things rather than only thinking or talking about them (Westernick, n.d.). The first manual training high school was founded in 1880 by Professor Calvin M. Woodard. The school was housed at Washington University in St. Louis, Missouri, and offered a combination of academic courses and shop work.

Some educators perceived manual training as a substitute for apprenticeship. However, Woodard argued that manual training was more likely to provide a symmetrical development of the mind and body, unlike the old systems of general education (Roberts, 1957). Venn noted that "manual training was *not* conceived of as vocational training. Rather, it was an attempt to infuse new vitality into old curricula, to rouse student interest in school programs, to promote more sensible occupational choices" (p. 49). The success of the Manual Training School at Washington University served as a springboard for other manual training high schools in the United States.

The major influence of the development of organized manual training programs in the United States was the Russian system of manual training. Victor Della Vos, director of the Moscow Imperial Technical, was instrumental in designing the Russian system of manual training. Vos became widely known for his combination of both theoretical and practical approaches to education (Schenck, 1984). The Russian system of manual training was introduced to the United States through a Russian exhibit in 1876 at the Centennial Exposition at Philadelphia. Historians suggested that the exhibit was well received and appreciated by American educators such as John D. Runkle, president of the Massachusetts Institute of Technology (MIT). Runkle did not hesitate to adapt Victor Della Vos's system of "instruction shops" as a vital part of the mechanical arts and engineering curricula at MIT (Hogg, 1999).

The Russian system comprised the following eight fundamental principles (Bennett, 1937; Scott, 2014), some of which you can still see evidence of in CTE today:

1. Each industrial/mechanical art (e.g., joinery, blacksmithing, locksmithing) was taught in a separate shop of instruction.
2. Each shop of instruction was designed with as many work areas and tools as there were students to receive instruction simultaneously.
3. Models of courses were designed based on the level of difficulty of the exercises and were given to students in a logical sequence.

4. Models were made from drawings, and each student was provided with a drawing that was mounted on a varnished cardboard.

5. Drawings were developed by students for elementary drawing under the guidance of a drawing instructor who received instructions for the drawing from the shop supervisor.

6. No student was allowed to start a new model until successful completion of the previous model with a minimum grade of three (good) or "C."

7. Early or first exercises were accepted if dimensions were partially correct; later exercises had to be of precise dimension. However, the same marks given to students at different periods of the course were relative to the instructional sequence and high quality of work.

8. All instructors had to be very knowledgeable of their specialty. Therefore, constant practice was necessary for instructors to stay current in their fields and serve as instructors of authority.

Philosophical Views of Selected Scholars' Contributions to Early CTE Curriculum Development

Booker T. Washington

Booker T. Washington was the most influential CTE leader of his time (1856–1915). He encouraged minorities to elevate themselves by earning their education through participation in a rigorous curriculum in CTE at the Tuskegee Institute. Washington was often referred to as the "prophet of practical" by his peers. Thus, practical demonstrations were encouraged to support theory and practice. Denton (1993) noted that "Washington believed that all training, deriving its meaning and purpose from real purpose problems, could be extended toward the elevation of individual and community life when the student left Tuskegee" (pp. 108–109).

Washington argued for the total curriculum (agriculture to religion) at the Tuskegee Institute to align with his pragmatic philosophy of self-help (Denton, 1993). Parnell noted (1985), "he believed that 'The Intellectuals,' as he called them, understood theories but were not knowledgeable enough in practical matters to become well-educated artisans, businessmen, and property owners" (p. 58).

Washington's philosophy for Tuskegee's CTE program was based on the following principles (Hall, 1973; Scott, 2014):

- Educating students for the immediate conditions of their environment.
- Teaching students the value of working with their hands.
- Correlating or connecting the different branches of education.
- Learning by doing.

During Washington's tenure at Tuskegee Institute:

> Academic classes coordinated their work with the students' occupational training. English compositions, for example, should be written about how to shoe a horse or make a mattress, and mathematical problems should be derived from practical things like land measurements, building requirements, or soil composition. Conversely, occupational students should know how to write, speak, and read well; they were required to write monthly compositions relating to their training, take written and oral exams, and make oral presentations dealing with their occupations. (Denton, 1993, p. 108)

There was a deep historical and philosophical rivalry between W. E. B. Du Bois and Washington during the early 19th century concerning "the academic versus the practical." Dr. W. E. B. Du Bois (1868–1963) was a Harvard-educated scholar and author who was a central figure in the founding of the NAACP (Gordon & Schultz, 2020). These two great leaders disagreed on strategies of social and economic progress for minorities. Du Bois favored the classical education curriculum that was designed to liberate the mind through rigorous academic subjects. On the other hand, Washington strongly promoted a curriculum in vocational/industrial education over liberal arts education. This separation between liberal arts and CTE still exists in many places today, but CTE educators have taken great strides to better integrate academic and technical skills into their curriculum in recent years to eliminate the need for students to choose between the two approaches to education.

John Dewey

John Dewey (1859–1952), another prominent education philosopher of the late 19th and early 20th century, believed that CTE had exploration values and provided an opportunity for workers to attain social and cultural competency, as well as the skills of their occupation. Thus, he argued that CTE was for everyone, and everyone could benefit. Dewey also perceived CTE as a danger of becoming too "rote, mechanical, and slavish" (Wonacott, 2003, p. 6). Miller and Gregson (1999) stated that "John Dewey attempted to influence schools to hold a philosophical view that would influence practices to be different from the past. He wanted educators to give careful thought to educational programming and practice based on a unifying philosophic position" (p. 25).

Based on his progressive educational philosophy, Dewey was an ardent supporter of reform efforts that were more likely to include experiential and/or contextualized learning, project-based instruction, problem-based instruction, and curriculum integration. He argued that traditional liberal education did not provide the relevant skills for living in the age of science (Calhoun & Finch, 1982; Miller & Gregson, 1999). However, Dewey's educational philosophies provided the foundation for liberal arts in the United States.

Charles Prosser

Charles A. Prosser (1871–1952) was a lawyer and educator. Two of his most prominent early roles included serving as the associate commissioner of education for Massachusetts and as the executive director of the National Society for the Promotion of Industrial Education, where his purpose was to advocate for the passage of federal legislation to support CTE programs. He had a pragmatic philosophy and believed that occupational experiences should play a key role in the education of workers and that practice and theory within CTE should go hand in hand. He also suggested that the educational environment should be as much like the workplace as possible (Gordon & Schultz, 2020).

One of the lasting legacies of Charles Prosser is the set of 16 theorems that were influential in the development and evolution of CTE in the early 20th century (Gordon & Schultz, 2020). These 16 statements outlined how he believed programs should be operated and were instrumental in creating the language of the Smith-Hughes Act of 1917, which provided significant resources for CTE programs.

VOICES FROM THEORY

Charles Prosser's Sixteen Theorems (Prosser & Allen, 1925):

1. Vocational education will be efficient in proportion as the environment in which the learner is trained is a replica of the environment in which he must subsequently work (p. 194).
2. Effective vocational training can only be given where the training jobs are carried on in the same way with the same operations, the same tools and the same machines as in the occupation itself (p. 195).
3. Vocational education will be effective in proportion as it trains the individual directly and specifically in the thinking habits and the manipulative habits required in the occupation itself (p. 197).
4. Vocational education will be effective in proportion as it enables each individual to capitalize his interest, aptitudes and intrinsic intelligence to the highest possible degree (p. 198).

---

5. Effective vocational education for any profession, calling, trade, occupation or job can only be given to the selected group of individuals who need it, want it, and are able to profit by it (p. 198).

6. Vocational training will be effective in proportion as the specific training experiences for forming right habits of doing and thinking are repeated to the point the habits developed are those of the finished skills necessary for gainful employment (p. 199).

7. Vocational education will be effective in proportion as the instructor has had successful experience in the application of skills and knowledge to the operations and processes he undertakes to teach (p. 200).

8. For every occupation, there is a minimum of productive ability which an individual must possess in order to secure or retain employment in that occupation. If vocational education is not carried to that point with that individual, it is neither personally or socially effective (p. 200).

9. Vocational education must recognize conditions as they are and must train individuals to meet the demands of the 'market' even though it may be true that more efficient ways of conducting the occupation may be known and that better working conditions are highly desirable (p. 202).

10. The effective establishment of process habits in any learner will be secured in proportion as the training is given on actual jobs and not on exercises or pseudo jobs (pp. 202–203).

11. The only reliable source of content for specific training in an occupation is in the experience of masters of that occupation (p. 203).

12. For every occupation there is a body of content which is peculiar to that occupation and to which has practically no functional value in any other occupation (p. 204).

13. Vocational education will render efficient social service in proportion as it meets the specific training needs of any group at the time that they need it and in such a way they can most effectively profit by the instruction (p. 206).

14. Vocational education will be socially efficient in proportion as in its methods of instruction and its personal relations with learners it takes into consideration the particular characteristics of any particular group which it serves (p. 207).

15. The administration of vocational education will be efficient in proportion as it is elastic and fluid rather than rigid and standardized (p. 208).

16. While every reasonable effort should be made to reduce per capita cost, there is a minimum below which effective vocational education cannot be given, and if the course does not permit this minimum per capita cost, vocational education should not be attempted (p. 209).

Differences in Philosophical Views of Charles A. Prosser and John Dewey

Philosophical controversy existed in the 19th century concerning the relevance of including vocational education in the public school curriculum. Scott (2014) wrote that "two conflicting philosophies fed the controversy. On the one hand were the philosophical views of Charles Prosser, who favored a type of vocational essentialism, and on the other the views of John Dewey, who was a proponent of the progressive philosophy" (p. 443). The following comparison of their views on how CTE programs were to be implemented into the curriculum highlights their fundamental differences (Gordon & Schultz, 2020, p. 43):

Philosophical Criteria

- **Teaching *Style and Methodologies***
  Prosser: Sequential, begins with basic facts. Instructors have strong industrial experience.
  Dewey: Begins with problem solving—results in knowledge base. Instructors have strong educational experience.

- **Administrative Structure**
  Prosser: Seeks advice from industrial leaders, planner, implementer; is cost effective.
  Dewey: Facilitator of personal choices, adviser.

- **Personal/School Philosophies**
  Prosser: Accents the needs of industry.
  Dewey: Accents the needs of individuals.

- **Benefits of the Program**
  Prosser: Students gain marketable skills to become productive society members.
  Dewey: Students gain life skills and adaptability skills.

- **Transferability of Skills**
  Prosser: Transfer occurs naturally between similar tasks. Transfer is not focused.
  Dewey: Transfer is the focus of a broad education.

- **Training to Work Transition**
  Prosser: Facilitated through current equipment and instructors with an industrial background.
  Dewey: Facilitated through focus transfer.

- **Development of Problem-Solving Skills**
  Prosser: Acquisition of a base of knowledge precedes problem-solving skills.
  Dewey: Instruction begins with problem-solving skills.

- **Major Goal of the School**
  Prosser: To meet the needs of industry and prepare people for work.
  Dewey: To meet the needs of individuals and prepare people for life.

- **Influencing Factors on School Success**
  Prosser: Follow Prosser's Sixteen Theorems.
  Dewey: Follow guidelines in Dewey's Democracy and Education (Dewey, 1916).

- **School Climate**
  Prosser: Individualized differences are recognized, and all people and types of work are seen as having value.
  Dewey: Individualized differences are equalized.

- **Adequate Supplies, Space, and Equipment**
  Prosser: Schools must have adequate supplies, space, and equipment.
  Dewey: Schools need to have adequate supplies, space, and equipment, but students may use transfer skills to cover deficiencies.

- **Personal Motivations**
  Prosser: Vocational education should be reserved for those who are motivated and can benefit from it.
  Dewey: Vocational education is for everyone, and everyone can benefit.

Labaree (2010) suggested that, at the time, Prosser's philosophical views won over Dewey's views concerning the role of CTE programs in the public school curriculum and helped to pass the Smith-Hughes Act of 1917. According to Miller and Gregson (1999):

> The leadership of Prosser and the many early supporters of vocational education gave rise to ideas that would establish the ideals and practices that would guide the development of vocational education in its first half-century as part of America's school system. (p. 24)

VOICES FROM THE FIELD

Dr. Barton Washer—Assistant Commissioner, Office of College and Career Readiness, Missouri Department of Elementary and Secondary Education

For whom is CTE intended? Prosser vs. Dewey

While the John Dewey and Charles Prosser career and technical education (CTE) debates in the early 1900s may not be true judicial case law, many CTE stakeholders believe the "Dewey vs. Prosser" debates that impacted the Smith-Hughes Act of 1917 still impact CTE curriculum, instructional delivery, and student audiences today just like historical judicial case law impacts court arguments and decisions in current and future cases. But unlike judicial case law, where a decision may render winners and losers, could there be multiple winners in the Dewey vs. Prosser debate if they occurred today? And even if the debates occurred in the early 1900s, can CTE still benefit from both Prosser and Dewey's views today? And what if their main differences simply originated from their different philosophies of education?

On one side of the "For Whom is CTE Intended" issue was Prosser, who suggested that career and technical education should be only for those students who need it the most and that the pragmatic skills taught by industry-trained educators should focus solely on the needs of business and industry since we should be preparing "those" students for work. And Prosser also advocated that the "other" group of students should learn certain core academic content like the Great Works and other liberal arts content.

Perhaps an example comparing both student groups could be that we are preparing students to enter the workforce directly after the completion of their technical training, and the other group of students is preparing for academic careers by going to college. And given the needs of society at any given time, perhaps these two different curricula should be taught in totally different environments, or maybe even in different schools. Because industry is an important contributor to society, two forms of education (one vocational education, one liberal arts education) are needed. Philosophically speaking, perhaps this person aligned with an essentialist philosophy.

And perhaps Dewey was on the other side of the "For Whom is CTE Intended" issue and suggested that all students should take CTE courses within one educational system and not be split into two separate educational systems. That we educate students for life rather than for work, and students should be able to apply their learning to solve immediate and future problems for themselves through a comprehensive societal emphasis and not just focus on the needs of business and industry.

So maybe learning is focused on the needs of the students and not necessarily on the needs of business and industry. And while business and industry needs should be addressed, maybe those needs are addressed in a more progressive sense where all students should understand the impact of career and technical education on society, but not where their rights as students and citizens were infringed upon by the needs of business and industry. Philosophically, perhaps this person aligned with a progressive philosophy.

As reported by Scott and Sarkees-Wircenski (2008) and many other scholars on the history and philosophy of career and technical education, Prosser was an Essentialist. Translated, this meant that CTE was fine for a certain group of students who studied in schools that mirrored industry, who were educated to go to work and meet the needs of industry. Dewey, a progressivist, believed that all students should be educated for life through one educational system using a "problems-based" approach to focus on the needs of the learner. While Prosser's *Sixteen Theorems* provided the Essentialist philosophical base for CTE, Dewey's *Democracy and Education* was a competing Progressivist philosophical argument that framed the debate between the two in an attempt to answer the question "For Whom is CTE Intended?" As the executive secretary of the National Society for the Promotion for Industrial Education, Prosser's Sixteen Theorems ultimately "won" the debate in the early 20th century.

While Prosser's Sixteen Theorems are still influencing CTE today, Dewey's progressivist approach may be influencing many 21st century CTE movements as well. Many believe that Dewey's impact on the entire American educational system is also up for debate, but this editorial remains in the context of CTE and how his philosophy may be impacting CTE in 2022. These impacts may include increased CTE graduation requirements for high school students in many states, decentralizing CTE into comprehensive high schools rather than only shared-time CTE centers, problem-based learning initiatives, contextual learning, multi-teacher collaboration, and continued postsecondary education for all students, regardless of their educational goals.

So for whom is CTE intended? What do YOU and your colleagues believe? And how does the "Prosser vs. Dewey" debate impact your answers? Have fun with this conversation, but never underestimate the impact of our personal philosophies on our answers to these questions.

Impact of Federal Legislation on CTE Curriculum

The Smith-Hughes Act of 1917

Historical CTE federal legislation in the United States started appearing in the early 1900s. The first landmark legislation was Public Law (P. L.) 64-347, which became known as the Smith-Hughes National Vocational Education Act. This act was signed into law on February 23, 1917. The act was sponsored by Sen. Hoke Smith and Rep. Dudley Hughes, both from Georgia. Funding was authorized for secondary and postsecondary CTE curricula addressing the occupational areas of agriculture, home economics, and trades and industry. In addition, funds were provided for CTE teacher training.

There was an urgent need for this legislation because of the growing number of immigrants, the problems of urbanization, the increase in automation, and the narrow curricula offered at the high school level that was geared primarily to classical education and unsuitable for the masses (Moore, 2017; Sarkees-Wircenski & Wircenski, 1999; Scott, 2014). The Smith-Hughes Act laid the foundation for over a century of federal investments in CTE, but its structure also contributed to the separation of CTE and academic instruction highlighted by early education philosophers. It required 50 percent of students' time to be spent in the shop, 25 percent on related subjects, and 25 percent on academics (Imperatore & Hyslop, 2017). According to Finch and Crunkilton (1979), "The Smith-Hughes Act and subsequent federal legislation have had profound effects on the public vocational and technical curriculum" (p. 4).

The Vocational Education Act of 1963

The year 1963 was the most significant in the legislative history of CTE since the passage of the 1917 Smith-Hughes Act. While several smaller CTE bills were passed in the intervening years, the Vocational Education Act of 1963 (P. L. 88-210), which was signed into law by President Lyndon B. Johnson, marked a new era for CTE. This act declared the federal government's commitment to CTE as a necessary program for the United States (Scott, 2014) and expanded CTE programs to people of all ages and in all communities across the country (Imperatore & Hyslop, 2017). Funding was increased and distributed based on student population and per capita income, rather than CTE discipline area, and funds were set aside for specific purposes or populations.

As the Vocational Education Act of 1963 was further amended in 1968 and 1976, the focus on expanded access and equity within CTE grew, including for students with disabilities, students who were economically disadvantaged, and women, among others. Additional activities, such as expanded career guidance, research, accountability, and program evaluation, were also added to the legislation over time.

Perkins Legislation

The following brief overview of Perkins (I-V) legislation is synthesized from historical research conducted by selected scholars (Gordon & Schultz, 2020; Gray & Herr, 1998; Hyslop, 2018; Imperatore & Hyslop, 2017; Sarkees-Wircenski & Wircenski, 1999; Scott, 2014; Stone & Lewis, 2012). The 1984 reauthorization of the Vocational Education Act of 1963 was the first version of that law to carry the name of Carl D. Perkins, the long-term representative from Kentucky who served as the chair of the U.S. House of Representatives Committee on Education and Labor for 17 years and was a strong proponent of strengthening educational opportunities for all students. It became known as the Perkins Act. Each version of the law since has carried his name, and thus the four reauthorizations of this Act in 1990, 1998, 2006, and 2018 are typically referred to as Perkins II, III, IV, and V respectively.

Carl D. Perkins Vocational Education Act of 1984 (PL 98-524)

This amendment to the Vocational Education Act of 1963 followed amendments made in 1976. As mentioned above, it was known as the Perkins Act and was concerned with two major goals, one economic and one social. The economic goal was to improve the skills of the labor force and prepare adults for job opportunities. The social goal was to provide equal opportunities for adults in vocational education. This goal is traceable to the Smith-Hughes Act. This act was one of the most comprehensive in attempting to meet the vocational education needs of special populations and included single parents and homemakers, criminal offenders, and individuals participating in programs designed to eliminate sex bias and stereotyping.

The Carl D. Perkins Vocational and Applied Technology Act of 1990 (PL 101-392)

The next update to the federal CTE law was made in 1990 and known as Perkins II. Some major components of the act were:

- Emphasized accountability and required each state to create a set of core standards and performance measures that would serve as a benchmark for evaluations of CTE programs.

- Required each state to conduct an initial assessment of vocational programs.
- Authorized funds for Tech Prep programs, which were to integrate vocational and academic content and connect secondary and postsecondary education levels.
- Emphasized career guidance and counseling.
- Reduced set-asides for special populations.
- Increased funds to local recipients and required minimum grant levels.

The Carl D. Perkins Vocational and Technical Education Act of 1998 (PL 105-332)

The 1998 act updated the 1990 Perkins Act and was known as Perkins III. In this act, Congress required states and local school districts to provide more information on student achievement, program completion, placement in postsecondary education, and improved gender equity in program offerings through an enhanced accountability system. Perkins III also built on the academic integration and alignment efforts of the 1990 act, with a significant focus on academic achievement of CTE students. Almost all of the remaining focus on special population set-asides and smaller funding streams was eliminated, with a focus on directing even more funds to local recipients.

The Carl D. Perkins Career and Technical Education Improvement ACT of 2006 (PL 109-270)

The 2006 act, or Perkins IV, had several key themes. One was that, for the first time, the federal legislation used the term "career and technical education" rather than "vocational education" to reflect the evolution of the field over the prior century. The law also included specific requirements for programs of study that linked academic and technical content across secondary and postsecondary education, prioritizing linkages between learner levels and across the curriculum. Accountability also continued to be a key component of the legislation, as Perkins IV expanded earlier requirements to include a new local accountability model and additional performance indicators.

Strengthening Career and Technical Education for the 21st Century Act of 2018 [Perkins V] (PL 115-224)

Perkins V was passed in 2018 and currently governs the federal investment into CTE programs across the country. This law was significantly shaped by the Great Recession and included greater focus on working more closely with employers to address the skills gap and align programs to labor market needs. The focus on academic achievement that was front and center in the 1990 and 1998 reauthorizations was still there, but there was also an enhanced emphasis on technical and employability skills, including constructs like industry certifications and work-based learning. In addition, some of the most substantive changes in the Perkins V legislation include:

- *Data-driven decision making*: The most significant change in the law was the requirement for a new comprehensive local needs assessment (CLNA) at the local level to better connect data, funding, and planning decisions.
- *Revised accountability indicators*: The law adds specificity to the accountability system through a new definition of a "CTE concentrator," which determines who is included in accountability reporting. In addition, accountability indicators are streamlined to reduce the burden on local systems.
- *Enhancing efforts to serve special populations*: Perkins V returns to a priority from much earlier legislation with enhancements to requirements around supporting underrepresented and special population students, including a new purpose of the law, expanded definitions, a new set-aside focused on student recruitment, and specific requirements for data disaggregation and use.

Perkins V also provides an important opportunity to expand opportunities to younger students (especially grades five through eight) to explore, choose, and follow CTE programs of study and career pathways to earn credentials of value, and career counseling and career development activities are important components of the law.

Summary

This chapter provided a useful understanding of the historical perspectives of CTE curriculum development in America. A historical understanding results in a greater awareness of curricular changes that influenced the growth of today's CTE programs. The chapter includes an overview of apprenticeship and manual training, philosophical views of selected scholars' contributions to early CTE curriculum development, and differences in the philosophical views of Charles A. Prosser and John Dewey. This chapter ended by discussing the timeline and impact of federal legislation on CTE curriculum development within a historical context.

References

Bennett, C. A. (1937). *History of manual and industrial education 1870 to 1917*. Chas. A. Bennett Co., Inc.

Calhoun, C. C., & Finch, A. V. (1982). *Vocational education: Concepts and operations* (2nd ed.). Wadsworth Publishing Company.

Denton, V.L. (1993). *Booker T. Washington and the adult education movement*. University Press of Florida.

Dewey, J. (1916). *Democracy and education*. Macmillan.

Finch, C. R., & Crunkilton, J. R. (1979). *Curriculum development in vocational and technical education: Planning, content, and implementation*. Allyn and Bacon, Inc.

Gordon, H. R. D., & Schultz, D. (2020). *The history and growth of career and technical education in America* (5th ed.). Waveland Press, Inc.

Gray, K. C., & Herr, E. L. (1998). *Workforce education: The basics*. Allyn and Bacon

Hall, C. W. (1973). *Black vocational technical and industrial arts education: Development and history*. American Technical Society.

Hawkins, L., Prosser, C. A., & Wright, J. C. (1951). *Development of vocational education*. American Technical Society.

Hogg, C. L. (1999). Vocational education: Past, present, and future. In A. J. Paulter, Jr. (Ed.), *Workforce education: Issues for the new century* (pp. 3–20). Prakken Publications, Inc.

Hyslop, A. (2018). *Perkins V: The official guide to the Strengthening Career and Technical Education for the 21st Century Act*. Association for Career and Technical Education.

Imperatore, C., & Hyslop, A. (2017). CTE Policy Past, Present, and Future: Driving Forces Behind the Evolution of Federal Priorities. *Peabody Journal of Education*, *92* (2), 275–289.

Labaree, D. F. (2010). *How Dewey lost*. https://web.stanford.edu/%7Edlabaree/publications/How_Dewey_Lost.pdf

Lerman, R. I., & Rauner, F. (2012). Apprenticeship in the United States. In A. Barabash & F. Rauner (Eds.), *Work and education in America: The art of integration* (pp.175–193). Springer Science Business Media B.V.

Miller, M. D., & Gregson, J. A. (1999). A philosophic view for seeing the past of vocational education and envisioning the future of workforce education: Pragmatism revisited. In A. J. Paulter, Jr. (Ed.), *Workforce education: Issues for the new century* (pp. 21–34). Prakken Publications, Inc.

Moore, G. (2017). The Smith-Hughes Act: The road to it and what it accomplished. *Techniques*, *92*(2), 16–21.

Parnell, D. (1985). *The neglected majority*. The Community College Press.

Prosser, C. A., & Allen, C. R. (1925). *Vocational education in a democracy*. The Century Company. https://www.google.com/books/edition/Vocational_Education_in_a_Democracy/NQQtAAAAMAAJ?hl=en&gbpv=0

Roberts, R. W. (1957). *Vocational and practical arts education: History, development, and principles*. Harper & Brothers.

Sarkees-Wircenski, M., & Wirecenski, J. L. (1999). Legislative review of workforce education. In A. J. Paulter, Jr. (Ed.), *Workforce education: Issues for the new century* (pp. 35–44). Prakken Publications, Inc.

Schenck, J. P. (1984). *The life and times of Victor Karlovich Della-Vos* (ED297137). ERIC. https://files.eric.ed.gov/fulltext/ED297137.pdf

Scott, J. L. (2014). *Overview of career and technical education* (5th ed.). American Technical Publishers, Inc.

Scott, J. L., & Sarkees-Wircenski, M. (2008). *Overview of career and technical education* (2nd ed.). American Technical Publishers, Inc.

Stone, J. R., III, & Lewis, M. V. (2012). *College and career ready in the 21ˢᵗ century: Making high school matter.* Teachers College Press.

Thompson, J. F. (1973). *Foundations of vocational education: Social and philosophical concepts.* Prentice-Hall, Inc.

Venn, G. (1964). *Man, education, and work: Postsecondary vocational and technical education.* American Council on Education.

Westernick, D. (n.d.). *Manual Training Movement.* http://www3.nd.edu/~rbarger/www7/manualtr.html

Wonacott, M. E. (2003). *History and evolution of vocational and career technical education.* https://files.eric.ed.gov/fulltext/ED482359.pdf

Chapter 2

■

CAREER & COLLEGE READINESS

Alisha Hyslop—Association for Career & Technical Education
Edward C. Fletcher Jr.—The Ohio State University
Michelle L. Conrad—University of Central Missouri
Howard R. D. Gordon—University of Nevada, Las Vegas, National Institute for Automotive Service Excellence

Introduction

In the 21st century, it is clear that high school graduates need some type of postsecondary credential—whether it be a certificate, associate, baccalaureate, or graduate degree—to be competitive in our knowledge-based, global economy. To that end, there has been a paradigm shift in national dialogue around secondary education, focusing on preparing students to be both college and career ready—and this is the case for all learners, regardless of their socioeconomic status, gender, ethnic and racial background, and/or (dis)ability (Castellano et al., 2017).

While preparing students to be college and career ready is the major aim of K-12 schools across the country, there remains little consensus of what this commitment entails. Many educational stakeholders believe college and career readiness translates into increasing the rigor and standards of the K-12 curricula and focusing on more student core academic (e.g., English and mathematics) course taking (Achieve, 2016; Chester, 2018; McClarty et al., 2018; National Center on Education and the Economy, 2007). This perspective seems to equate college ready with career ready (Stone & Lewis,

2012). Others define college and career readiness as the preparation of students for college—without the need for remediation (National Center on Education and the Economy, 2007).

Stone and Lewis (2012) provided an alternate and comprehensive definition for college and career readiness. Their definition encompassed the need for high school students to graduate with proficient academic knowledge, as well as employability and technical skills. A similar definition was developed by the Association for Career and Technical Education in 2010 and emphasized that career readiness

> involves three major skill areas: core academic skills and the ability to apply those skills to concrete situations in order to function in the workplace and in routine daily activities; employability skills (such as critical thinking and responsibility) that are essential in any career area; and technical, job-specific skills related to a specific career pathway (p. 1).

In alignment with the new college and career readiness paradigm, CTE administrators have sought to recalibrate their curricula to better help students obtain skills across all three paradigms.

Policy Landscape

The federal policy landscape has also shifted in response to the national dialogue around college and career readiness. As mentioned in chapter 1, the Carl D. Perkins Career and Technical Education Act of 2006 (Perkins IV) was the first federal CTE Act to acknowledge the name change from "vocational education" to "career and technical education." The change in name signified the transition from a stigmatized field to one that embraced a new vision for the preparation of students—both college and careers (Fletcher & Zirkle, 2009; Giani, 2019). Perkins IV also introduced the concept of a "program of study" to create stronger pathways between secondary and postsecondary education and the workforce.

In 2018, Perkins V continued to emphasize preparing students for postsecondary education and the workforce. The goal of that legislation is to provide "individuals with rigorous academic content and relevant technical knowledge and skills needed to prepare for further education and careers in current or emerging professions, which may include high-skill, high-wage, or in-demand industry sectors or occupations" (The Strengthening Career and Technical Education for the 21st Century Act, 2018, p. 4). For example, Perkins V added accountability metrics related to high school student participation in work-based learning and industry certification attainment, as well as earning early postsecondary credits—further emphasizing the dual mission of secondary CTE to focus on college and career readiness. The 2018 Perkins Act also continued to emphasize the need for programs of study, building on work done in Perkins IV (Hyslop, 2018).

Programs of Study

Both Perkins IV and Perkins V emphasize expanded opportunities for students to explore, choose, and follow CTE programs of study (POS) to earn Industry-Recognized Credentials (IRCs). A program of study is defined in Perkins V (2018) as

> …a coordinated, nonduplicative sequence of academic and technical content at the secondary and postsecondary level that—
>
> (A) incorporates challenging State academic standards, including those adopted by a State under section 1111(b)(1) of the Elementary and Secondary Education Act of 1965;
> (B) addresses both academic and technical knowledge and skills, including employability skills;
> (C) is aligned with the needs of industries in the economy of the State, region, Tribal community, or local area;
> (D) progresses in specificity (beginning with all aspects of an industry or career cluster and leading to more occupation-specific instruction);
> (E) has multiple entry and exit points that incorporate credentialing; and
> (F) culminates in the attainment of a recognized postsecondary credential (p. 12).

Under the Perkins Act, each local school district has to implement at least one full program of study, and many states have moved toward requiring all Perkins-funded programs to meet the program of study's requirements—and in some cases, for all CTE programs in the state to meet these requirements.

The program of study requires collaboration across levels of education for students to build technical, academic, and employability knowledge and skills in a coordinated sequence. A secondary-postsecondary sequence of courses should reflect academic content to fulfill the state's high school graduation requirements, postsecondary general education requirements, and academic content that supports the program of study's technical content. The course sequence should be a coordinated and non-duplicative progression, aligning courses taken from one level to the next, and students should be able to progress without requiring remedial coursework (Imperatore & Hyslop, 2018).

Course sequences should be mapped with both academic and CTE courses within a program of study. Introductory courses at the secondary level should teach foundational knowledge and skills for the career pathway and should allow students to earn postsecondary credit. Figure 2.1 provides an example of how this coordination could be represented to stakeholders.

Figure 2.1 Program of Study Example: Construction Trades

Career Options	Education Level	Required Credits for Graduation	Area of Focus Coursework		
• Carpenter • Cement Mason • Electrician • HVAC • Heavy Equip Operator • Home Builder • Home/Building • Inspector • Insurance Adjuster • Material Manager • Metal Worker • Millwright • Painter • Pipe Fitters • Project Manager • Roofer • Telecom Line Installer/Repair • Welder	**High School**	English = 4 Math = 3 Science = 3 Social Studies = 3 Physical Education = 1 Health = .5 Personal Finance = .5 Fine Arts = 1 Practical Arts = 1 Focused Electives = 4 General Electives = 5 **26 credits to graduate**	Courses selected must equal 4.0 credits: • Intro Engineering & Design (PLTW) • Civil Eng. Arch (PLTW) • Metal Technology—LSHS only • Furniture Making—LSH/LSN • Woodworking Tech—LSHS only • Adv. Materials & Processing Tech • CCE Internship (2 credits) • Industrial Engineering I/II @ Herndon • Welding/Metal Fabrication I & II @ Herndon • Construction Technology @ Herndon	• Machine Tool Technology—LSHS only • Advanced Concepts in CAD • ~Auto & Home Care • ~Basic Electricity/Electronics • ~Materials & Processing Tech • ~Power & Energy Technology	

	Education Level	Required Credits for Graduation	Community College Majors	College/University Majors	Other Options
	Postsecondary	Gain education, training and work experience to further your career!	Associate Degree: • Applied Science • Industrial Technologies Construction Management	Bachelor/Graduate Degree: • Construction Engineering Tech • Construction Management • Safety/Health/ Environmental Mgmt.	Certificates (less than 2 yr): • Carpentry • On-the-Job Training • Union Apprenticeship • Print Reading Certification

	Education Level	Sample Occupation	Degree Required	Entry-Level/Experienced (Salary based on info missourieconomy.org)	Employment Outlook (Through 2018)
	Outlook	Construction Manager	Bachelor	$46,000 - $100,800	Growing
		Electrician	Long-term On-the-Job-Training	$32,400 - $63,400	Growing
		Plumber, Pipe-fitter	Long-term On-the-Job-Training	$32,600 - $65,000	Growing
		Carpenter	Long-term On-the-Job-Training	$32,800 - $57,000	Growing

Note: ~Denotes .5 credits per semester @ Denotes off-campus course equals 3.0 credits per year

Courses in the program of study should progress to become more occupationally specific, particularly at the postsecondary level, for entry into the field and for career advancement. Standards for academic, employability, and technical skills should be built throughout the program of study. These standards should be continually validated with industry partners and incorporate academic knowledge and skills (English, math, science, etc.), employability skills (communication, problem solving, time management, teamwork, etc.), and the technical knowledge and skills for the field.

After programs of study were originally introduced in the Perkins Act in 2006, the U.S. Department of Education, Office of Career, Technical, & Adult Education (OCTAE) created a Program of Study Design Framework to support states in their implementation of the new construct. The OCTAE Design Framework includes 10 elements to guide states in creating and implementing comprehensive programs of study.

Figure 2.2 Program of Study Design Framework

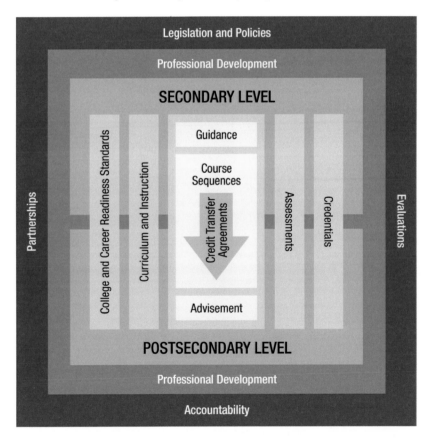

The framework elements include (Perkins Collaborative Resource Network, 2021):

- *Legislation and Policies:* Provides resources and establishes formal procedures for program of study (POS) development and ensures opportunities for all learners to participate.
- *Partnerships:* Link to existing state workforce initiatives and identify and validate the skills taught within a POS.
- *Professional Development:* Supports curriculum alignment and ensures teachers and faculty have necessary content knowledge and teaching skills.
- *Accountability and Evaluation Systems:* Ensure strategies to gather and utilize data to evaluate and improve the POS.
- *College & Career Readiness Standards:* Define what students should know and be able to do to enter and advance in the POS.
- *Course Sequences:* Ensure non-duplicative sequences of secondary and postsecondary courses to progress in the POS.
- *Credit Transfer Agreements:* Provide opportunities for secondary students to earn postsecondary credit as seamlessly as possible.
- *Guidance Counseling and Academic Advisement:* Help students make informed choices about a POS.
- *Teaching and Learning Strategies:* Integrate academic and technical learning with needed employ-ability skills for success in the POS. Contextualized learning through work-based, project-based, and problem-based approaches, as well as through Career & Technical Student Organizations (CTSOs), should be utilized.
- *Technical Skill Assessments:* Ensure entry and advancement in the POS; these should be industry recognized where available and appropriate.

VOICES FROM RESEARCH

Do CTE programs benefit students?

According to Nat Malkus (2019), Senior Fellow and Deputy Director of Education Policy Studies at the American Enterprise Institute, "by most accounts, we have moved past the 'voc-ed' stereotypes. Some rigorous evidence has shown specific CTE programs have boosted student outcomes, and more generally, students concentrating in CTE courses boast increased graduation rates and higher earnings" (p. 2).

To answer this question, Malkus (2019, p. 6) described 30 years of CTE course taking by examining representative samples of US high school graduates in selected years from 1982 to 2013. Here are the findings:

- Since CTE has changed dramatically in recent decades, studies finding some or no benefits to CTE quickly become outdated.
- States also differ substantially in the types of CTE offered and the policy surrounding those offerings and the labor market contexts, meaning any lessons from one study might not transfer broadly.
- CTE delivered in more focused programs, such as dual enrollment, career academies, or regional CTE centers, may have benefits that do not materialize in the regular high school programs in which most students take CTE classes.
- There is limited and circumstantial evidence of differential benefits across courses of study.
- Where evidence of benefits has been found, it tends to be in more focused and coherent CTE delivery systems.
- Career academies, which are like CTE-focused schools within a school, have been shown in one causal study to produce income benefits, and others suggest graduation increases.
- CTE-focused schools, some of which are explicitly described as high quality, and others explicitly described as unremarkable, have also produced benefits.
- Some CTE programs, particularly those that are coherently organized to produce labor market readiness, can have material benefits for students.
- Increasing CTE program coherence and its alignment to labor market needs is probably the best way to improve CTE's results.

ACTE Quality Program of Study Framework

In 2015, amid the "college and career readiness" movement, the Association for Career and Technical Education (ACTE) recognized the variety of perspectives contributing to the national catchphrase "high-quality career and technical education" (Imperatore & Hyslop, 2015). Lacking a comprehensive framework for local implementation left states, organizations, and stakeholders with differing perspectives on qualifying "high quality." While the OCTAE Program of Study Framework could serve as a foundation, it lacked focus on some key elements related to classroom-based curriculum and instruction and was focused more on systems. To help fill the gap, ACTE embarked on a multiphase project from 2015 through 2018 to identify the specific characteristics of a high-quality program of study and to determine the most important characteristics for evaluation purposes (Imperatore & Hyslop).

The 2018 ACTE Quality CTE Program of Study Framework was the result of the project and serves as a definition of "high-quality CTE." The framework was designed to apply to "individual, local CTE programs of study spanning secondary and postsecondary education" (Imperatore & Hyslop, 2018, p. 1). The resulting framework included 12 elements and 92 criteria that were designed to be as mutually exclusive as possible (Imperatore & Hyslop). Criteria are not repeated across the framework even if they apply to multiple topics, so it is important to consider the framework holistically for a complete picture. The 12 elements include (Imperatore & Hyslop, 2018):

- **Element 1: Standards-aligned and Integrated Curriculum**
  This element of the framework addresses the development, implementation, and revision of a program of study's curriculum, including relevant knowledge and skills taught in the program and the standards on which they are based. Particular emphasis is included in this section on including academic, technical, and employability skills; utilizing employer input to inform curriculum; integrating knowledge and skills through authentic scenarios; regular review and update processes; and public availability.

- **Element 2: Sequencing and Articulation**
  This element addresses course sequencing, knowledge and skill progression, and alignment and coordination across courses in a program, as well as across learner levels, such as from secondary to postsecondary education. This element is often seen as encompassing many of the structural components that make up the "program of study" definition in Perkins, including multiple entry and exit points and recognized postsecondary credentials. It also emphasizes opportunities for students to earn postsecondary credits while in high school or stackable credentials and broader coordination across career pathways systems.

- **Element 3: Student Assessment**
  This element addresses the types and quality of assessments used in the program of study, including the types of knowledge and skills that should be assessed. It includes significant focus on the use of classroom-based assessments, including formative and summative assessments, validity and reliability, alignment with program standards and curriculum, and using multiple forms of assessment. It also emphasizes assessing the full range of students' academic, technical, and employability knowledge and skills. Finally, the element also includes preparing students for assessments that lead to credentials, such as industry certifications.

- **Element 4: Prepared and Effective Program Staff**

  This element addresses the necessary qualifications and professional development of CTE program staff, including certification and licensing requirements, the appropriate knowledge and skills, and access to professional development across the entire framework. In addition, educator support and time for collaboration are included, as well as the goal for CTE staff to demonstrate leadership and commitment to the profession.

- **Element 5: Engaging Instruction**

  This element addresses instructional strategies that will support student attainment of relevant knowledge and skills outlined in the curriculum and standards and focuses on a student-centered learning environment that builds a culture of respect and meets the needs of diverse learners. It includes a focus on project-based learning and related instructional approaches, as well as contextualized learning and the connection between academic and technical knowledge and skills.

- **Element 6: Access and Equity**

  This element addresses CTE program promotion, student recruitment, and supports to ensure access and equity for all student populations, particularly those that have historically been underrepresented in CTE programs. It focuses on how each element of the program, including career guidance, facilities and equipment, curriculum, instruction, materials and assessments, should be free from bias, inclusive, accessible, and nondiscriminatory, and there should be actions to support success and eliminate barriers to student participation in various program elements.

- **Element 7: Facilities, Equipment, Technology, and Materials**

  This element addresses the alignment, appropriateness, and safety of the physical and material components of a CTE program. It includes a focus on ensuring these components are reflective of current industry trends, aligned with curriculum and standards, meet occupational safety and health standards, and that there are processes in place for their safe use and for maintenance and updates or replacement as necessary, as well as for maximizing student access.

- **Element 8: Business and Community Partnerships**

  This element addresses business and community partnership recruitment, partnership structure, and the activities partners should be engaged in. While it does not suggest one specific model of partnership, it focuses on partner outreach, diversity of partners, and having a formalized, structured approach to partnership building. It also suggests partners should be involved in helping ensure the program meets current and future workforce needs, supporting students' and teachers' extended learning, offering tangible financial or in-kind support, advocating for and promoting the program, and helping to evaluate the effectiveness of the program.

- **Element 9: Student Career Development**
  This element addresses strategies that help students gain career knowledge and engage in education and career planning and decision-making. It includes a focus on comprehensive career development activities that are coordinated and sequenced, personalized education and career plans for each student, and alignment with relevant standards. This element also describes the types of information students should have access to around further education and training options, regional occupational trends, job search and placement services, and the information that career development professionals need to support students.

- **Element 10: Career and Technical Student Organizations**
  This element addresses CTSOs and the activities they should engage in as an integral, intra-curricular part of the instructional program, including how they reinforce relevant academic, technical, and employability skills. It also describes how CTSOs should provide opportunities for students to interact with business professionals and participate in relevant competitive events, community service activities, and leadership development activities; be aligned with relevant national, state, and local standards; and be led by dedicated CTE staff.

- **Element 11: Work-based Learning**
  This element addresses the delivery of a continuum of work-based learning activities involving sustained, meaningful interactions with industry or community professionals that foster in-depth, firsthand engagement with the tasks required in a given career field. It describes how work-based learning should align with relevant standards and with students' education and career goals to develop and reinforce technical, academic, and employability skills and how it should be structured with clear requirements and procedures before, during, and after the experience.

- **Element 12: Data and Program Improvement**
  This element addresses access to data, and the collection, reporting, and use of data for continuous evaluation and program improvement, including data required for formal state and

federal reporting, as well as other data of interest to program quality. Of particular importance is how educators can access and share data and a formal process for the use of data for program improvement.

While the elements and associated criteria were designed to be as mutually exclusive as possible, career and technical educators should know that all the elements are interrelated and work together to create high-quality CTE programs. Standards-aligned and integrated curriculum serves as the first element in the quality program of study framework and is clearly the most directly related to the program's curriculum, but the other 11 elements all influence CTE curriculum as well.

Consider the following examples:

- A welding program with only five welding bays (Element #7: Facilities, Equipment, Technology, and Materials) will limit the amount of practice time students can receive and might influence the pacing or sequence of the curriculum.
- Having a national award–winning FBLA chapter (Element #10: Career and Technical Student Organizations) requires significant time and effort and is likely the result of significant integration of CTSO activities into the program's curriculum.
- A local airport looking to expand the number of aviation maintenance positions (Element 8: Business and Community Partnerships) might shape the courses offered and shift the curriculum to focus on specific knowledge and skills in that pathway.
- Dual-credit opportunities for a Health Science program with a local community college (Element 2: Sequencing and Articulation) impact course sequencing and require close collaboration between secondary and postsecondary faculty to ensure curriculum is aligned but not duplicative.
- A shared time center that does not receive IEPs from sending schools until November (Element 6: Access and Equity) will have a challenging time making appropriate decisions about program curriculum to meet the needs of students with disabilities.

Each of the elements is going to influence the curricular plans an instructor creates and should be considered in the development of high-quality CTE curriculum.

High-Quality CTE Curriculum Defined

The ACTE quality program of study framework then serves as a guide for defining high-quality CTE curriculum. Each chapter in this text will include a connection back to the ACTE Quality Program of Study Framework to reinforce how high-quality CTE curriculum is needed to produce high-quality CTE programs of study. High-quality curriculum then, for the purposes of this text, needs to be clearly defined based on this perspective.

In education, a general definition of high-quality curriculum may be *the set of actual experiences and perceptions relating to the improvements of skills and strategies in thinking critically, solving problems, working collaboratively, communicating well, writing more effectively, reading more analytically, and conducting high-quality research* (Brown, 2006; Glatthorn, Boschee, & Whitehead, 2009, p. 5; Hass, 1987). While CTE falls into this broad educational definition, high-quality CTE curriculum is:

- Based on industry-validated technical standards, with alignment to academic core subjects, incorporates employability skills, and reflects the latest advances in the industry.
- Developed, reviewed, and revised with employer input, based on in-demand and emerging careers, and is publicly available and accessible to all stakeholders.
- Allows for student career exploration and application of knowledge and skills in authentic learning situations, including the integration of CTSOs and work-based learning opportunities (Godbey & Gordon, 2019).
- Considers diverse students' cultural backgrounds and developmental needs.
- Incorporates relevant equipment, technology, and materials.
- Includes assessments that are aligned to program standards and appropriate to students' level of knowledge and skill attainment.

Summary

A high-quality CTE program of study is based on a standards-aligned and integrated curriculum that incorporates academic, technical, and employability skills. Across educational levels, these knowledge and skills should be coordinated and sequenced to support students' progress in earning credentials that lead to career goals. Perkins V emphasizes the mission of college and career readiness, but more importantly, it causes educators to consider the important role of programs of study and career skills needed beyond those used in a classroom environment.

References

Achieve, Inc. (2016). *The college and career readiness of U.S. high school graduates.* https://www.achieve.org/publications/college-and-career-readiness-us-high-school-graduates

Association for Career and Technical Education. (2010). *What is "Career Ready"?* https://www.acteonline.org/wp-content/uploads/2018/03/Career_Readiness_Paper_COLOR.pdf

Brown, D. F. (2006). It's the curriculum, stupid: There's something wrong with it. *Phi Delta Kappan, 87*(10), 777–783.

Carl D. Perkins Career and Technical Education Act of 2006, 20 U.S.C. § 2301 *et seq.* (2006). https://www.congress.gov/109/plaws/publ270/PLAW-109publ270.pdf

Castellano, M., Richardson, G. B., Sundell, K., & Stone, J. R., III. (2017). Preparing students for college and career in the United States: The effects of career-themed programs of study on high school performance. *Vocations and Learning, 10*, pp. 47–70. https://doi.org/10.1007/s12186-016-9162-7

Chester, M. (2018). Foreword: "A toast to Sofia and Hector's future." In K. L. McClarty, K. D. Mattern, & M. N. Gaertner (Eds.), *Preparing students for college and careers: Theory, measurement, and educational practice* (p. vii). Routledge.

Fletcher E. C. Jr., & Zirkle, C. (2009). The relationship of high school curriculum tracks to degree attainment and occupational earnings. *Career and Technical Education Research, 34*(2), 81–102. https://doi.org/10.5328/CTER34.2.81

Giani, M. S. (2019). Does vocational still imply tracking? Examining the evolution of career and technical education curricular policy in Texas. *Educational Policy, 33*(7), 1002–1046. https://doi.org/10.1177/0895904817745375

Glatthorn, A. A., Boscee, F., & Whitehead, B. M.(2009). *Curriculum leadership: Strategies for development and implementation* (2nd ed.). SAGE Publications, Inc.

Godbey, S., & Gordon, H. R. D. (2019). Career exploration at the middle school level: Barriers and opportunities. *Middle Grades Review, 5*(2), 1–8.

Hass, G. (1987). *Curriculum planning: A new approach* (5th ed.). Allyn and Bacon.

Hyslop, A. (2018). *Perkins V: The official guide to the Strengthening Career and Technical Education for the 21st Century Act.* Association for Career and Technical Education.

Imperatore, C., & Hyslop, A. (2015, July). *Defining high-quality CTE: Contemporary perspectives on CTE quality.* Association for Career and Technical Education. https://www.acteonline.org/wp-content/uploads/2018/03/ACTE_Contemporary_Perspectives_on_CTE_Quality_FINAL.pdf

Imperatore, C. & Hyslop, A. (2018, October). *2018 ACTE quality program of study framework.* Association for Career and Technical Education. https://www.acteonline.org/wp-content/uploads/2019/01/HighQualityCTEFramework2018.pdf

Lee's Summit R-7 (LSR7). (2021). *Career and educational planning guide.* https://sites.google.com/lsr7.net/lscepg/career-paths

Malkus, N. (May 2019). *The evolution of career and technical education: 1982-2013.* American Enterprise Institute. https://www.aei.org/research-products/report/the-evolution-of-career-and-technical-education-1982-2013/

McClarty, K., Gaertner, M., & Mattern, K. (2018). Introduction. In K. McClarty, K. Mattern, & M. Gaertner (Eds.), *Preparing students for college and careers: Theory, measurement, and educational Practice* (pp. 1–8). Routledge.

National Center on Education and the Economy. (2007). *Tough choices or tough times: The report of the new commission on the new skills of the American workforce.* Jossey-Bass.

Perkins Collaborative Resource Network. (2021). *Programs of study.* U.S. Department of Education, Office of Career, Technical, & Adult Education. https://cte.ed.gov/initiatives/octaes-programs-of-study-design-framework

Stone, J. R. III., & Lewis, M. V. (2012). *College and career ready in the 21st century: Making high school matter.* Teachers College Press.

Strengthening Career and Technical Education for the 21st Century Act, 20 U.S.C. § 2301 (2018). https://www.govinfo.gov/content/pkg/PLAW-115publ224/pdf/PLAW-115publ224.pdf

Chapter 3

■

CURRICULUM DESIGNS

Michelle L. Conrad—University of Central Missouri

Introduction

Over the years, educators have often asked small children this question: "What do you want to be when you grow up?" This is followed by excited answers of firefighter, nurse, doctor, police officer, etc. Somewhere over the years, a shift happens in those students. Students aren't excited to learn, and the excited answers turn into, "I don't know." Do they realize there are so many options that it is difficult to decide? Do they realize the training that is needed for each field? Do they get so lost in math and English that learning has lost its meaning?

How this shift happens is unclear, but the fact that it exists has significant importance for CTE. CTE has grown from its historical roots in apprenticeship to prepare students for career and college readiness and as such has a primary concern on career exploration, planning, and preparedness. As we consider ways to design curriculum, it follows that we must consider how well these components are built into the curriculum.

This chapter begins by addressing the differences between curriculum and instructional design and then explores competency-based education, before jumping into design frameworks. Design frameworks, including Backwards Design, ADDIE, Systematic Curriculum Instructional Development

(SCID), Successive Approximations Model (SAM), and Universal Design for Learning (UDL), are then described with attention to how these are utilized in career and technical education programs.

Curriculum Design vs. Instructional Design

As we consider curriculum design, we must also think about instruction. Curriculum is often thought of as being conducted prior to instruction, being a "macro" level activity, where instruction is the "micro" activity of planning for specific learning experiences (Finch & Crunkilton, 1999). Curriculum development or design has been defined as beginning with an assessment of educational outcomes, determining the skills needed to achieve the outcomes, and then planning for sequential skill development from previously learned skills to those yet to be developed (Collins & O'Brien, 2011). Instructional design then is seen as the process of using specific instructional actions or methods to create desired changes in knowledge and skills for specific content and learners (Collins & O'Brien).

While curriculum design and instructional design may have slightly different technical meanings, we know while curriculum is being designed, we must think through the instruction of that curriculum, and while we are instructing, we need to be thinking about the end goal of our designed curriculum (Finch & Crunkilton, 1999). Over the years, as instructional design has emerged as a technological field for eLearning and industry training, the two have merged. We discuss instructional and curriculum design almost synonymously.

In CTE, whether curriculum or instructional design, we begin with technical, academic, and employability standards. While these are explored in more detail in future chapters of this text, it is necessary to consider the influence of being standards or competency driven. "Competency based" is a phrase often heard in CTE, so examining this concept provides context for understanding design frameworks in CTE.

Competency-based Education

Competency-based education (CBE) may also be known as proficiency-based or mastery-based education. It first appeared in the 1960s with Bloom's (1968) concept of learning for mastery. CBE faded away through the end of the 1990s, as the emphasis in education shifted to standards-based curriculum and test-based accountability. Starting about 2000, a second wave of CBE, focused on personalized and student-centered learning, took precedence (Evans et al., 2019). Technologies and new delivery methods, such as flipped classrooms, MOOCs, and Badges emerged, and at the same time, policymakers were concerned with the high costs of continued education. CBE is seen as a way to bridge the gap between education and employers (Johnstone & Soares, 2014).

According to Evans and colleagues (2019), the five elements of high-quality CBE include:

1. Students advance when they demonstrate mastery;
2. Competencies are communicated in explicit and measurable learning objectives;
3. Assessments are meaningful and create a positive learning experience for students;
4. Students receive timely and individualized support for their learning needs; and
5. Learning objectives (emphasizing competencies) include application and creation of knowledge, as well as skill and disposition development.

CBE focuses on what students should know and be able to do with their education and proposes that learning outcomes and competencies focus on applied learning, intellect, broad and specialized knowledge, and civic learning (Johnstone & Soares, 2014). By removing time barriers and promoting individual responsibility for learning, CBE promotes the idea that all students can learn if given time and opportunities to demonstrate mastery (Evans et al., 2019; Springer, 2019). CBE also views instructors as guides and caring individuals who not only educate students but serve as mentors (Springer, 2019).

As mentors in a CBE-framed program, educators should be willing to engage in discussion on the content and competencies being developed, even if it means being challenged by students in regard to the content from time to time. CBE instructors are also willing to discuss the students' lives beyond school and empathetically listen and respond to students' difficult experiences. Educators are also open to providing for special needs the learner may have in order to demonstrate the required knowledge and skills (Springer, 2019).

So, why talk about CBE in a CTE curriculum book? CTE has promoted real-world application and personalized learning for years! Consider the ways in which CTE programs provide contextualized learning for students, high-quality experiential learning opportunities, and authentic measurements of student learning. CTE prepares students for college and careers through real-world and project-based learning, all founded on standards-based learning objectives (Schneider, 2015). As with any educational approach, CBE can be supported through a variety of educational design frameworks, a few of which are explored in the rest of the chapter.

Backwards Design

Understanding by design, also known as "backwards design," was developed by Grant Wiggins & Jay McTighe (1998). The focus is on designing curriculum, assessment, and instruction by developing an understanding of important ideas in students. In order to plan for understanding, they describe three stages of planning or "backwards design" (Wiggins & McTighe, 2005).

Wiggins & McTighe's (2005) Stages of Backwards Design:

- **Stage 1: Identify desired results.**
  What should students know or be able to do at the end of the instruction? This stage starts with looking at national, state, or local standards and curriculum expectations. As a curriculum designer, there will be more content than there is time, so by examining standards and expectations, choices can be made about the priorities for the curriculum.

- **Stage 2: Determine acceptable evidence.**
  How will we know if students have met the learning goals? A curriculum designer should consider the assessment evidence needed to document and validate if student learning has occurred. This means to first "think like an assessor" (p. 18) before planning curriculum.

- **Stage 3: Plan learning experiences.**
  What knowledge (facts, concepts) and skills (processes, procedures) will students need in order to achieve the intended results? This stage involves thinking through the instructional activities, sequence of lessons, and resources needed to effectively teach and for students to learn.

Backwards design calls for thinking about the "big ideas" of the curriculum and prioritizing those for student learning. In CTE, we often do not do this alone, but rather with industry partners. With those partners, we explore a variety of questions. What are the most important ideas for students just starting in the field? What knowledge and skills are most foundational? Then the CTE curriculum designer builds on that knowledge through the program of study to arrive at more specific elements of the curriculum.

Rather than instructors "covering" content, with a goal of teaching for understanding, there is a greater emphasis on students working to "uncover" the content. Students need to become investigative or inquiry driven in order to fully understand the big ideas of the content and understand how those big ideas transfer to other situations (Wiggins & McTighe, 2005).

To more deliberately build a quality instructional plan, Wiggins & McTighe (2005) suggest using the WHERETO acronym:

W — Where is the unit headed & Why?

H — Hook students at the start & Hold their attention

E — Equip students with experiences, knowledge, and resources to meet learning goals.

R — Rethink big ideas, Reflect on progress, and Revise as needed

E — Evaluate students' progress and allow students to self-assess

T — Tailor to individual talents, interests, and needs

O — Organize curriculum for depth of understanding

Designing curriculum in a backwards design approach is not without its detractors. There are critics who believe that "understanding" is perceived as linear and that understanding can be achieved by design. Critics also have concerns with the use of "assessment" and "evaluation" as synonyms (Cho & Trent, 2005). Assessment traditionally "referred to collecting and interpreting information to guide classroom decision-making," and evaluation meant "the process of making judgments about the quality or goodness of a performance or a course of action" (Cho & Trent, p. 115). Are these really the same concepts?

If we think about how we use formative assessment in a classroom to assist in learning, the idea of thinking like an "assessor" should not be about the end goal, but rather the process of getting there. Some may say this is a semantic distinction, but it is a power shift in thinking of the role of the instructor in the learning and assessment process.

A third criticism is a lack of concern with the complex cultural environment. If the "end goals" focus on student assessment measures, then how can teachers focus on connecting knowledge and skills to student interests and needs? Critics argue that backwards design treats students as passive knowledge consumers, rather than considering students as cultural, value-laden, and able to construct knowledge of their own (Cho & Trent).

While backwards design fits within the CTE framework of training students to earn industry credentials, additional frameworks can be explored to consider employability demands of business and industry.

Analysis, Design, Development, Implementation, and Evaluation (ADDIE)

ADDIE is used to describe a systematic approach to instructional development, but there is no singular model. Rather, ADDIE is a term that refers to a variety of models that share common structures (Molenda, 2015). ADDIE has been used to design educational programs, as well as corporate and military training (Hur & Suh, 2010). The process of analysis, design, development, implementation, and evaluation is sequential, but also iterative (Molenda). Each of these components of ADDIE has distinctive characteristics.

Analysis is the process of examining needs, including prior learning, general learning styles, and the content area. Stakeholders' perspectives are also taken into account. Surveys, observations of the environment, and task analyses are some of the methods that could be used for the analysis phase (Braxton et al., 2000; Hur & Suh, 2010).

The design phase includes specifying learning objectives, outlining content, exploring assessment strategies, and planning instruction (Braxton et al., 2000; ELM Learning, 2019; Hur & Suh, 2010). Based on the learning objectives, designers develop test items to measure learning and then develop instructional strategies (Hur & Suh).

Development is the process of creating the actual learning materials. Course content is developed by dividing the content into sections (modules or units) to then develop or select learning activities, instructional guides, assessments, projects, and assessments (ELM Learning, 2019; Hur & Suh, 2010; Braxton et al., 2000).

Implementation is when teachers deliver the instruction. Recording feedback and considering assessment data occurs during this phase as well (Braxton et al., 2000; ELM Learning, 2019; Hur & Suh, 2010).

The final phase is evaluation. This phase includes determining the quality and effectiveness of the instruction (Braxton et al., 2000; Hur & Suh, 2010). This phase also includes evaluating if the goals identified in the analysis phase were accomplished (ELM Learning, 2019). Although this is the last phase, evaluation should be built throughout all phases in the ADDIE model (Braxton et al.; Hur & Suh).

While the ADDIE model is widely accepted as a process for design, it is important to note that there is no real theory or creator of the model (Molenda, 2015). It has also been criticized for being too slow, too linear, and too subject to becoming misdirected (Gordon & Zemke, 2000; Wyrostek & Downey, 2016).

Systematic Curriculum Instructional Development (SCID) Model

SCID is a version of ADDIE with additional components detailed in each phase, for a total of 23 components (Wyrostek & Downey, 2016). SCID was developed at the Center on Education and Training for Employment at the Ohio State University and provides additional structure and procedures for each phase of the ADDIE model (Norton, 1993; Norton, 1998). The main phases include curriculum analysis, curriculum design, instructional development, training implementation, and program evaluation. Each phase contains a number of individual tasks to consider, providing more detail to assist curriculum developers through the process.

While all the phases are critical to the curriculum development process, the program evaluation phase provides feedback for the other four phases (Norton, 1993; Norton, 1998). The job analysis section in the curriculum analysis phase references a specific job analysis approach that works well within the SCID framework. That approach is called the Developing A CUrriculUM (DACUM) approach. DACUM is a systematic strategy that employs the knowledge and experiences of "expert workers" in a career field to determine content for curriculum in that career field (Finch & Crunkilton, 1979; Wyrostek & Downey, 2016). More information on DACUM is provided in chapter 4.

The following details the major components of the SCID five phases (Norton, 1993; Norton, 1998).

Curriculum Analysis:

1. Conduct needs analysis.
2. Conduct job analysis.*
3. Conduct task verification.
4. Select tasks for training.
5. Conduct standard task analysis.
6. Conduct literacy task analysis.

Curriculum Design:

1. Determine training approach.
2. Develop learning objectives.

3. Develop performance measures.
4. Develop a training plan.

Instructional Development:

1a. Develop a competency profile.
2a. Develop learning guides/ modules
    OR
1b. Develop a curriculum guide.
2b. Develop lesson plans.
3. Develop supportive media.
4. Pilot-test/revise materials.

Training Implementation:

1. Implement a training plan.
2. Conduct training.
3. Conduct formative evaluation.
4. Document training.

Program Evaluation:

1. Conduct summative evaluation.
2. Analyze information collected.
3. Initiative corrective actions.

Just winging it seems to be a popular method of planning for the classroom; however, this style of "curriculum planning" is neither planning nor effective. In the end, it ends up costing the instructor time and energy due to last-minute assignment creation. It does not prepare the students for future coursework or employment. If the instructor has to be gone due to illness or some other unforeseen event, the students have little "real" work and end up with a wasted day.

There is an alternative! Careful, thoughtful curriculum planning sets both the students and the instructor up for success! When instructors and instructional leadership take the time to carefully plan out the curriculum, something amazing happens. The students are prepared to move on to next levels, and the instructor actually has more time and less stress. When the instructor is gone, instructional time is not lost! This is a win for everyone!

Successive Approximations Model (SAM)

SAM is another design approach developed from ADDIE. Seeing ADDIE as too linear, inflexible, and time consuming, especially for e-Learning environments with adult learners, the SAM approach was developed. It includes an iterative process, providing opportunities to test and revise throughout the process (Jung et al., 2019). SAM consists of three simple main phases: preparation, design, and development. Figure 3.1 provides a model for understanding SAM.

SAM begins with the preparation phase by gathering all relevant background information and knowledge. This can include exploring an organization's background, prior instruction, and other program materials (Wyrostek & Downey, 2016). An initial preparation meeting serves as a "savvy start," providing those involved an opportunity to review the background information and determine initial ideas for content design (Jung et al., 2019).

Design, prototyping, and evaluation rotate in small steps as an iterative design process. The design is the development of an idea or ideas for organizing the background information and knowledge into a coherent sequence. A prototype is a means of communicating among team members by making ideas visible. These can take the form of a sketch, website layout, or an outline. Once developed, the prototype provides an opportunity for reactions and feedback (Allen, 2012; Allen Interactions, 2021).

Figure 3.1 The Successive Approximations Model (SAM)

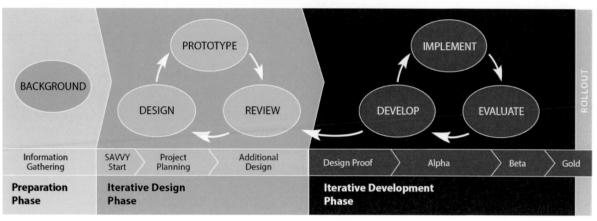

From "SAM: Successive Approximations Model," by Dr. Michael Allen and Allen Interactions, 2021.
(https://www.alleninteractions.com/services/custom-learning/sam/elearning-development)
Copyright 2021 by Allen Interactions. Reprinted with permission.

Similar to the design phase, development, implementation, and evaluation rotate as an iterative process through the development phase. The design proof from the design phase is the first part of the development phase, allowing for feedback and modifications to the development as content is utilized (Jung et al., 2019). Through iterative cycles, content is created and implemented to produce a series of approximations until the final product is produced (Allen, 2012; Allen Interactions, 2021).

In both the iterative design and development phases, the process must support collaboration, be efficient, and be manageable (Wyrostek & Downey, 2016). SAM focuses on learning experiences and opportunities to practice throughout the development of the curriculum (Allen, 2012).

Universal Design for Learning (UDL)

UDL emerged originally from the field of architecture as a way to promote environmental and product designs for use by all people and at the same time, meet the requirements of the Americans with Disabilities Act (ADA). These principles established a framework for design standards, which the Center for Applied Special Technology (CAST) applied to curricular reform in education (OCALI, n.d.). UDL embraces the idea that all curriculum design and development can be accessible for all learners (Kennette & Wilson, 2019).

While often utilized for students with disabilities or students with culturally diverse backgrounds, UDL benefits all learners, including those with disabilities, no identified disabilities, or extraordinary abilities (Kennette & Wilson, 2019; Posey, 2021; Sarkees-Wircenski & Scott, 2003). The focus of UDL is on learning goals, so rather than focusing on how to adapt a particular lesson for each student, the focus is on how to change the design of the assessments, methods, and materials (Kennette & Wilson; Posey). UDL does not mean "dumbing down the curriculum." Rather, it provides alternatives to diversifying instruction (Sarkees-Wircenski & Scott). UDL consists of three principles: multiple means of engagement, representation, and action and expression.

- *Multiple means of engagement*: How can all students be engaged in learning? Students are provided choice and autonomy in learning, which can optimize relevancy and value in what they are learning. Options are also considered for varying demands and resources to challenge each learner. Collaboration and cooperation foster community. Self-assessment and reflection help students to learn self-regulation skills (CAST, 2018).

- *Multiple means of representation*: In what ways can information be presented to reach all learners? Recognizing that some students are auditory learners, some kinesthetic, and others visual, information is displayed in multiple ways. This can include pictures and videos or other multimedia, along with charts, text, or symbols. Options for comprehending information are also provided by highlighting patterns, big ideas, and relationships among content (CAST, 2018).

- *Multiple means of action and expression*: How can students show what they know? Action and expression involve exploring options for timing and pacing of learning, how to use assistive technology, and multiple ways to demonstrate learning. Checklists or calendars can be used for tracking progress toward goals, and time is allocated for practice and skill building. Demonstration of knowledge can be through a variety of formats, including narrative writing, posters, multimedia, etc. (CAST, 2018).

Increased choice and authentic assessment are also components of project-based learning. Both have been shown to increase engagement in students. Research has found that engagement in learning also increases student motivation (Kennette & Wilson, 2019).

{))) **VOICES FROM THE FIELD**

Abraham Ewing—Woodshop & Manufacturing Teacher, ConVal Regional High School, Peterborough, NH

Universal Design for Learning (UDL) has changed the way I teach. It's helped me reflect on what I was already doing well and justify that to myself and my administration. For example, from working in industry and coaching, I knew that building culture in the classroom was going to be really important. But before learning about UDL, I didn't really have a way to explain how my class culture connected to the learning. Now, I see that what I was doing was building a culture that minimized threats and distractions. By increasing the autonomy in my class, I was empowering students to make choices, and that helped them learn.

UDL also helped me improve as a teacher. Since I started using it, I've seen the number of nontraditional students (in my case, females) taking my class increase every year. Right now, 40 percent of my class is female. That's significant because when I first started, I'd maybe get a couple of girls enrolled each year. I think it's again because of the class culture. UDL has helped me promote high expectations for all the learners in my class, but also make sure I provide support, prompts, guides, coaching, and even peer mentors to ensure all learners have what they need to achieve the goal.

Summary

Curricular and instructional design can have different meanings, but over the years have almost merged because of the significant interaction between the two. This chapter started with an overview of competency-based education which has a significant influence on CTE curriculum. Curriculum design frameworks, including Backwards Design, ADDIE, Systematic Curriculum Instructional Development (SCID), Successive Approximations Model (SAM), and Universal Design for Learning (UDL) were explored for use within CTE programs. Whether we use one design framework or a combination of frameworks, CTE curriculum developers should be intentional in their design approach and consider both learner and employer needs.

ACTE's Quality CTE Program of Study Framework Connection

The concepts in this chapter related to the following elements of the *Quality CTE Program of Study Framework* developed by the Association for Career and Technical Education (read more about the framework in chapter 2; Imperatore & Hyslop, 2018):

- **Element 1: Standards-aligned and Integrated Curriculum**
  This element of the framework addresses the development, implementation, and revision of a program of study's curriculum, including relevant knowledge and skills. Many of the curriculum design frameworks discussed in this chapter include a focus on program or course standards and on ensuring curriculum is developed and designed with the input of employers or other experts.

- **Element 2: Sequencing and Articulation**
  This element addresses course sequencing, knowledge and skill progression, and alignment and coordination across courses in a program, as well as across learner levels, such as from secondary to postsecondary education. Designing curriculum means coordinating the program of study to best teach the content, from broad foundational knowledge and skills to more specific depth of knowledge and skills. Utilizing curricular designs allows non-duplicative and vertically aligned programs of study to prepare students.

- **Element 3: Student Assessment**
  This element addresses knowledge and skills that should be assessed through CTE programs and the types and quality of assessments used. Utilizing curricular designs ensures that assessments are aligned to program standards and are appropriate for students' current level of knowledge and skill attainment. Assessments provide instructors with information on student attainment of knowledge and skills in the curriculum.

- **Element 5: Engaging Instruction**
  This element addresses instructional strategies that will support student attainment of relevant knowledge and skills. Program of study instruction is driven by the curricular content. Designing curriculum in ways that allow for engaging instructional approaches, such as project-based, inquiry-based, or challenge-based learning, and emphasizes cross-disciplinary collaboration, allows students to achieve learning objectives in an authentic, contextualized manner.

References

Allen Interactions. (2021). *SAM: The successive approximations model.* https://www.alleninteractions.com/services/custom-learning/sam/elearning-development

Allen, M. (2012). *Leaving ADDIE for SAM: An agile model for developing the best learning experiences.* American Society for Training & Development.

Braxton, S., Bronico, K., & Looms, T. (2000). *Instructional system design* (ISD): *Using the ADDIE model.* https://www.lib.purdue.edu/sites/default/files/directory/butler38/ADDIE.pdf

CAST. (2018). *Universal design for learning guidelines version 2.2* [graphic organizer]. https://udlguidelines.cast.org/

Cho, J., & Trent, A. (2005). "Backward" curriculum design and assessment: What goes around comes around, or haven't we seen this before? *Taboo: Journal of Culture & Education, 9*(2), 105–122.

Collins, J. W., & O'Brien, N. P. (2011). *The Greenwood dictionary of education* (2nd ed.). Greenwood.

ELM Learning. (2019). *What is ADDIE? Your complete guide to the ADDIE model.* https://elmlearning.com/instructional-design-addie-model/

Evans, C. M., Graham, S. E., & Lefebvre, M. L. (2019). Exploring K-12 competency-based education implementation in the northeast states. *NASSP Bulletin, 103*(4), 300–329.

Finch, C. R., & Crunkilton, J. R. (1979, April 8–12). *Review and critique of strategies for determining career education curriculum content* [Paper presentation]. Annual Meeting of the American Educational Research Association, San Francisco, CA, United States. https://files.eric.ed.gov/fulltext/ED178696.pdf

Finch, C. R., & Crunkilton, J. R. (1999). *Curriculum development in vocational and technical education: Planning, content, and implementation.* Allyn and Bacon.

Gordon, J., & Zemke, R. (2000). The attack on ISD. *Training, 37*(4), 42. https://performancexdesign.files.wordpress.com/2011/03/gordon_attack-on-isd.pdf

Hur, J. W., & Suh, S. (2010). The development, implementation, and evaluation of a summer school for English language learners. *The Professional Educator, 34*(2), https://files.eric.ed.gov/fulltext/EJ988199.pdf

Imperatore, C. & Hyslop, A. (2018, October). *2018 ACTE quality program of study framework.* Association for Career and Technical Education. https://www.acteonline.org/wp-content/uploads/2019/01/HighQualityCTEFramework2018.pdf

Johnstone, S. M., & Soares, L. (2014). Principles for developing competency-based education programs. *Change: The Magazine of Higher Learning, 46*(2), 12–19.

Jung, H., Kim, Y. R., Lee, H., & Shin, Y. (2019). Advanced instructional design for successive e-learning: Based on the successive approximation model (SAM). *International Journal on E-Learning, 18*(2), 191–204.

Kennette, L. N., & Wilson, N. A. (2019). Universal design for learning (UDL): What is it and how do I implement it? *Transformative Dialogues: Teaching & Learning Journal, 12*(1), 1–6.

Molenda, M. (2015). In search of the elusive ADDIE model. *Performance Improvement, 54*(2), 40–41.

Norton, R. E. (1993, June 9–11). SCID: *Model for effective instructional development* [Paper presentation]. Mid-America Competency-Based Education Conference, Bloomington, MN, United States.

Norton, R. E. (1998). *Quality instruction requires high quality materials: SCID.* ERIC Opinion Paper, https://files.eric.ed.gov/fulltext/ED359338.pdf

OCALI. (n.d.). *History of UDL.* https://www.ocali.org/project/learn_about_udl/page/udl_history

Posey, A. (2021). *Lesson planning with universal design for learning.* Understood. https://www.understood.org/en/school-learning/for-educators/universal-design-for-learning/lesson-planning-with-universal-design-for-learning-udl

Sarkees-Wircenski, M., & Scott, J. L. (2003). *Special populations in career and technical education.* American Technical Publishers, Inc.

Schneider, C. (2015). *Integrating career technical education with competency-based education.* Aurora Institute. https://aurora-institute.org/cw_post/integrating-career-technical-education-with-competency-based-education/

Springer, S. B. (2019). Forty years: Where is competency-based education? *Adult Learning, 31*(2), 54–56.

Wiggins, G., & McTighe, J. (1998). *Understanding by design.* Association for Supervision & Curriculum Development.

Wiggins, G., & McTight, J. (2005). *Understanding by design* (2nd ed.). Association for Supervision & Curriculum Development.

Wyrostek, W., & Downey, S. (2016). Compatibility of common instructional models with the DACUM process. *Adult Learning, 28*(2), 69–75.

PART II

■

CURRICULUM CONTENT

 ## CHAPTER 4: PARTNER ENGAGEMENT IN CURRICULUM DEVELOPMENT

Chapter 4 introduces the U.S. Chamber of Commerce Foundation's Talent Pipeline Management initiative as a method utilized by industry to solve worker shortages. The chapter then explores the philosophical basis and introspection as educator-focused strategies for determining curriculum content and approaches, which can be utilized to engage business and industry, such as Developing A CurriculUM, Task Analysis, All Aspects of an Industry, Critical Incident Technique, and the Delphi Method. Using the resources provided in this chapter will assist in engaging business and industry partners, as well as in validating CTE curriculum.

 ## CHAPTER 5: TECHNICAL STANDARDS

Chapter 5 explains the importance of technical standards and how these are an essential component of CTE curriculum to ensure there are no mismatches between the education provided in the program and industry needs. In addition, the chapter emphasizes the importance of advisory board involvement in determining the technical skills to be taught, as well as national technical skills frameworks, including the Career Clusters framework and the Common Career Technical Core (CCTC). The authors emphasize that the standards to be taught must align seamlessly with the technical facility and equipment in order to promote the transfer of learning. Applying the information provided in this chapter is essential to advancing high-quality CTE programming.

 ## CHAPTER 6: ACADEMIC CORE INTEGRATION

Chapter 6 emphasizes the importance of integrating academic content into CTE curriculum and instruction to promote greater comprehension of academic core concepts (i.e., reading, writing, listening, speaking, mathematics, and science), as well as their application in real-world contexts. The chapter further provides an overview of the national standards initiatives and resources for the academic core in CTE, as well as helpful strategies for approaching academic core integration efforts.

 ## CHAPTER 7: EMPLOYABILITY SKILLS

Chapter 7 examines career development and exploration as a component of career readiness and explains how career and technical educators are in a favorable position to aid guidance and counseling professionals within schools. The chapter further explores several models for career readiness, including 21st Century Skills by Battelle for Kids, the Career Ready Practices by Advance CTE, and Employability Skills as defined by the U.S. Department of Education. This chapter emphasizes the essential role of CTE in developing employability skills in students and how this is critical to preparing a globally competent workforce. Applying the information provided in this chapter is essential to advancing high-quality CTE programs.

Chapter 4

■

PARTNER ENGAGEMENT IN CURRICULUM DEVELOPMENT

Michelle L. Conrad—University of Central Missouri

Introduction

When we consider how CTE differs from other educational endeavors, we must consider the role of business and industry partners actively engaging with educators to strengthen programs. Employer input to the curriculum ensures alignment with industry standards and prepares students for careers, as well as furthering their education (Imperatore & Hyslop, 2018). Too often there is a disconnect between schools and the community. Business and industry representatives sometimes don't feel comfortable seeking out ways to get involved in education, despite the fact they need qualified and prepared employees. Finding ways for community members to offer input that connects instruction to the real world better prepares students for the workplace (Pawlowski & Meeder, 2012).

There are a variety of ways and reasons to engage employers, but for the alignment of curriculum in a program of study, the goal is to engage employers in helping to determine the appropriate content. To engage employers, a number of processes directly involving industry input into designing curriculum exist; these processes often start with industry standards. Figuring out which standards are foundational, which are more specialized, and how the standards build through a program of study, should be guided by a formal process.

Too often CTE content is determined by a person or school's philosophy or by instructors thinking solely about their own perspective. Although these strategies have a place in curriculum development, more formal strategies employed to determine or validate the curriculum strengthen the final product. This chapter will begin with an overview of the U.S. Chamber of Commerce Foundation's Talent Pipeline Management initiative as a way industry is attempting to solve worker shortages. Then it will explore both the philosophical basis and introspection as educator-focused strategies for determining curriculum content and review approaches involving industry to determine curriculum content. Approaches introduced will include Developing a CurriculUM, Task Analysis, All Aspects of an Industry, Critical Incident Technique, and the Delphi Method.

Talent Pipeline Management

What is Talent Pipeline Management (TPM)?

- Establishes a framework for employer engagement
- Provides clear roles and direction for stakeholders
- Emphasizes how employers need to get involved
- Provides a common language for employers and educators to partner
- Furnishes a process to analyze workforce needs and challenges.

Since primary goals of CTE are to acclimate students to a career field and to equip students with knowledge and skills needed for success, there is "no substitute for connecting with local companies and finding out what knowledge and skills they want new employees to have" (Pawlowski & Meeder, 2012, p. 5). The U.S. Chamber of Commerce Foundation has developed a major initiative for business and industry to take a more active role in worker development, Talent Pipeline Management (TPM). TPM is a framework and a process. It provides "a systematic framework for how employers can engage effectively in producing information, facilitating partnerships, managing performance, and improving outcomes in career pathways" (U.S. Chamber of Commerce Foundation, 2018, p. 5). TPM is also a comprehensive process for employers to analyze their workforce needs and challenges. The framework helps employers get organized to become better partners with education and training providers and delivers a return on investment in a way that might be missing in most partnerships (U.S. Chamber of Commerce Foundation, 2018). TPM allows employers to get organized around workforce needs to establish effective partnerships with CTE.

Philosophical Basis

A person's philosophy is basically what a person believes. Just as the Dewey vs. Prosser debates explored in chapter 1 had an influence on curriculum, so, too, do educators and stakeholders' philosophical beliefs today. An educational philosophy may be made up of several beliefs, which contribute to the philosophical make-up of the curriculum (Finch & Crunkilton, 1999). If we look around at general education offerings, it is not difficult to see how teachers', administrators', and school board members' personal philosophies have provided a basis for curriculum (Finch & Crunkilton, 1979).

Philosophy certainly finds its way into the CTE curriculum as well. For example, if an institution or school district has strategic goals to better meet the needs of women or an urban population, these belief statements can serve as a foundation for curriculum content and the approach taken to instruction (Finch & Crunkilton, 1979). Another example of the influence of philosophy is in the choice of a design model, as not all instructional design models support competency-based education, a fact which could be detrimental to CTE curriculum (Wyrostek & Downey, 2016).

If we take a philosophical basis to curriculum development, then we would start by identifying and agreeing on all belief statements. Once shaped into a philosophy, content is identified to align with this philosophy. If one of our belief statements is that education prepares students for employment, then our curriculum should evolve to focus on how curriculum content relates to the work environment. And if it doesn't relate to the work environment, it should be questioned (Finch & Crunkilton, 1999).

A strength of the philosophical basis is that if the educational community firmly believes in the belief statements and how those can benefit students, it can permeate an educational institution. The weakness, especially for CTE, is that a philosophical basis may not provide specific competencies for preparing students for the workforce (Finch & Crunkilton, 1999).

Introspection

Introspection means "examining one's own thoughts and feelings," either as an individual or a group (Finch & Crunkilton, 1979). A group of teachers might reflect on what they feel should be included in the curriculum based on their previous employment or teaching experiences (Finch & Crunkilton, p. 4). Introspection may begin with a review of relevant literature and examining new trends within a field and often involves considering current CTE programs and curriculum. One or more instructors may reflect on what they remember from past experience. Once this "introspection" process is complete, a content outline is developed to serve as the basis of the curriculum (Finch & Crunkilton, 1999).

Although this process is used by many faculty and teachers, especially those just starting as career and technical educators, it is not necessarily valid. CTE instructors come from industry, so they will naturally make choices on the importance given to particular content. It is important, however, to gain a variety of inputs. Working with a group of instructors to utilize introspection collectively can serve to keep bias to a minimum, but again, is not necessarily valid for the scope of the curriculum content. Using an advisory committee of professionals in a particular field to review the curriculum and validate it can help with the validity problem of developing curriculum through introspection (Finch & Crunkilton, 1999).

VOICES FROM THE FIELD

Leone Herring—Missouri ProStart Coordinator, National Restaurant Association; Former Director, Family Consumer Science and Human Services, Missouri Department of Elementary & Secondary Education

I consider CTE curriculum development and use from two points of view—one, as a state department of education director, and the other, as a state coordinator of an industry-developed program and former business owner in that industry. This combination makes developing CTE curriculum a more meaningful process for me. So, when asking industry representatives for their input and expertise...

Be organized. Care should be taken to make sure the time requested is well planned, so usable information and advice are collected. This information should be carefully considered and used in the development of the curriculum. It is also important to keep an open mind when asking industry representatives for their opinions. Educators sometimes use the information-gathering process to validate their opinions on what should be taught, not as a practical method to learn about a specific industry's training needs. Listen to what is being communicated. Their time is "money." Educational jargon and acronyms can be confusing and create gaps in understanding. Jargon can sometimes interfere with collecting the type of industry insight desired to develop a curriculum that truly prepares students to work in that industry's environment.

By bringing together a group of industry representatives from all levels of that industry, we have been able to identify the skills needed to be successful in that industry. How should skills be taught and evaluated? How should educators be trained to deliver experiences to teach these skills? How should industry be positioned to support the program being developed? What steps should be used to implement the program into the educational environment? How does developing a good work ethic, including coming to work on time, personal hygiene, and remaining drug free, contribute to success?

Cultivating industry input and support is necessary to the development of curriculum that meets industry needs.

Developing a Curriculum (DACUM)

A variation of introspection is the Developing a CurriculUM (DACUM) approach. DACUM utilizes introspection, but does so in a way that relies on business and industry experts in a systematic process. In DACUM, expert business and industry partners identify and validate knowledge, skills, and dispositions needed for success in a particular job or career (Wyrostek & Downey, 2016). Typically, 10 to 12 experts or resource people from a particular field come together for a one- to two-day workshop where a facilitator documents the analysis and discussion to create a curriculum profile (Finch & Crunkilton, 1999; Wyrostek & Downey).

Typically a DACUM workshop begins with a committee orientation to the task to be accomplished. The facilitator then guides the group to review written documents. This may include previously developed curriculum, industry standards, or specific certification or IRC requirements. Once the group reviews existing materials, general areas of competence within the field are identified. For example, in automotive technology, general areas of competence may include General Suspension and Steering Systems Diagnosis or Suspension Systems Diagnosis and Repair.

Once general areas are identified, specific skills and behaviors for each general area can be detailed. The general and specific skills and behaviors can then be organized into a meaningful sequence, and levels of competence for each skill can be identified based on real-world situations. The resulting curriculum profile (See Figure 4.1 for an example) is typically a single sheet that presents the skills of an entire occupation (Finch & Crunkilton, 1999).

Figure 4.1 Example Curriculum Profile: Suspension Systems Diagnosis and Repair

0	1	2	3	4	5	6	Suspension Systems Diagnosis and Repair	Priority	Notes:
							1. Diagnose short and long arm suspension system noises, body sway, and uneven ride height concerns; determine necessary action.	P-1	
							2. Diagnose strut suspension system noises, body sway, and uneven ride height concerns; determine necessary action.	P-1	
							3. Remove, inspect, and install upper and lower control arms, bushings, shafts, and rebound bumpers.	P-2	
							4. Remove, inspect and install strut rods and bushings.	P-2	
							5. Remove, inspect, and install upper and/or lower ball joints.	P-1	
							6. Remove, inspect, and install steering knuckle assemblies.	P-2	
							7. Remove, inspect, and install short and long arm suspension system coil springs and spring insulators.	P-3	
							8. Remove, inspect, install, and adjust suspension system torsion bars; inspect mounts.	P-3	
							9. Remove, inspect, and install stabilizer bar bushings, brackets, and links.	P-2	
							10. Remove, inspect, and install strut cartridge or assembly, strut coil spring, insulators (silencers), and upper strut bearing mount.	P-1	
							11. Remove, inspect, and install leaf springs, leaf spring insulators (silencers), shackles, brackets, bushings, and mounts.	P-3	
							12. Other:		

There are differing opinions on whether instructors should be included in the DACUM process, as it is based on an occupational analysis of industry experts. Some suggest having instructors included as ex officio members or bringing in the instructors afterward to organize, sequence, and detail the instruction. Many CTE teachers, however, have valid industry experience, and given their understanding of the learners, may also provide a valuable perspective in the process.

Advantages of using a DACUM approach is that it takes a relatively short period of time to develop, it incorporates business and industry partners in an engaging conversation about the skills and behaviors needed in the field, and educator involvement can be varied based on needs (Finch & Crunkilton, 1999). A limitation to this method is that career exploration or career awareness is not a focus, as it is specific for occupational skills and behaviors, and some may see the one-workshop approach as lacking an opportunity for reflection or for sequencing reconsideration (Finch & Crunkilton, 1979).

 VOICES FROM THE FIELD

Chelsea McCreary—Audio, Video, Technology, and Film, Teacher Ola High School McDonough, Georgia

The importance of an advisory board is immeasurable. The need for an outside of education voice is imperative to the success of our program. Community leaders and stakeholders in the community serve as a vital role in the "beyond" education piece of our standards.

Task Analysis

Task analysis is a process where actual worker tasks are identified and verified. Key to the process is the involvement of workers who complete an interview or survey on the work they do (Finch & Crunkilton, 1979; Finch & Crunkilton, 1999). The process also allows skills or work activities to be broken down into smaller components to be taught (Collins & O'Brien, 2011). While there are several ways a task analysis may be conducted, all tend to be thorough and systematic, with five consistent components. These components are:

• *A literature review focused on identifying existing job or task lists.*
  A review of relevant literature determines what skills or job tasks have already been examined. From this review, a consolidated list of tasks and equipment employed within a career area can be created. Task lists can be developed for one job or several jobs from the consolidated list. It is up to the curriculum developer to determine the scope of the analysis and how it relates to the curriculum being developed. If the scope includes related jobs within a career cluster, tasks, as well as equipment lists, can be identified for relevant curricular components of similar career areas.

- *Creation of a career inventory, a survey made of the initial list or lists.*
  Combining these initial lists into an inventory or survey to be completed by those working in the field gives the curriculum developer a tool to use with workers as they identify their work tasks. Equipment can also be incorporated into the tool, so workers can identify items used on the job. Within the survey, tasks can be grouped within headings dependent on the career field. Workers can then select a task based on a particular job or even the time spent on doing particular tasks. The curriculum developer needs to note that this part of the process will result in a list of tasks that a worker must perform, without taking into account the importance of any one task or the time that tasks could take to complete.

- *Formation of a sample of workers from the field.*
  A sample of workers can then be selected to participate in the data collection phase. The final worker sample should be representative of the population in order to ensure that the results can be generalized. Research sampling procedures provide a strong approach for identifying a representative sample.

- *Data collection.*
  Data on work tasks is then gathered from the sample of workers. To make sure that the final task list or lists are as credible and complete as possible, it is important to consider return rates. To facilitate a good return rate, the curriculum developer may need to work with professional organizations within the field, or secure support for worker participation from the employers of workers.

- *Analysis of the data provided by the workers.*
  Collected information on job tasks can then be statistically analyzed for inclusion on the final task list. In determining the task list that will be used in developing curriculum, the level and focus of the CTE program need to be considered; the final task list can depend on the level of employment the program is preparing students to enter. High school CTE programs will need to utilize those entry-level positions students can obtain, where a community college CTE program may be preparing students for higher-level positions (Finch & Crunkilton, 1999).

Task analysis has great value in identifying content for career preparation curricula and has been shown to effectively identify technical skills. Task analysis can, however, be an expensive process, depending on the availability of workers to interview or survey. Additionally, career exploration tasks are not always identified through this process (Finch & Crunkilton, 1979).

All Aspects of Industry (AAOI)

According to Perkins V, "the term 'all aspects of industry' means strong experience in, and comprehensive understanding of, the industry that the individual is preparing to enter" (Hyslop, 2018, p. 15). "All Aspects" curriculum is designed to provide context around where technical skills are used. Students are exposed to broad themes such as global marketing, arts and media, or health and safety, which allow curriculum to be developed with content that is meaningful for the broad theme (Collins & O'Brien, 2011; Finch & Crunkilton, 1999). In a program of study, the curriculum begins within the broader career cluster or theme and progresses to more occupation-specific instruction (Hyslop, 2018).

It is important that the broad content area is defined in comprehensive terms, which is where All Aspects enters the curriculum process. Embracing the Career Clusters model is one way to embrace the All Aspects approach, but it could also be defined by a local CTE program with input from stakeholders (Finch & Crunkilton, 1999; Kansas CTE, n.d.). All Aspects curriculum needs to embrace three areas: the school, the workplace, and the community. More basic knowledge and skills, such as math, science, history, and English, are integrated with other theme-related technical knowledge and skills to make learning more relevant to students (Finch & Crunkilton, 1999).

From the All Aspects perspective, a curriculum developer should consider a number of questions, including (Finch & Crunkilton, 1999):

- Does the theme align with the needs of the students who will be enrolled?
- Does it build on employers' strengths so they can contribute to the curriculum?
- Does it link and build upon community resources?

All Aspects considers the breadth and depth of curriculum to first focus on broader worker activities so workers can function in a variety of workplace contexts and to then become more specific for specific jobs and tasks. In this way, the program of study moves from simple to more advanced (Collins & O'Brien, 2011; Finch & Crunkilton, 1999).

Critical Incident Technique

The Critical Incident Technique is an approach to teaching that highlights critical incidents to use as a basis for analysis, discussion, problem solving, and learning (Collins & O'Brien, 2011; Hughes et al., 2008). First developed by John Flanagan in 1954, the Critical Incident technique has been seen as a useful tool to observe human behavior in work settings (Finch & Crunkilton, 1979). A critical incident is:

> any observable human activity that is sufficiently complete in itself to permit inferences and predictions to be made about the person performing the act. To be critical, an incident must occur in a situation where the purpose or intent of the act seems fairly clear to the observer and where its consequences are sufficiently definite to leave little doubt concerning its effects (Flanagan, 1954, p. 1).

Although use of the Critical Incident Technique may seem limited for CTE programs, its application serves as a firm foundation for identifying nontechnical, affective skills (Finch & Crunkilton, 1979). Flanagan intended that utilizing the Critical Incident Technique would underpin practical problem solving (Hughes et al., 2008). Its utility is in isolating those important values and attitudes students must demonstrate for success in the career field (Finch & Crunkilton, 1979).

The five-step process for the Critical Incident Technique includes:

1. *Defining the activity to be studied.* In this step, the curriculum developer creates a brief, clear statement that indicates the activity objective and what the activity is expected to accomplish.
2. *Developing a plan for data collection.* The goal of this step is to establish a plan to identify the critical behaviors. The plan should include four components: situation, relevance, extent, and observers.
3. *Collecting the data.* Not surprisingly, this involves having individual interviews or direct observations of workers to collect data based on the critical incidents related to the activity being studied.
4. *Analyzing the data.* The collected data should be classified to identify critical behaviors of the worker(s).
5. *Interpreting and reporting the data.* The results of the analysis should result in a discussion of the findings, including a set of critical behaviors that define the activity. (Hughes et al., 2008)

Through this process, researchers can identify similarities, differences, and patterns to how and why workers engage in the activity. Emerging patterns then uncover those situations that demonstrate both positive and negative behaviors (Collins & O'Brien, 2011; Hughes et al., 2008). Critical behavior themes in the data can then "serve as a foundation for curriculum content that focuses on developing appropriate attitudes and values" (Finch & Crunkilton, 1999, p. 158).

Examples might include why workers are calling in sick on Mondays; why individuals are being placed on jobs, but then being fired quickly; or why workers are not taking initiative on the job. Workers can complete a form for when these incidents occurred, what led to the incidents, exactly what the workers did or failed to do, and how the incidents contributed to the situation being studied. While this approach may not directly identify technical content, this type of affective educational content allows appropriate values and attitudes to be infused throughout the curriculum and the entire educational experience (Finch & Crunkilton, 1999).

Delphi Method

Originally developed by the RAND corporation to predict alternate defense futures, the Delphi technique has been found as a useful tool to set priorities, establish goals, and forecast emerging occupations (Collins & O'Brien, 2011; Finch & Crunkilton, 1999). Basically, the technique begins by determining a sample or samples of experts from the field who are knowledgeable in the curricular area. This group is asked to respond individually to several rounds of survey questions. In each iteration, the respondents learn the distribution of all of the responses from the previous set of questions and have an opportunity to change or explain their answers. The process continues with additional iterations until a consensus is reached. The respondents never meet face to face, so the group is never biased by the perspective of one person (Collins & O'Brien, 2011; Finch & Crunkilton, 1999).

The resulting product is a consensus on educational needs (Collins & O'Brien, 2011). Often, however, there is more content identified than time to teach the material, so a curriculum developer must establish a way to determine the most relevant content for the curriculum and educational time. The Delphi process can also consume a considerable amount of time and relies on participants who can dedicate time to read and respond to the surveys. Originally a Delphi process was conducted through mailed surveys that had to be returned; however, internet or web-based surveys have streamlined the process. The Delphi technique is especially useful for emerging occupations that have few workers or instructors (Finch & Crunkilton, 1999).

Putting Strategies into Practice

These strategies all have a place in developing curriculum, but the curriculum developer needs to determine which processes to utilize based on time, cost, and validity needs. The philosophical basis works best to identify the goals of a community but is less useful to identify career exploration or technical skills content. Task analysis might be used to focus on specific aspects of an occupation, but it does not incorporate the emerging trends of a career field in the same way as a Delphi approach would. And while task analysis and the Delphi method may identify technical skills, these may not be as effective as All Aspects of Industry to identify broader skills for younger students to explore careers or to identify academic skills needed across multiple careers. Strategies are not mutually exclusive, and multiple strategies have the greatest potential for high-quality content. Figure 4.2 provides an overview of which strategies may work best, given particular situations.

Figure 4.2 Curriculum Determination Strategies

Strategy	Ease of Data Collection	Objectivity	Validity	Cost	Time	Application to CTE Curriculum			
						Career Exploration	Academic Integration	Technical Skill Identification	Employability/ Affective Skill Identification
Philosophical Basis	+	-	?	+	+	?	?	-	?
Introspection	+	-	?	+	+	?	?	?	?
DACUM	?	+	+	?	+	-	?	+	?
Task Analysis	-	+	+	-	-	-	?	+	?
All Aspects of Industry	?	?	?	?	?	+	+	+	+
Critical Incident Technique	-	?	+	-	-	-	?	?	+
Delphi Method	-	+	+	?	-	+	?	+	?

While there may not be one "best" approach to determining curricular content for every situation, using a combination of strategies to engage business and industry partners provides an opportunity to validate CTE curriculum.

Summary

Engaging employers in determining appropriate curriculum content is a necessary part of CTE programs. Utilizing formal processes that begin with industry standards and assist employers in connecting the curriculum to their own talent requirements creates opportunities for partners to be directly involved in creating the skilled workforce needed. Validating personal and school philosophies through a formal stakeholder process ensures students will be prepared for the workforce and emerging careers. No matter the process selected, involving industry partners in a formalized, structured approach allows the curriculum to be validated for local, regional, and state workforce needs.

ACTE's Quality CTE Program of Study Framework Connection

The concepts in this chapter related to the following elements of the *Quality CTE Program of Study Framework* developed by the Association for Career and Technical Education (read more about the framework in chapter 2; Imperatore & Hyslop, 2018):

- **Element 1: Standards-aligned and Integrated Curriculum**
  This element of the framework addresses the development, implementation, and revision of a program of study's curriculum, including relevant knowledge and skills. Ensuring that curriculum is developed with employer input to prepare students for both further education and in-demand and emerging careers is foundational to ensuring program quality.

- **Element 2: Sequencing and Articulation**
  This element addresses course sequencing, knowledge and skill progression, and alignment and coordination across courses in a program, as well as across learner levels, such as from secondary to postsecondary education. Utilizing content determination strategies that include business and industry partners allows a sequence of courses and student competence to build throughout a CTE program of study. Collaborating to ensure the program of study meets the needs of employers is a necessary component of CTE curriculum development.

- **Element 8: Business and Community Partnerships**
  This element addresses business and community partnership recruitment, partnership structure, and the activities partners should be engaged in. A formal, structured approach to coordinating CTE curriculum development and feedback ensures the program of study is informed by employer and community needs. Partners who identify, validate, and review curriculum, as well as support extended learning opportunities, ensure the effectiveness of the program of study in preparing students for further education and careers.

References

Collins, J. W., & O'Brien, N. P. (2011). *The greenwood dictionary of education* (2nd ed.). Greenwood.

Finch, C. R., & Crunkilton, J. R. (1979, April 8–12). *Review and critique of strategies for determining career education curriculum content* [Paper presentation]. Annual Meeting of the American Educational Research Association, San Francisco, CA, United States. https://files.eric.ed.gov/fulltext/ED178696.pdf

Finch, C. R., & Crunkilton, J. R. (1999). *Curriculum development in vocational and technical education: Planning, content, and implementation*. Allyn and Bacon.

Flanagan, J. C. (1954). The critical incident technique. *Psychological Bulletin, 51*(4). https://www.apa.org/pubs/databases/psycinfo/cit-article.pdf

Hughes, H., Williamson, K., & Lloyd, A.(2007). Critical incident technique. In S. Lipu, (Ed.). *Exploring methods in information literacy research* (pp. 49–66). Centre for Information Studies.

Hyslop, A. (2018). *Perkins V: The official guide to the Strengthening Career and Technical Education for the 21st Century Act*. ACTE.

Imperatore, C. & Hyslop, A. (2018, October). *2018 ACTE quality program of study framework*. Association for Career and Technical Education. https://www.acteonline.org/wp-content/uploads/2019/01/HighQualityCTEFramework2018.pdf

Kansas CTE. (n.d.). *All aspects of an industry*. https://www.ksde.org/Portals/0/CSAS/CSAS%20Home/CTE%20Home/Instructor_Resources/FinalAllAspects.pdf

U.S. Chamber of Commerce Foundation. (2020). *TPM resource guide: A compendium for high-quality CTE*. https://www.uschamberfoundation.org/reports/tpm-curriculum

U.S. Chamber of Commerce Foundation. (2018, June 4). *TPM Academy Curriculum*. https://www.uschamberfoundation.org/reports/tpm-curriculum

Wyrostek, W., & Downey, S. (2016). Compatibility of common instructional models with the DACUM process. *Adult Learning, 28*(2), 69-75. doi:10.1177/1045159516669702

Chapter 5

■

TECHNICAL STANDARDS

Kemaly Parr—Murray State University
Larae Watkins—University of Central Missouri
Michelle L. Conrad—University of Central Missouri
Mark D. Threeton—Pennsylvania State University

Introduction

Every industry has some way of defining what quality work looks like: the practices, the skills, the end products of the work, the expectations for the way things are done. In welding, there are the American Welding Society Standards for different types of welders and roles within the welding industry. Automotive professionals follow the National Institute for Automotive Service Excellence Educational Foundation standards, which include standards in many different facets of automotive service, as well as standards for programs and instructors who teach aspiring professionals.

Many standards are tied to certifications within career fields. NCLEX certifies nursing professionals and provides the standards that individuals must achieve to take their certification exams. Cisco has established a number of computer networking certifications, all with their own learning standards. State CTE websites will include the IRC accepted. CTE curriculum is driven by these industry standards.

This chapter will first focus on employer involvement to determine the technical skills to teach. This will be followed by an overview of national technical skills frameworks, including the Career

Clusters framework and the Common Career Technical Core (CCTC). Technical standards are the foundation for CTE curriculum and ensure the alignment of education to industry needs.

Employer Involvement

Engaging business and industry partners in determining content is necessary for local, regional, and state employment needs (Pawlowski & Meeder, 2012). Formal engagement strategies were explored in the previous chapter, but let's begin here by reviewing the important role advisory boards or similar formal groups made up of employer partners play in a successful program. Advisory board engagement provides an opportunity for important decisions regarding expenditures of funds and curricular needs. If you need to establish an advisory board, Figure 5.1 provides a list of common questions and ideas to consider as part of your advisory board plan.

Figure 5.1 Checklist for Advisory Board Planning

☐ Interview an administrator or fellow teacher at your school to discuss the protocol for advisory board meetings.

☐ Discuss the history of the advisory board for your program.

☐ Are advisory board meetings program-specific or general across the school or district?

☐ When are advisory board meetings held for your program? (day of the week, time of day, time of year, how often—spring and fall)

☐ Where is the committee meeting held? If outside of your classroom or lab, do you include a tour of your facility?

☐ Is there a general format?

☐ Is there food at the meetings? Who gets the food? When will the food be set up, how, and where? Who takes care of cleaning up after the meeting?

☐ Does the meeting room need to be rearranged? If so, who will set up and when will set up occur? Who will take care of rearranging after the meeting?

☐ Where does the budget for the meeting come from? What funds are designated for the meeting?

☐ Who attends the meeting (list your stakeholders)? Are there specific people in your building that always attend?

☐ What emails or announcements will be sent for the meeting (including frequency and type)?

☐ Who records the minutes? Who will share the minutes with stakeholders and how?

☐ Where are minutes to be kept and by whom?

☐ Discuss online attendance components if applicable.

☐ Will a parking pass and directions for obtaining a pass be needed?

☐ How long will the meeting be?

☐ Will name tents be created?

☐ How will attendance be taken? Will a sign-in sheet be created for attendance?

☐ Signage in the building: Who will create the directional signs, put them up, and take them down?

☐ When will signage be displayed (an hour before meeting, etc.)?

☐ Is there a sample agenda you may use?

☐ How are introductions handled?

☐ What data will you share at the meeting (enrollment numbers, industry certifications, CTSO participation, etc.)?

☐ Where do you get data to share at the meeting?

☐ Create a presentation for the advisory board meeting.

☐ What slides will be included?

- Welcome
- Agenda
- Data
- CTSO highlights

Advisory Board Stakeholders

One of the first steps in convening an advisory board is to designate a stakeholder list. Over half of the board should be made up of business and industry professionals. The other members could include a postsecondary representative, a student in the program, a parent of a student in the program, an administrator at the school, and a graduate of the program (Kentucky Department of Education [KDE], 2020; Pawlowski & Meeder, 2012).

Invitations should be sent asking stakeholders to participate as advisory committee members. Determining availability follows so that dates and times for meetings can be established. Make sure to send reminder emails about one month, one week, one day, and one hour before the meeting; include an agenda so members know what to be prepared to discuss. Following the meeting, be sure to distribute minutes and a reminder of the next scheduled meeting. Check in periodically with stakeholders who did not make it to the meeting or any members who were given a task. Figure 5.2 provides important details regarding successful advisory boards.

Figure 5.2 Successful Advisory Board Recommendations

1. 6–10 members
2. Members should include teachers in the program, an administrator, a student, a parent, a graduate of the program, a postsecondary representative, and at least 50 percent of the membership should be industry professionals
3. Advisory board emails include invitations to join the board, scheduling requests and confirmation emails, reminder emails at one week, one day, and one hour before a meeting.

 VOICES FROM THE FIELD

Matt Pratt—Machine Tool Instructor/WCHS Girls Soccer, Webster County Area Technology Center, Kentucky

Advisory boards in CTE pathways are a must for a program to succeed. They provide day-to-day knowledge and changing procedures that help you keep up and change lessons based on real-time data in industry. This helps the teachers and the students stay relevant. Then, when the students are ready to complete the pathway, they can step into their careers ahead, instead of behind.

Industry professionals are interested in their future employees, so bringing these individuals together as vested partners only strengthens a CTE program. Taking time to structure advisory board participation, as described in the previous chapter, allows for input on the skills needed in the workforce, as well as an opportunity for partners to network with each other, consider resources they could provide, or identify work-based learning opportunities for students. These types of community partnerships help to align CTE programs with local industry job offerings and partners in training students for real-world learning.

Industry Standards

Industry professionals who serve on advisory boards are most familiar with the technical skills for their industry. Starting the curriculum discussion with a focus on industry standards is often a logical place to begin. Professional standards, such as the American Welding Society Standards, the National

Institute for Automotive Service Excellence Educational Foundation standards, the National Council of State Boards for Nursing, and many others drive much of the content of the CTE curriculum. Some industries also have more clear education standards; for example, the National Consortium of Health Science Educators has developed the National Health Science Standards and Objectives (NCHSE, 2021), and the National Business Education Association developed and routinely updates the NBEA Business Education Standards (NBEA, 2021).

While these industry standards may not be specific for the level of students being taught, Industry-Recognized Credentials (IRCs), as well as any state and national CTE standards, will be derived from these. IRCs are credentials indicating that a student has demonstrated competence in content and performance standards for a specific occupational area or cluster of related occupational areas (Missouri Department of Elementary and Secondary Education [Missouri DESE], 2021). As discussed in chapter 2, a quality CTE program of study should lead to one or more recognized postsecondary credentials, which can include an industry certification, a professional license, an apprenticeship certificate, or a postsecondary certificate or degree (Imperatore & Hyslop, 2018).

The latest version of the Carl D. Perkins Career and Technical Education Act (Perkins V) promotes this, and employers increasingly look for graduates with some kind of credential, whether that credential is a certification, a license, an associate degree, a baccalaureate degree, or even a graduate degree. In working with your advisory committee as you develop your curriculum, use the standards that are recognized in your field to guide your content. Keep on top of any changes in your field, because just as curriculum grows and changes, industry standards adapt and change to meet the changing demands of the workplace.

 VOICES FROM THE FIELD

Andrea Heisner—Health Science Teacher McCracken County High School Paducah, KY

Aligning my lessons with technical and academic standards is critical. By doing this, I'm able to prepare my students for real-world experience. I align with standards to help students prepare for careers outside of high school and to earn certifications in their career pathways.

National Career Clusters Framework

The National Career Clusters Framework was initiated in 1996 as an organizing tool for CTE programs, curriculum design, and instruction. While not replacing industry standards, the Career Clusters provide a common language and structure for CTE programs across the wide range of current and potential career fields. They allow CTE teachers and students to see across a range of related career fields to develop programs of study aligning with a broad range of occupations, as well as with industry-specific standards.

There are 16 Career Clusters, representing 79 Career Pathways (See Figure 5.3). A Career Cluster contains occupations in similar fields that require similar skills. Education plans can be focused on obtaining knowledge and competence for success within a particular pathway within the cluster (National Center for ONet Development, 2021). The 79 pathways also allow for alignment between K-12 education, postsecondary education, and employment opportunities (Perkins Collaborative Resource Network [PCRN], 2021). A career pathways system then "is about the coordination of people and resources" (PCRN, para. 1).

Since its development, the National Career Clusters Framework has been used throughout the country to organize career preparation programs and assist in helping students explore career options. At the time of publication of this text, however, the framework is being updated to ensure its relevance for the needs of learners and the workplace. An updated framework is scheduled to be released in late 2022.

Figure 5.3 16 Career Clusters

1. Agriculture, Food, and Natural Resources	11. Information Technology
2. Architecture and Construction	12. Law, Public Safety, Corrections, and Security
3. Arts, A/V Technology, and Communications	13. Manufacturing
4. Business Management and Administration	14. Marketing
5. Education and Training	15. Science, Technology, Engineering and Mathematics
6. Finance	16. Transportation, Distribution, and Logistics
7. Government and Public Administration	
8. Health Science	
9. Hospitality & Tourism	
10. Human Services	

Common Career Technical Core

While technical standards are largely founded on industry-specific and industry-developed technical content, a successful CTE program also includes broader sets of technical standards, which are common across all careers within a career cluster and across all the career clusters. The CCTC fills this gap, providing a set of benchmarks for what students should know and be able to do once they've completed a full program of study in a CTE field. CCTC development was a state-led initiative, which involved representatives from business and industry, secondary and postsecondary educators, and other key CTE stakeholders. In all, the rigorous process included over 3,500 individuals from across the CTE stakeholder community (Advance CTE, 2021).

The CCTC comprises two main sections: Career-Ready Practices and Career Cluster and Pathway Standards. The 12 Career-Ready Practices are those skills that enable an individual to be career ready and are applicable across all Career Clusters and Pathways. The Career-Ready Practices were developed by looking at all the Career Clusters and Pathways and describing employability skills from a CTE perspective. The 12 Career-Ready Practices are listed in Figure 5.4.

Figure 5.4 Career-Ready Practices

1. Act as a responsible and contributing citizen and employee.
2. Apply appropriate academic and technical skills.
3. Attend to personal health and financial well-being.
4. Communicate clearly, effectively, and with reason.
5. Consider the environmental, social, and economic impacts of decisions.
6. Demonstrate creativity and innovation.
7. Employ valid and reliable research strategies.
8. Utilize critical thinking to make sense of problems and persevere in solving them.
9. Model integrity, ethical leadership, and effective management.
10. Plan education and career paths aligned to personal goals.
11. Use technology to enhance productivity.
12. Work productively in teams while using cultural/global competence.

The Career Cluster and Pathway standards then provide a set of benchmark standards for each of the 16 Career Clusters and their related Career Pathways. These standards do not replace industry standards, but rather complement them by providing an agreed-upon basic set of standards across states and regions within the country. As students may move around the state or the country, the Career Cluster–based standards should remain a consistent reference point for students, as well as the teachers they work with (Advance CTE, 2014).

VOICES FROM THE FIELD

Chelsea McCreary—Audio, Video, Technology, and Film, Teacher Ola High School McDonough, Georgia

Currently, in lower-level courses, I follow standards-based learning. The expectation is that the Georgia Department of Education (GaDOE) standards are following in conjunction with our pacing guide. The Henry County Board of Education designated one or two teacher representatives to compile and write a pacing guide that aligns with the GaDOE standards. This pacing guide is put in place to keep all content teachers on the same schedule. From the pacing guide (that aligns with the GaDOE standards), teachers have the freedom to design their own lesson plans.

Personally, I use the standards and the pacing guide (along with a textbook) to build my lessons. The standards help make a mental checklist of items that need to be mastered prior to moving to the next-level course. The standards and pacing guide also align with the NOCTI End of Pathway Assessment for my course.

Technical Skills in Curriculum

Technical or pathway standards provide a comprehensive snapshot of the content that should be taught. Some states and CTE programs will align directly to the industry standards, while other states and programs will align to the CCTC, while others will develop their own CTE program standards. The location of these technical standards documents may vary from state to state, but can customarily be found on the state's Department of Education website.

When creating lesson plans, the technical or pathway standards documents are critically important. Each lesson should outline the academic, employability, and occupational skills that students will learn. Individual lessons should then build into the unit plan, curriculum map, and ultimately, the program of study.

Let's consider a Foundations of Technical Careers course (Missouri DESE, in press) with technical skills based on the CCTC standards for the Architecture and Construction Career Cluster (National Association of State Directors of Career Technical Education Consortium, 2012, pp. 5–6). An "Electrical Concepts" unit of instruction might be aligned, as shown in Figure 5.5. Notice the "coding" in the column to the left, which corresponds with the CCTC Standards as found in the CCTC.

Figure 5.5 CCTC Alignment: Electrical Concepts Unit

Career/Technical Knowledge and Skills	
AC-a, AC-MO-a	Use vocabulary, symbols, and formulas common to architecture and construction.
AC-b, AC-CST-i, AC-CST-h, AC-DES-f, AC-MO-c, AC-MO-d, MN-f, MN-HSE-a, MN-LOG-b, MN-MIR-a, MN-PPD-a, MN-QA-f, TD-c, TD-HSE-b, TD-LOG-a, TD-OPS-a, TD-SYS-a, TD-SYS-b, TD-WAR-a	Use industry-related skills to create and manage a project and use equipment.
AC-d, AC-DES-e, MN-a, TD-a	Evaluate the nature and scope of the different career clusters and their role in society and the economy.
AC-f, AC-CST-e, AC-DES-c, AC-DES-d, AC-DES-h	Read, interpret, and use technical drawings, documents, and specifications to plan a project.
AC-g, MN-d, TD-f	Describe career opportunities and means to achieve those opportunities in each of the career clusters and their specific pathways.
AC-DES-b, AC-DES-g, MN-LOG-a, MN-PRO-d, MN-QA-c, TD-SAL-b	Use effective communications skills and strategies (listening, speaking, reading, writing, and graphic communication) to work with clients and colleagues.

From this unit plan, however, the student learning objectives for one of the lessons in this unit, "Electrical Concepts," might look like those in Figure 5.6. While the learning objectives for the lesson are not identical to the standards in the unit plan, we can see that the lesson objectives were derived from those standards. These objectives also include the condition, the performance, and the criterion, which will be discussed further in Chapter 12.

Figure 5.6 Student Learning Objectives: Electrical Concepts Lesson

At the end of this unit, students will be able to:

- Explain the basics, as outlined in course notes, of:
  - Electrical theory, including the charges of protons, neutrons, and electrons
  - AC/DC theory
  - Multimeter functions, including setting the multimeter to test basic AC/DC circuits
- Identify basic (AC/DC) circuits, symbols, simple wiring diagrams, and color coding with 100 percent accuracy.
- Build and test basic working DC circuits (using a multimeter).

Technical Facilities and Equipment

While technical standards and the CCTC are essential to anchoring curriculum to the industry, it is also critical to highlight the importance of having a well-established CTE learning environment, which simulates the actual working conditions as closely as possible. For example, it would be very difficult for an instructor to teach the American Welding Society Standards in the curriculum without a suitable technical laboratory and appropriate welding apparatus. Similarly, an instructor couldn't be expected to successfully teach the National Institute for Automotive Service Excellence Educational Foundation standards solely through lecture in a classroom setting. Therefore, to best promote the transfer of learning, the standards to be taught must align seamlessly with the facility.

Beyond just the learning environment itself, this also includes providing the appropriate tools, equipment, machines, and other apparatuses, which parallel the standards found within the designated industry. As they say, there is no substitute for the real thing. With this adage in mind, a wise career and technical educator works diligently with their advisory board to affirm that the learning environment and applicable apparatus align well with the industry standards and curriculum that are to be taught. The following crosswalk (Figure 5.7) is provided to assist career and technical educators in aligning curriculum to the learning environment and related apparatus.

Figure 5.7 Curriculum and Facilities Crosswalk

Program Type: Building Construction Operations		
Instructional Content to be Taught	Tools, Equipment, and Supplies Needed for the Unit	Type of Space Required in the Facility
Laboratory Safety	Safety glasses, hardhat, steel-toe boots, OSHA Job Site Analysis Handout	Laboratory Setting with Large Table for Demonstration
Fall Protection	OSHA 1926 Construction Safety Standards Book, Safety Harness and Lanyard	Classroom with Seating for 30 and Laboratory Setting for Demonstration and Harness Inspection Activity

Facilities and equipment availability can also impact curriculum. Each student in a program needs to have time to learn and use equipment, which can be dependent on availability. For example, if a welding lab only has five bays, but there are 12 students, rotating projects and time in bays may be necessary, impacting the instruction and the time needed for particular units of instruction. CTE curricular planning needs to take into consideration the learners' needs, as well as the physical space and equipment.

Summary

CTE programs provide students with opportunities to acquire skills, develop strategies for success, and master industry competencies. Teachers need to align technical standards across all aspects of the program. Extending learning beyond the classroom, students should be provided with opportunities to explore careers, gain experience in their communities, participate in CTSOs, engage in lab activities and work-based learning, and integrate their learning experiences. Tying it all together, teachers should be able to demonstrate how student learning accomplishes practical and theoretical knowledge and skills needed for their future careers (NBPTS, 2014).

Technical standards, along with the advice of engaged employer partners through an advisory board, drive CTE curriculum to ensure students are prepared for the local, state, and national workforce.

ACTE's Quality CTE Program of Study Framework Connection

The concepts in this chapter related to the following elements of the *Quality CTE Program of Study Framework* developed by the Association for Career and Technical Education (read more about the framework in chapter 2, Imperatore & Hyslop, 2018):

- **Element 1: Standards-aligned and Integrated Curriculum**
  This element of the framework addresses the development, implementation, and revision of a program of study's curriculum, including relevant knowledge and skills. The program of study should be developed with employers to ensure that students are prepared for both further education and emerging careers. Curriculum should be based on industry standards and regularly reviewed by an advisory committee or similar group of employers.

- **Element 7: Facilities, Equipment, Technology, and Materials**
  This element addresses the alignment, appropriateness, and safety of the physical and material components of a CTE program. Facilities, equipment, technology, and materials in the program of study should reflect industry requirements and align to curriculum standards and program objectives. Access to relevant facilities, equipment, technology, and materials allows for flexible curriculum delivery models.

- **Element 8: Business and Community Partnerships**
  This element addresses business and community partnership recruitment, partnership structure, and the activities partners should be engaged in. As mentioned in the chapter, advisory boards are an important component of determining appropriate technical standards. Employers should be used to ensure the program meets current and future workforce demand and skill needs by identifying, validating, and reviewing curriculum and standards.

References

Advance CTE. (2021). *The career ready practices*. https://careertech.org/career-ready-practices

Advance CTE. (2014, July). *The common career technical core, programs of study & industry-based standards*. https://careertech.org/sites/default/files/CCTC-IndustryStandards.pdf

Imperatore, C. & Hyslop, A. (2018). *2018 ACTE quality CTE program of study framework*. Association for Career & Technical Education. https://www.acteonline.org/wp-content/uploads/2019/01/HighQualityCTEFramework2018.pdf

Kentucky Department of Education. (2020). *Guidelines for An Advisory Committee*. https://education.ky.gov/CTE/perkins/Documents/Perkins_V_Advisory_Committee_2020.pdf

Missouri Department of Elementary and Secondary Education (2021). *Technical skills attainment & industry recognized credentials*. https://dese.mo.gov/college-career-readiness/career-education/technical-skills-attainment-industry-recognized-credential

Missouri Department of Elementary and Secondary Education. (in press). *Foundations of technical careers course (year 1), electrical concepts (unit 4)*. Pathways to skilled technical careers.

National Association of State Directors of Career Technical Education Consortium. (2012). *Common Career Technical Core*. Advance CTE. https://cte.careertech.org/sites/default/files/CCTC_Standards_Formatted_2014.pdf

National Business Education Association (NBEA). (2021). *Business education standards*. https://nbea.org/page/BusinessEdStandards

National Center for O*NET Development. *O*NET online*. https://www.onetonline.org/

National Consortium for Health Science Education (NCHSE). (2021). *National health science standards and objectives*. https://healthscienceconsortium.org/standards/

Pawlowski, B. & Meeder, H. (2012). Building advisory boards that matter: A handbook for engaging your business partners. Association for Career and Technical Education.

Perkins Collaborative Resource Network (PCRN). (2021). *Career pathways systems*. https://cte.ed.gov/initiatives/career-pathways-systems

Chapter 6

■

ACADEMIC CORE INTEGRATION

Larae Watkins—University of Central Missouri
Kemaly Parr—Murray State University
Michelle L. Conrad—University of Central Missouri

Introduction

Almost every educator knows "academic core" classes are English, math, science, and social studies, and every state has graduation requirements for high school students to earn these credits. Some students, however, find these courses theoretical and difficult to understand. We hear students say, "Why do I need to know this?" And while our teaching colleagues are well educated and understand their content, contextualizing that content can be difficult. In CTE, however, we know there is a reason for everything we teach. Our industry partners have communicated these reasons directly to us. Students need to know how to communicate, speak appropriately to clients and coworkers, and apply math skills to solve real-world problems.

Although the standards initiative has been focused at the K-12 educational level, postsecondary educators often recognize the consequences of students who are not yet prepared for continued education and also need to incorporate and reinforce academic core concepts in their curriculum. Being prepared to integrate academic core concepts, no matter the educational level being taught, better prepares students for their careers. Whether your state is a Common Core state or has its own academic standards, finding ways to integrate academics into the CTE curriculum allows students to better understand those academic core concepts, as well as how to apply their learning in real-world situations. This chapter will provide an overview of national standards initiatives, provide some examples and resources for the academic core in CTE, and end with strategies for approaching academic core integration efforts.

National Standards Initiatives

Standards are used in many industries to communicate that something is good enough for a particular purpose or that it has reached a level of excellence. Safety standards communicate if products can be trusted, or star systems communicate how good something might be (Cambridge Assessment, 2017). In education, standards communicate a description of "what is to be learned and taught (the curriculum) and the results of assessments" (Cambridge Assessment, para. 3). Academic core standards are set by grade level, beginning in kindergarten and continuing through high school graduation (Lee, 2021).

In the United States, education is a state responsibility, so each state's department of education sets its own standards. Although the federal government does not set academic core standards, federal laws, such as the Every Student Succeeds Act (ESSA), can have an influence (Lee, 2021). As a CTE instructor, having an understanding of these standards assists in finding ways to integrate core academic concepts into CTE curriculum, as well as opportunities to contextualize theoretical concepts for student learning.

 VOICES FROM THE FIELD

Matt Pratt—Machine Tool Instructor/WCHS Girls Soccer, Webster County Area Technology Center, KY

I integrate technical and academic skills as much as I can to show the students that we use traditional math in manufacturing, as well as how I was taught in the field to simplify processes due to time constraints on the job. They realize at that moment that there is ALWAYS another way to approach life, school, and career.

Common Core State Standards

The Common Core State Standards are arguably some of the most well-known and controversial educational standards put forth in recent memory. The Common Core State Standards are a set of mathematics and English language arts/literacy standards that outline what a student "should know and be able to do at the end of each grade" (CCSS Initiative, 2021, para. 2). The Common Core began in 2009 as an initiative of the Council of Chief State School Officers (CCSSO) and the National Governors Association (NGA) and was conceptualized as a way to create a set of consistent learning goals across states. The standards were designed through a collaboration among teachers, administrators, and other experts across states (CCSS Initiative; Lee, 2021). The Common Core State Standards define the knowledge and skills students should attain in math and ELA throughout their K-12 education to graduate from high school prepared to succeed in entry-level careers, college courses, and workforce training (CCSS Initiative).

Next Generation Science Standards

The Next Generation Science Standards (NGSS) were also a state initiative developed to identify core scientific and engineering ideas, practices, and concepts that all students should master by the end of high school in order to be career and college ready. When students graduate from high school, more jobs will require skills in science, technology, engineering, and mathematics (STEM) than in the past. Developed by science teachers, administrators, and professionals across 26 states, the NGSS provides standards to prepare students for our rapidly changing world (NGSS, 2021a). Scientific literacy is critical to the ability of the United States to continue innovating and creating jobs for the future (NGSS, 2021b).

National Curriculum Standards for the Social Studies

The National Council for the Social Studies (NCSS) defines social studies as:

> ...the integrated study of the social sciences and humanities to promote civic competence. Within the school program, social studies provides coordinated, systematic study drawing upon such disciplines as anthropology, archaeology, economics, geography, history, law, philosophy, political science, psychology, religion, and sociology, as well as appropriate content front he humanities, mathematics, and natural sciences (NCSS, 2021, para. 3).

Learning in social studies helps people make informed decisions as citizens of a culturally diverse and democratic society (NCSS, 2021). The NCSS standards provide a framework for curricular planning in prekindergarten through the 12th grade around 10 themes that organize knowledge "about the human experience in the world" (NCSS, para. 7).

State Standards

The United States needs to be prepared to compete in the world, and rigorous standards, designed so that students do not need remedial education when they enter postsecondary programs, are necessary. Ensuring an environment of high-quality standards allows K-12 teachers to focus on the skills students need to be successful as they move from grade level to grade level. While many states utilize national standards as their state standards, other states have used these to guide the development of state-specific standards. Each state provides access to its standards through a state department of education website (U.S. Department of Education, 2021).

Curriculum and assessment systems are set around these state standards. Teachers are then empowered to monitor their students' progress and adjust instruction to ensure every learner is on track for career and college readiness. The most important characteristic of strong state standards is that they ensure student learning is aligned with the demands of the real world (U.S. Department of Education, 2021). Whether your state utilizes national or state academic core standards, the CTE curriculum needs to include an alignment to these.

When we consider alignment to standards in curriculum, "codes" may be used to indicate where alignment exists; sometimes the comparison between the curriculum and the standards is referred to as a "crosswalk." Another way to think of this is from the perspective of how your CTE content area standards reflect these academic core standards or how you can incorporate these academic core concepts into your CTE curriculum. Each set of standards includes instructions for how to "code" the standards, so others understand what standard is being referenced. For example, in the Common Core State Standards for English language arts, the standards are identified by their strand (Reading for Information [RI], Reading for Science & Technology [RST], Writing [W], etc.), grade level (K, 1, 2, etc.), and number (CCSS, 2010). RST.11-12.4 then refers to Reading for Science & Technology, grades 11–12, and the fourth standard, which reads, "Determine the meaning of symbols, key terms, and other domain-specific words and phrases as they are used in a specific scientific or technical context relevant to grades 11–12 texts and topics" (CCSS, 2010, p. 62). When aligning curriculum with standards of any type, make sure that the coding being used is accurate for the standards being referenced, so your alignment is clear.

Academic Core in CTE

Resources already exist to assist teachers in identifying the connections between their content areas and academic core standards. Some national organizations have aligned their standards to English, math, and science standards, such as the National Association of Agricultural Educators (NAAE) alignment of the Agricultural, Farm, and Natural Resources standards to national academic standards for English language arts, mathematics, science, and financial literacy (National Council of Agricultural Education, 2012).

CTE instructors can also consult their state departments, which may have already aligned CTE content standards to academic core standards. For example, the Nevada Practical Nursing Standards are aligned with the Nevada Science and English language arts standards, as shown in Figure 6.1. Another example, in Figure 6.2, is the California Standards for Energy, Environment, & Utilities, aligned to the Common Core State Standards.

Figure 6.1 Nevada Practical Nursing Standards Crosswalk

Performance Indicators	Nevada Academic Content Standards
8.1.1	**Science: HS-Biological Evolution: Unity and Diversity** HS-LS4-4 Construct an explanation based on evidence for how natural selection leads to adaptation of populations.
8.1.2	**English Language Arts: Reading Standards for Literacy in Science and Technical Subjects** RST.11-12.8 Evaluate the hypotheses, data, analysis, and conclusions in a science or technical text, verifying the data when possible and corroborating or challenging conclusions with other sources of information.
8.2.4	**English Language Arts: Reading Standards for Literacy in Science and Technical Subjects** RST.11-12.3 Follow precisely a complex multistep procedure when carrying out experiments, taking measurements, or performing technical tasks; analyze the specific results based on explanations in the text.

Figure 6.2 California Energy, Environment, & Utilities Standards Alignment

ENERGY, ENVIRONMENT, AND UTILITIES	PATHWAYS		
	A. Environmental Resources	B. Energy and Power Technology	C. Telecommunications
TechnologyGeometry – G-SRT – Similarity, Right Triangles, and Trigonometry			
Apply trigonometry to general triangles			
11. (+) Understand and apply the Law of Sines and the Law of Cosines to find unknown measurements in right and non-right triangles (e.g., surveying problems, resultant forces).			C3.0
Geometry – G-PCC – Polar Coordinates and Curves			
Graph polar coordinates and curves.			
1. Be familiar with polar coordinates. In particular, determine polar coordinates of a point given in rectangular coordinates and vice versa. (CA Standard Trigonometry - 15.0)	A2.0		
Number and Quantity – N-Q – Quantities			
Reason quantitatively and use units to solve problems			
1. Use units as a way to understand problems and to guide the solution of multi-step problems; choose and interpret units consistently in formulas; choose and interpret the scale and the origin in graphs and data displays.	A6.0		
2. Define appropriate quantities for the purpose of descriptive modeling.	A2.0, A6.0		
3. Choose a level of accuracy appropriate to limitations on measurement when reporting quantities.	A2.0, A6.0		
Number and Quantity – N-VM – Vector and Matrix Quantities			
Represent and model with vector quantities			
1. (+) Recognize vector quantities as having both magnitude and direction. Represent vector quantities by directed line segments, and use appropriate symbols for vectors and their magnitudes (e.g., v, |v|, ||v||, v).			C3.0
3. (+) Solve problems involving velocity and other quantities that can be represented by vectors.			C3.0

Even though the state and national level alignments are extremely helpful, the CTE curriculum on a local level also should identify the core academic standards integrated within the existing content. For example, Figure 6.3 is the first page of a local unit plan for a skilled technical sciences unit on precision measurement.

Figure 6.3 Foundations of Technical Careers, Precision Measurement Unit Plan

STANDARDS ADDRESSED				
Career/Technical Knowledge and Skills		**Academic Knowledge and Skills**		
AC-b, AC-CST-i, AC-CST-h, AC-DES-f, AC-MO-c, AC-MO-d, MN-f, MN-HSE-a, MN-LOG-b, MN-MIR-a, MN-PPD-a, MN-QA-f, TD-c, TD-HSE-b, TD-LOG-a, TD-OPS-a, TD-SYS-a, TD-SYS-b, TD-WAR-a	Apply industry-related skills in using tools.	Mathematics		
		1.6A	Communicate precisely with clear definitions.	
		1.6B	Use symbols consistently and appropriately.	
		1.6C	Carefully specify units of measure and label axes.	
AC-g, MN-d, TD-f	Describe career opportunities and means to achieve those opportunities in each of the career clusters and their specific pathways.	2.1B	Change from one unit to another in the same measurement system.	
		2.2C	Change from one measurement system to another.	
		2.1J	Identify mistakes in calculations.	
AC-DES-a, MN-PPD-b, MN-PRO-a, MN-QA-b, TD-b, TD-MNT-b, TD-LOG-b, TD-SAL-a	Justify design solutions through research documentation and data analysis.	Communication Arts		
		1d	Read informational texts, charts, and manuals closely and use specific information to address a question or solve a problem.	
AC-DES-b, AC-DES-g, MN-LOG-a, MN-PRO-d, MN-QA-c, TD-SAL-b	Use effective communication skills and strategies (i.e., listening, speaking, reading, writing, and graphic communication) to work with clients and colleagues.	1e	Read informational text and recipes independently and proficiently.	
		5a	Acquire and accurately use a range of career-related words and phrases in speaking and writing.	
Employability/Soft Skills				
2a.	Uses the knowledge and skills acquired through experience and education to be more productive			
8d.	Carefully considers the options to solve the problem			
11a.	Finds and maximizes the productive value of existing and new technology to accomplish workplace tasks and solve workplace problems			
11b.	Demonstrates flexibility and adaptability in acquiring and using new technology			
11c.	Demonstrates proficiency with widely used technology applications			
11d.	Understands the inherent risks of technology applications and takes actions to prevent or mitigate these risks			

Notice in this example (Figure 6.3), the technical skills are identified, as well as academic and employability skills. Since this is a local curriculum, it also includes local strategies to code the standards utilized.

Documents such as these can assist instructors in several ways. Alignment documents allow educators to communicate with administrators how their curriculum reinforces core academic knowledge and skills. CTE instructors are also able to provide contextualized examples to core academic teachers through these documents. While CTE instructors are often looking to find academic connections within their curriculum, core academic teachers are often looking for real-world connections to contextualize learning in their classrooms. By providing crosswalks or curricular alignment, CTE instructors have a basis for sharing examples with academic core instructors, and that sharing becomes a starting point for conversations about how to further collaborate.

Another benefit, and quite possibly the most important reason to document where academic connections exist, is to intentionally reinforce core academic knowledge and skills for students. Students need to understand how their core academic content can be applied in the real world, and CTE offers many opportunities to engage students through real-world projects and assignments. Students can engage in CTE programs of interest that lead to careers, while understanding how to use core academic knowledge and skills. The result is students who graduate career and college ready.

Academic Integration Strategies

CTE teachers are often content experts in their fields and hired for their level of content expertise, so integrating academic standards into curriculum may present challenges at first. Spending the time to integrate academic standards, however, can have significant benefits for students. Consider terminology as one example. The word "dressing" has multiple meanings depending upon the context. "Dressing" in health care may refer to "dressing a wound." "Dressing" in culinary arts may mean a salad dressing or turkey dressing for a Thanksgiving meal. "Dressing" in childcare may be putting clothing on a child. "Dressing the stone" in masonry refers to a concept of squaring a stone.

Who can best teach terminology then? When the context matters, the vocabulary should be taught based on the situation for which it is being used, and students can develop an understanding based on the specific situation. Additionally, as we will explore in future chapters, students learn in different ways, so when the teacher has the ability to explain the academic connections within the real-world context of CTE, students are helped to better understand both the academic connection and the CTE content.

Numerous strategies can be utilized to integrate academics. To provide a starting point, four established strategies are briefly explored here, including collaborating with an academic core instructor, Math-in-CTE, utilizing online materials, and an online training option through the ACTE CTE Learn community.

Collaborating with Core Academic Instructors

The process of integrating academic standards can be utilized as an opportunity to reach out to other instructors, especially the academic core teachers, for collaborative projects. This collaboration enables instructors to make connections between their curricula that they otherwise would not be able to do. Students in both the CTE programs and the academic core classes can then see benefits, as practical applications and real-world situations are also shared with those academic core instructors. Projects can even be built between programs and courses. Academic core instructors who know their standards can assist CTE instructors to readily identify the core concepts in their curriculum and how academic core standards might be met using CTE content.

VOICES FROM THE FIELD

J.T. Payne—Agriculture Teacher and FFA Advisor Henderson County High School Henderson, KY

Technical standards are the bedrock of my classroom instruction and provide an outline of course content. At least one of each lesson's learning targets is directly tied to technical standards. Academic standards assist me in determining methods of instruction. For example, the technical standard for my veterinary science course might be centered around administering injections, but academic standards challenge the educator to go a step further and integrate math skills to determine proper dosage. I have found that core content teachers are amazed at the academic integration in CTE and jump at any opportunity to partner with vocational classes.

Math-in-CTE

Math-in-CTE is an approach states and districts have used to formalize the collaboration process between mathematics and CTE instructors. The formal process, developed by the National Research

Seven Elements of a Math-Enhanced CTE Lesson

(Stone et al., 2007, pg. 2)

1. Introduce the CTE Lesson.
2. Assess students' math awareness as it relates to the CTE lesson.
3. Work through the math example embedded in the CTE lesson.
4. Work through related, contextual math-in-CTE examples.
5. Work through traditional math examples.
6. Students demonstrate their understanding.
7. Formal assessment.

Center for Career and Technical Education, was to prepare CTE math teacher teams to collaborate in the creation of mathematics-embedded CTE curriculum. The Math-in-CTE structure uses a seven-element pedagogic framework. Over a five-day workshop, teacher teams first review foundational curriculum documents to identify math concepts embedded in CTE programs. For example, a health occupations math team could identify the use of proportions and ratios in the preparation of medicines. Teacher teams would then use the seven elements to refine math-embedded CTE lessons to be implemented by the CTE teacher in the context of the CTE lesson (Stone et al., 2008). Many states and districts utilize the Math-in-CTE model and include training opportunities for teachers, as well as access to units and lessons that have been developed previously and are available online.

ACTE CTE Learn Training

Originally developed to help CTE teachers understand the CCSS and learn how to integrate these into CTE curriculum, ACTE established training modules for "C.O.R.E. Education." The modules are housed within the ACTE CTE Learn community in the free resources section (ACTE, 2021). While C.O.R.E. was originally developed for the CCSS, the process can work to help CTE instructors integrate any core academic standards into their curriculum. The acronym C.O.R.E. represents four steps in a curriculum integration process:

1. *Collaborate:* Communicate content expectations vertically up and down the grade spectrum and across subject areas through educator collaboration.
2. *Orient:* Orient curriculum to the standards by matching current CTE content to academic standards and identify assumptions about what students should already know or be able to do.
3. *Relate:* Translate standards to key questions in student-friendly language so we can relate the CTE content to the academic standards. Identify the gaps between key questions and current activities.

4. *Enhance:* Access resources to enhance curriculum. Add or expand course content to support key questions previously developed and determine assessments that measure depth of understanding for those key questions of both CTE and academic core content (ACTE, 2021).

The C.O.R.E. Education online learning modules can be accessed for free through the CTE Learn online community and include ongoing communities of teachers sharing ideas, lessons, and other resources.

Other Online Materials

While collaborating with core content teachers is ideal, sometimes it is not possible. Several educational organizations have online resource materials to help CTE teachers understand core academic standards and to explore existing core academic integrated lessons and activities.

One of these organizations is the Literacy Design Collaborative (LDC). The LDC began as a community of educators focused on closing achievement gaps by ensuring rigorous writing assignments. The LDC now creates writing assignments for most major content areas, allowing instructors to adapt instruction to include additional rigorous writing standards (LDC, 2021). While creating a log-in is required, the free curricular materials within the LDC library allow an educator to enhance reading and writing strategies and adapt these to their own lessons.

Another organization with free online resources for CTE and academic integration is Achieve, Inc. (2021), which includes resources of instructional tasks that demonstrate how CTE can leverage math content. The ThemeSpark website also allows teachers to build lesson plans from a rubric or standard and includes core academic lessons (EdCourage, Inc., 2021). A fourth online option is Lesson Planet, which has many lesson plans, lab resources, activities, and learning games, but does charge a small fee after the 10-day free trial period (EducationPlanet, Inc., 2021).

State websites may also provide useful information and resources for academic integration. A few that might be useful include the CTE Technical Assistance Center of New York, which offers curriculum and instructional resources; Florida's CPalms, which has an online toolbox of resources and interactive tools; and the Texas Education Agency, which offers descriptions and materials for innovative CTE courses (CTE TAC, 2021; Florida State University, 2019; Texas Education Agency, 2020). Instructors should check if their state offers resources for integrating academics into CTE programs.

Summary

Academic core integration has become a significant aspect of the CTE curriculum. In order to ensure that students are truly college and career ready when they leave a CTE program, it is our responsibility to help support student learning of academic content through its application within the CTE curriculum. Whether the core academic standards are from national initiatives or developed specifically by and for a state, knowing what those standards are is an initial step for CTE instructors.

Documenting the alignment between CTE content and academic standards is a part of the curriculum development process, not an add-on or afterthought. However, CTE teachers have a wealth of resources available to help with the integration process, and many curricular examples and integration strategies are available online. Integrating core academic standards may seem like a daunting task, but the benefit for students is significant in preparing them for career and college success.

ACTE's Quality CTE Program of Study Framework Connection

The concepts in this chapter related to the following elements of the *Quality CTE Program of Study Framework* developed by the Association for Career and Technical Education (read more about the Framework in chapter 2, Imperatore & Hyslop, 2018):

- **Element 1: Standards-aligned and Integrated Curriculum**
  This element of the framework addresses the development, implementation, and revision of a program of study's curriculum, including relevant knowledge and skills. Aligning CTE curriculum with the standards for core academic subjects allows students to integrate their knowledge and skills in authentic, contextual situations.

- **Element 5: Engaging Instruction**
  This element addresses instructional strategies that will support student attainment of relevant knowledge and skills. Ensuring that instruction emphasizes the connection between academic CTE knowledge and skills, including through cross-disciplinary collaboration, can enhance students' future education and career success and overall employability.

- **Element 4: Prepared and Effective Program Staff**
  This element addresses the necessary qualifications and professional development of CTE program staff. CTE and academic staff need to collaborate regularly to coordinate curriculum, instruction, assessment, and extended learning activities for student success. Working together to integrate academic knowledge and skills, CTE and core academic core teachers ensure relevancy and contextualized learning.

References

Achieve, Inc. (2021). *CCSS-CTE classroom tasks.* https://www.achieve.org/ccss-cte-classroom-tasks

Association for Career and Technical Education (ACTE). (2021). *ACTE online learning network.* https://www.ctelearn.org/

Cambridge Assessment International Education. (2017). *Standards in education.* https://www.cambridgeinternational.org/Images/271196-standards-in-education.pdf

Common Core State Standards (CCSS) Initiative. (2010). *Common core state standards for English language arts.* http://www.corestandards.org/wp-content/uploads/ELA_Standards1.pdf

Common Core State Standards (CCSS) Initiative. (2021). *About the standards.* http://www.corestandards.org/about-the-standards/

CTE Technical Assistance Center (CTE TAC) of New York. (2021). *Academic integration.* https://nyctecenter.org/instruction/academic-integration

EdCourage, Inc. (2021). *Fast, easy K-12 teacher tools to improve student learning with curriculum.* https://www.themespark.net/

EducationPlanet, Inc. (2021). *Lesson planet.* https://www.lessonplanet.com/search

Florida State University. (2019). *CPalms.* https://www.cpalms.org/

Imperatore, C. & Hyslop, A. (2018, October). *2018 ACTE quality program of study framework.* Association for Career and Technical Education. https://www.acteonline.org/wp-content/uploads/2019/01/HighQualityCTEFramework2018.pdf

Learning Design Collaborative (LDC). (2021). *Our story.* https://ldc.org/about-us/

Lee, A. M. (2021). *State standards: A guide for what you need to know.* Understood for All, Inc. https://www.understood.org/articles/en/state-academic-standards-what-you-need-to-know

National Council for Agricultural Education. (2012). *AFNR standards.* https://thecouncil.ffa.org/afnr/

National Council for the Social Studies (NCSS). (2021). *National curriculum standards for social studies: Introduction.* https://www.socialstudies.org/standards/national-curriculum-standards-social-studies-introduction

Next Generation Science Standards (NGSS). (2021a). *NGSS fact sheet.* https://www.nextgenscience.org/resources/ngss-fact-sheet

Next Generation Science Standards (NGSS). (2021b). *Understanding the standards.* https://www.nextgenscience.org/understanding-standards/understanding-standards

Stone, J. R., Alfeld, C., & Pearson, D. (2008). Rigor and relevance: Enhancing high school students' math skills through career and technical education. *American Educational Research Journal, 45*(3), p. 767–795. https://doi.org/10.3102/0002831208317460

Stone, J. R., Alfeld, C., & Pearson, D., Lewis, M., & Jensen, S. (2007). *Rigor and relevance: A model of enhanced math learning in career and technical education.* National Research Center for Career and Technical Education. https://www.sreb.org/sites/main/files/file-attachments/rigor_and_relevance_0.pdf?1630433486

Texas Education Agency. (2020). *Innovative courses—career and technical education.* https://tea.texas.gov/academics/learning-support-and-programs/innovative-courses/innovative-courses-career-and-technical-education

U.S. Department of Education. (2021). *College- and career-ready standards.* https://www.ed.gov/k-12reforms/standards

Chapter 7

■

EMPLOYABILITY SKILLS

Kevin S. Elliott—Pittsburg State University
Michelle L. Conrad—University of Central Missouri

Introduction

The Common Core State Standard initiative, launched in 2009 (CCSS, 2021), moved the phrase "career readiness" into mainstream educational conversations. The National Association of Colleges and Employers (NACE) defines career readiness as "the attainment and demonstration of requisite competencies that broadly prepare college graduates for a successful transition into the workplace" (NACE, 2021, para. 3). The Association for Career and Technical Education (ACTE) defines career readiness as involving:

> three major skill areas: core academic skills and the ability to apply those skills to concrete situations in order to function in the workplace and in routine daily activities; employability skills (such as critical thinking and responsibility) that are essential in any career area; and technical, job-specific skills related to a specific career pathway. These skills have been emphasized across numerous pieces of research and allow students to enter true career pathways that offer family-sustaining wages and opportunities for advancement (ACTE, 2010, para. 3).

So, when we consider what it means for a student to be "career ready," it goes beyond those technical and academic skills to the heart of what it means to be prepared for the workforce.

Employability skills as further defined by ACTE (2010) include "(but are not limited to) critical thinking, adaptability, problem solving, oral and written communications, collaboration and teamwork, creativity, responsibility, professionalism, ethics, and technology use" (para. 7). A variety of organizations have developed career or employability readiness "standards" that CTE programs can choose to utilize or that can serve as a starting point for creating their own.

This chapter will begin with an overview of career development and exploration as a component of career readiness. We will then explore four employability models, including 21st Century Skills by Battelle for Kids, the Career Ready Practices by Advance CTE, Employability Skills as defined by the U.S. Department of Education, and Global Competence by the Asia Society.

Career Development and Exploration

Workforce preparation begins first with having a knowledge of self, career interests, and skills. The American School Counseling Association (ASCA) sets standards that include career development and defines these as a way for school counseling programs to guide students to "understand the connection between school and the world of work and plan for and make a successful transition from school to postsecondary education and/or the world of work and from job to job across the lifespan" (ASCA, 2021, p. 3). Therefore, as part of career readiness, students need to understand how the career fields they select have broader knowledge and skills that can be applied throughout their lifespans and careers.

Through CTE programs, educators are in a unique position to complement guidance and counseling professionals' efforts to provide students with career guidance (ACTE, 2008). Online resources such as the Bureau of Labor Statistics (http://www.bls.gov), O*Net Online (http://online.onetcenter.org), or Career One Stop (http://www.careeronestop.org) can help students understand the full scope of the career field, including salary and job opening information, exploring career options not previously considered within the field, and learning more about skills and preparation options. Building these resources into CTE curriculum helps students learn how to adapt to the changing job landscape and allows students to locate and analyze information in the context of lifelong career planning (Loup et al., 2017). Relevant and rigorous educational programs that provide employability and career decision-making support and guidance, along with academic and technical skills, connect students' hopes and dreams to the realities of their futures (ACTE).

Models for Career Readiness

States, institutions, schools, or districts can choose to adopt an existing framework for employability skills or can work with business and industry partners to develop their own. If skills are significantly lacking as identified by local business partners, teaching and assessing particular skills can help students gain employment. The following four models include 21st-century skills, career-ready practices, employability skills, and global competence, and provide instructors frameworks for embedding career readiness into curriculum.

Twenty-First Century Skills

The P21 Framework for 21st Century Learning by Battelle for Kids (2020) provides a model for career and technical educators to integrate 21st-century skills into curriculum. Utilizing this framework with technical and academic knowledge allows educators to teach skills such as critical thinking, communication, and problem solving. The model, represented by a rainbow, represents elements for interconnected teaching and learning.

Figure 7.1 Framework for 21st Century Learning

© 2019, Battelle for Kids. All Rights Reserved.

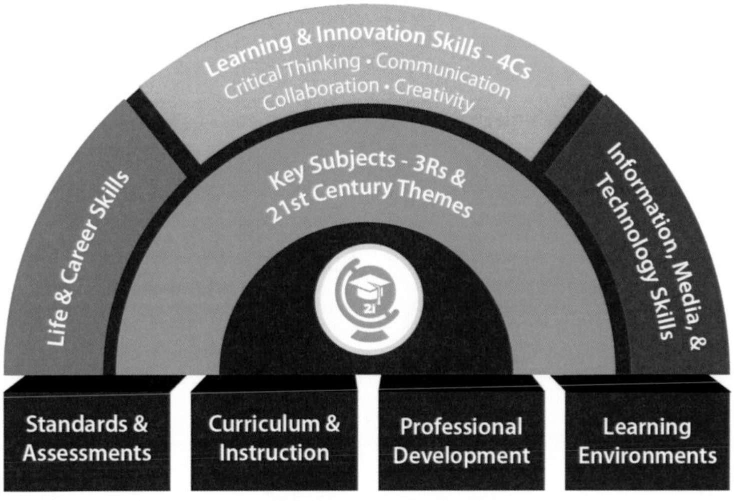

From "P21's Partnership for 21st Century Learning Frameworks and Resources," by Battelle for Kids, 2020.
(https://www.battelleforkids.org/networks/p21/frameworks-resources)
Copyright 2020 by Battelle for Kids. Reprinted with permission.

In the model, "Key Subjects—3Rs" and "21st Century Themes" include subjects such as English, world languages, arts, math, economics, science, history, government, etc. Across the top of the rainbow are three sets of skills—"Life & Career Skills," "Learning & Innovation Skills–4Cs," and "Information, Media, & Technology Skills" (Battelle for Kids, 2020).

"Life & Career Skills" include the ability for students to be flexible and adapt to change, take initiative and work independently, interact effectively with others and in diverse teams, be productive workers with the ability to hold themselves accountable, and lead and be responsible to others. Navigating complex work and life environments in our globally competitive world requires students to develop these life and career skills (Battelle for Kids, 2020).

"Learning & Innovation Skills—4Cs" include the four Cs of Critical thinking—Communication, Collaboration, and Creativity. Critical thinking involves the ability to reason effectively and solve problems. Communication involves the ability to articulate thoughts and ideas, listen effectively, and utilize communication for a variety of reasons. Collaboration means having the ability to work with diverse others effectively and respectfully. Creativity means the ability to create new ideas, demonstrate originality, and evaluate ideas to learn and improve.

"Information, Media, and Technology Skills" are those skills needed to live and work in a technological, media-driven society. Twenty-first-century workers should be able to access and evaluate information, as well as use and manage this information. Therefore, students should learn how to analyze media messages, as well as create media products through the use of technology. Collaboration across multiple cultures and countries has become possible through the use of technology. Students must be able to demonstrate appropriate use of digital technology for success (Battelle for Kids, 2020).

Career Ready Practices

The Career-Ready Practices (also explored in Chapter 5) were developed by Advance CTE in 2012 as part of the Common Career Technical Core (CCTC) Standards. Applicable to all careers and industries, the framework of 12 practices can be taught and observed across programs of study, educational levels, and learning environments.

The 12 practices include (Advance CTE, 2021):

1. Act as a responsible and contributing citizen and employee.
2. Apply appropriate academic and technical skills.
3. Attend to personal health and financial well-being.
4. Communicate clearly, effectively, and with reason.

5. Consider the environmental, social, and economic impacts of decisions.
6. Demonstrate creativity and innovation.
7. Employ valid and reliable research strategies.
8. Utilize critical thinking to make sense of problems and persevere in solving them.
9. Model integrity, ethical leadership, and effective management.
10. Plan education and career path aligned to personal goals.
11. Use technology to enhance productivity.
12. Work productively in teams while using cultural/global competence.

The practices can be "practiced" in a variety of settings, including classrooms/labs, workforce settings, CTSO activities, or adult learning environments (Advance CTE, 2021).

Employability Skills

The U.S. Department of Education developed the Employability Skills Framework as a set of abilities to cut across content areas for workforce development. Abilities are grouped into three broad categories, including applied knowledge, effective relationships, and workplace skills (Perkins Collaborative Resource Network [PCRN], 2021).

"Applied Knowledge" includes the integration of academic and technical skills, as used in the workplace. The two main areas within applied knowledge are applied academic skills, which include reading, writing, math, etc., and critical thinking skills, which enable workers to analyze, reason, think creatively, solve problems, plan, and organize (PCRN, 2021).

"Effective Relationships" include two main areas—interpersonal skills and personal qualities. Interpersonal skills allow an individual to collaborate with others or work independently, communicate effectively, contribute to workplace goals, and maintain a positive attitude. Workers can exercise leadership, respond to customer needs, respect differences, and resolve conflicts. Responsibility, flexibility, initiative, and self-discipline are the personal qualities identified as those that contribute to relationships. Personal qualities can also include demonstrating professionalism, integrity, and a willingness to learn (PCRN, 2021).

Figure 7.2 Employability Skills Framework

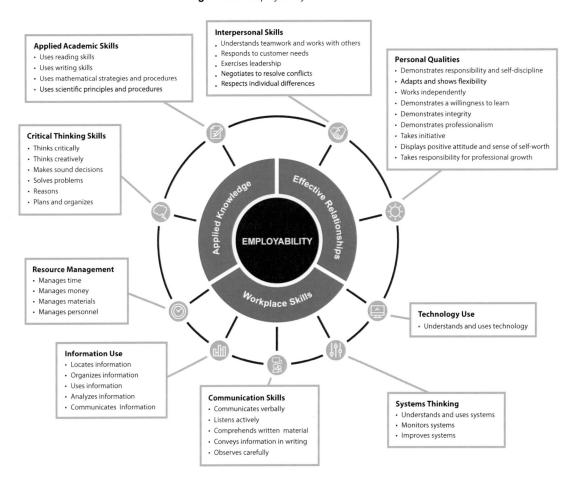

"Workplace Skills" are those needed by employees to complete work tasks. The five skills include (PCRN, 2021):

1. Resource management, which includes time, money, materials, or personnel management.
2. Information use, which means having the ability to locate, organize, use, analyze, and communicate information.
3. Communication skills, which allow employees to listen, comprehend, communicate verbally or in writing, and observe carefully.

4. Systems thinking, which allows an individual to understand, monitor, and improve systems.

5. Technology use, which is the ability to understand and utilize technology appropriately.

6. The U.S. Department of Education notes that defining, measuring, and building these skills can be challenging.

VOICES FROM THE FIELD

Terry Miller—Franklin County Career and Technology Center in Pennsylvania, Chambersburg, PA

One of the activities that all level 2 students participate in is a mock interview day. We bring in 25 to 30 people from business and industry to conduct the interviews. We look for five to six people from businesses that are related to each of our career academies (Construction, Health Sciences, Sales and Service, STEM and Manufacturing, and Transportation) to conduct the interviews. A rubric is used by the interviewers to score students. These rubrics, along with written feedback from the interviewer, are returned to the teachers, who then review the information with each student. Students are made aware that this is for practice but also that many of the interviewers are looking to hire co-op students.

Students are required to dress appropriately, prepare a résumé and cover letter, answer several questions from the interviewer, and prepare questions to ask at the interview. We conduct about 125 interviews from 8:30 to 12:00. The interviewers are then treated to a catered lunch prepared by our culinary students.

The benefits to this activity are:

1. Students are introduced to and practice an interview, many for the first time.

2. Students must communicate with someone they do not know. This brings many students out of their comfort zone and prepares them for self-reliance. Communication becomes more than just a text message. Students learn that appearance, eye contact, body language, and tone are important components of communication.

3. Students become aware that they are approaching the end of the beginning. They are no longer learning to become good students but rather good adults.

4. Business and industry stakeholders have an opportunity to interview the workforce of the future. They have an opportunity to adapt or prepare for the changes that are taking place within the workforce.

5. Stakeholders have an opportunity to see the results of the training that the CTC is providing to students. The CTC has an opportunity to see if what they are teaching is relevant to business and industry stakeholders.

6. The school becomes the facilitator of workforce development and engages all stakeholders in the process. The public relations benefit of the activity cannot be overestimated.

Global Competence

As our economy and job market becomes ever more internationally connected, CTE programs should consider global competencies needed for success, both in getting jobs, but also in being promoted within a career field. As defined by the Asia Society (Mansilla & Jackson, 2011), global competence is "possession of the knowledge, skills, and dispositions to understand and act creatively on issues of global significance" (p. xiii). This includes four domains of global competence (Asia Society, 2021):

Figure 7.3 Four Domains of Global Competence

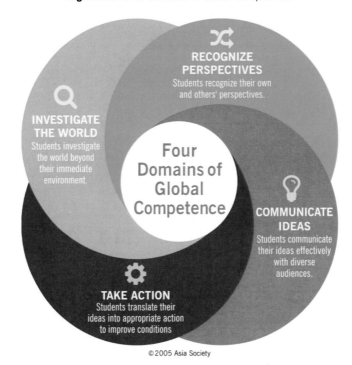

©2005 Asia Society

From "What is Global Competence" by the Center for Global Education, Asia Society, 2005. (https://asiasociety.org/education/what-global-competence) Copyright 2021 by the Asia Society. Reprinted with permission.

- *Investigate the World*: Students are engaged, curious, and interested in the world. They can ask and explore answers to globally significant "researchable" questions and problems. They can utilize information from a variety of local, national, and international sources and connect local problems to global concerns.
- *Recognize Perspectives*: Students recognize they have a perspective that others may or may not share. They can articulate a variety of viewpoints and understand how access to knowledge, technology, and resources can shape people's perspectives. They can also incorporate others' perspectives into their point of view.
- *Communicate Ideas*: Students understand that effective communication, both verbal and non-verbal, in culturally diverse settings is a key to working effectively in teams. They understand that audiences differ based on their place in the world (culture, faith, ideology, etc.). They are also technologically savvy in using technology to communicate with diverse audiences.
- *Take Action*: Students understand that they can make a difference in the world. They are able to recognize opportunities, alone or with others, to act ethically and creatively. They can assess the impact of their actions, taking into account a variety of perspectives and potential consequences.

Global competence is not a standalone set of skills but is embedded into employability skills. Working in a globally competitive economy means that students must have the employability skills to compete on an international scale. Whether working in domestic or international organizations, all companies have international influences or impacts. Consider where materials come from, where parts are made, where customers are located, or where employees come from. Thinking, communicating, and acting with an international perspective have become necessary for success in the global workforce (Asia Society, 2021).

State Perspective

The Kansas State Board of Education specifically identified goals for 21st-century teaching and learning. Through a P-20 advisory council, including policymakers, educators, and business leaders, the state has created a profile of the 21st-century learner. These profiles help define a vision for 21st-century learning in the state and assist educators to design or redesign schools or classrooms to prepare Kansas students for lifelong success (Kansas State Department of Education, 2008).

Profiles of the...

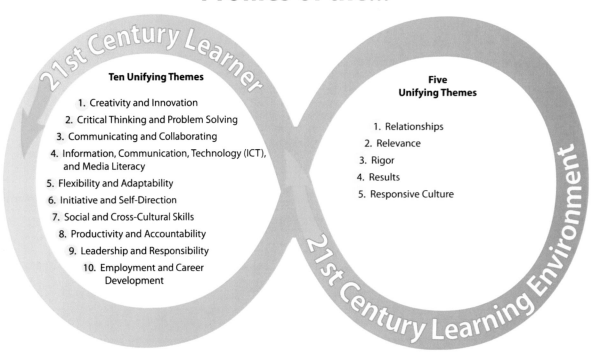

From "Profile of the 21st Century Learner and Profile of the 21st Century Learning Environment" by the Kansas State Department of Education, 2008. (https://community.ksde.org/Portals/25/Profile%20Bullets%2011-3-2008%20markup%20v5.pdf)—first page. In the public domain.

Curricular Planning

Just as we plan to teach technical content with embedded academic skills, instructors must plan for teaching and assessing employability skills. Many CTE programs utilize tools such as skills checklists, employability feedback forms, and employability rubrics to better reinforce employability expectations. These tools can be used by students as self-assessment opportunities or to provide feedback to each other, or these can be used by instructors for feedback or grading. Figures 7.4, 7.5, and 7.6 provide examples of these employability tools.

Figure 7.4 Tennessee Department of Education Employability Skills Checklist

Application of Academic and Technical Knowledge and Skills

☐ LITERACY: Read and comprehend relevant academic and technical texts

☐ MATH: Select and apply relevant mathematical concepts to solve problems and perform expected tasks

☐ INDUSTRY-SPECIFIC TECHNICAL SKILLS: Demonstrate industry-specific technical skills

☐ INDUSTRY-SPECIFIC SAFETY SKILLS: Demonstrate adherence to industry-specific safety regulations

Career Knowledge and Navigation Skills

☐ UNDERSTANDING CAREER PATHS: Plan and navigate education/career paths aligned to personal goals

☐ PLANNING: Develop and implement a personalized student learning plan

☐ REFLECTION: Reflect on experiences through creation of a personal portfolio

21st Century Learning and Innovation Skills

☐ CREATIVITY AND INNOVATION: Think creatively, Work creatively with others, Implement innovations

☐ CRITICAL THINKING & PROBLEM SOLVING: Reason effectively, Make judgments and decisions, Solve problems

☐ COMMUNICATION: Oral and written communications skills appropriate to the context, Listen effectively

☐ COLLABORATION: Exercise flexibility and willingness, assume shared responsibility, work with diverse teams

☐ INFORMATION LITERACY: Access and evaluate information, manage information accurately and ethically

☐ ICT (Information, Communications & Technology) LITERACY: Use technology effectively and appropriately

Personal and Social Skills

☐ INITIATIVE: Work independently; demonstrate agency, curiosity, and the ability to learn

☐ PROFESSIONALISM, ETHICS, AND INTERPERSONAL SKILLS: Demonstrate reliability, integrity, responsibility, proper etiquette, and ethical behavior

☐ CULTURAL AND GLOBAL COMPETENCE: Exhibit interpersonal and social skills that are respectful of cultural differences

☐ ADAPTABILITY AND FLEXIBILITY: Adapt flexibly to roles and responsibility; work effectively with ambiguity; change course as needed

☐ PRODUCTIVITY: Set goals and priorities and manage time and projects; exhibit punctuality, persistence, and precision and accuracy; complete projects to agreed-upon standards

From "Work-Based Learning Employability Skills Checklist" by the Tennessee Department of Education, 2016, Work-Based Learning Implementation Guide (https://documentcloud.adobe.com/link/review?uri=urn:aaid:scds:US:6b3bec4e-054a-41e9-8d93-897f40ff6931). In the public domain.

Figure 7.5 Employability Skills Assessment

Student: Employability Skills Self-Assessment

Student name: _____   School: _____

Career pathway/cluster (if applicable):   Grade: _____

_____

Please reflect and rate yourself on the skills being assessed at least twice during this WBL experience, in a first baseline review and in a second review near the end of the WBL experience. The feedback should happen every nine weeks. See Measuring and Reflecting Student Learning, page 12.*

0=No Exposure   1=Emerging   2=Developing   3=Proficient   4=Exemplary

EFFECTIVE RELATIONSHIPS	REVIEW 1	REVIEW 2	COMMENTS
Interpersonal skills			
☐ Teamwork			
☐ Customer service			
Personal qualities			
☐ Initiative			
☐ Adaptability			
☐ Professionalism			

WORKPLACE SKILLS	REVIEW 1	REVIEW 2	COMMENTS
Resource management			
☐ Manages time, money and personnel.			
Information use			
☐ Locates, organizes, analyzes, uses and communicates information.			
Communication			
☐ Verbal communication			
☐ Listening			
☐ Comprehends written material.			
☐ Conveys information in writing.			
Systems thinking			
☐ Understands, uses, monitors and improves systems.			
Technology use			
☐ Understands and uses technology.			

APPLIED KNOWLEDGE	REVIEW 1	REVIEW 2	COMMENTS
Applied academic skills			
☐ Academic application			
Critical thinking			
☐ Problem-solving			
☐ Creative thinking			
☐ Goal setting			

*Measuring and Reflecting Student Learning, Employability Skills Assessment, page 12, https://www.ksde.org/Portals/0/CSAS/CSAS%20Home/CTE%20Home/Measuring%20and%20Reflecting%20Student%20Learning%20%28002%29.pdf

WBL Department of Labor Fact Sheet https://www.dol.ks.gov/docs/default-source/workplace-laws-documents/kansas-work-based-learning-(002)-ef.pdf?sfvrsn=34008e1f_0

Liability agreement, Kansas WBL: Personalized Learning Plan, page 26.

Kansas State Department of Education | www.ksde.org   19

From "Kansas Work-Based Learning: Personalized Learning Plan" by Career, Standards and Assessment Services, Kansas State Department of Education, June, 2019. (https://www.ksde.org/Portals/0/CSAS/CSAS%20Home/CTE%20Home/Kansas%20Work-Based%20Learning_Personalized%20Learning%20Plan.pdf). In the public domain.

Figure 7.6 Essential Skills Awesome Careers Scoring Rubric for Employability Standards

Essential Skills Awesome Careers				Scoring Period			Student Name:	
Scoring Rubric for Employability Standards							Date of Completion:	
							Score out of 100 pts:	0
Criteria and Standards:	Descriptors:	20 Exceed Expectations Leader	18 Meets Expectations	15 Nearing Expectations/ Improving	10 Minimal Effort/ Not Near Expectations	Instructor Enter Score Below	Student Comments	Evaluator Comments
Instructions - hover over this box [1]			LINK TO EMPLOYABILITY STANDARDS					
Attendance & Personal Accountability (Employability Standards: 1a, 1c, 1d, 1e)	**Descriptor:** Absences, tardies, reliability and communication in situations where one is depended upon	Student is present, on time, communicates when needed, and may also come extra to help others/instructor	Student is absent or tardy no more than 1 time during month and communicates as needed. Work is complete	Student is absent or tardy no more than 2-3 times during grading period and communicates as needed. Most work is completed on time	Student is absent or tardy excessively (4 or more times during the grading period) and does not regularly complete work			
Critical Thinking & Creativity (Standards: 2b, 2c, 6a, 6d, 6e, 6f, 8a, 8c, 8d, 8e)	**Descriptor:** Applying appropriate skills under the right circumstances, demonstrating creativity and innovation, & utilizing critical thinking to make sense of problems and persevering in solving them	Student always displays excellent skills in Initiative, Goal Setting, Time Management, Personal Accountability, etc.	Student displays appropriate skills in Initiative, Goal Setting, Time Management, Personal Accountability, etc.	Student displays behavior that needs improvement in this area, including not completing multiple tasks in this grading period.	Student rarely or never shows skills in Initiative, Goal Setting, Time Management, Personal Accountability, etc.			
Integrity & Ethical Behavior (1f, 2a, 5a, 7a, 7b, 7c, 7d, 9a, 9d, 11d)	**Descriptor:** Acts as a responsible, contributing citizen, applies appropriate academic and technical skills, Considers the impact of their decisions, Employs valid and reliable strategies to situations, and models integrity, ethical leadership, and effective management	Student displays excellent ethical behavior and acts as a classroom leader in modeling and setting high expectations for peers.	Student displays ethical behavior under direct and indirect supervision	Student sometimes displays unethical behavior and/or has made a poor decision. An office referral may have happened during this grading period.	Student rarely displays ethical behavior and often makes very poor decisions.			
Interpersonal Skills (1b, 4d, 6b, 9c, 12a, 12b, 12c)	**Descriptor:** Contributing citizen through interactions with others, interaction with other with active listening, contributes ideas effectively in a group setting, positively impacts others, works productively in teams while using cultural/global competence	Student always displays exemplary interpersonal skills and takes on small or large leadership roles for his/her school or CTE program	Student displays appropriate skills in working with peers, adults or others	Student sometimes displays appropriate skills in working with peers, adults or others	Student rarely displays appropriate skills in working with peers, adults or others			
Communication & Technology (4a, 4b, 4c, 4e, 5b, 11b)	**Descriptor:** Communicating clearly, effectively and with reason, utilization of technology with the consideration of its social impact, and using technology to enhance productivity (safely)	Student always displays exemplary use of communication and technology. Acts as leader to others in its use	Student regularly displays exemplary use of communication and technology.	Student often displays exemplary communication & technology. However, student also has regular examples of misuse of communication or technology, but is working to get better	Student rarely displays adequate effort to improve in the use of communication and/or technology and makes frequent errors.			
	Total Points	100	90	75	50	0		
								LINK TO EMPLOYABILITY STANDARDS

https://drive.google.com/file/d/11PW5TLmEseIMuB-7v_SSkPlmi_tUzSj/view?usp=sharing

From Missouri Department of Elementary & Secondary Education, September 2021.

VOICES FROM THE FIELD

Bill Lieb—Automotive Instructor, Skills USA Adviser, The Career & Technology Center at Fort Osage, Independence, MO

Preparing students for careers beyond our programs starts in our programs. I believe we must model what the industry is expecting—professionalism, teamwork, and work ethic. For me, this starts with training students using the SkillsUSA Framework as a resource. I then have students evaluate themselves every three weeks with an employability rubric and then take a few moments to give feedback, just like a performance evaluation industry will give. I have found great success focusing on this part of students' development and teasing them with automotive-related activities. I have found, once established, program success and student engagement begin to really thrive.

Summary

Often CTE instructors will say that they "teach" employability skills, but without a solid plan to scaffold and assess this learning, efforts can fall flat. Building career exploration and development into CTE curriculum supports student career decision-making and planning. Utilizing the variety of models available for employability skill integration into CTE curriculum allows educators opportunities to reinforce the skills and behaviors employers want in the workplace. These models can guide the local discussion about employability skills to tailor checklist and rubric development for particular industries or state and local needs.

Integrating employability skills into CTE curriculum takes as much planning as integrating technical and academic skills. Using employability tools consistently through classroom expectations, lab activities, CTSO events, and work-based learning opportunities provides consistent communication and feedback to students on the skills and behaviors they need to demonstrate. Whether preparing college students or high school graduates for the workplace, the need to teach and for students to learn employability skills is vitally important to prepare a globally competent workforce.

ACTE's Quality CTE Program of Study Framework Connection

The concepts in this chapter related to the following elements of the *Quality CTE Program of Study Framework* developed by the Association for Career and Technical Education (read more about the framework in chapter 2, Imperatore & Hyslop, 2018):

- **Element 1: Standards-aligned and Integrated Curriculum**
  This element of the framework addresses the development of a program of study curriculum, including relevant knowledge and skills. The third criterion states that the CTE curriculum incorporates employability skill standards, such as skills in problem solving, critical thinking, teamwork, communications, and workplace etiquette. High-quality CTE programs should plan a curriculum that integrates workplace skills.

- **Element 3: Student Assessment**
  This element addresses knowledge and skills that should be assessed through CTE programs. In curricular planning in CTE, faculty need to ensure appropriate placement of both formative and summative assessments for scaffolding learning from the students' current knowledge level and continuing to build employability knowledge and skills. Curricular planning for high-quality CTE programs should include attention on how to appropriately assess employability skills students need for workplace success.

- **Element 9: Student Career Development**
  This element addresses strategies that help students gain career knowledge and engage in education and career planning and decision-making. Comprehensive career development is coordinated throughout the program of study, including within CTE courses and curriculum. As mentioned in the chapter, career readiness and workforce preparation begins with students having a knowledge of self, career interests, and skills.

References

Advance CTE. (2021). *The career ready practices.* https://careertech.org/career-ready-practices

American School Counselor Association (ASCA). (2021). *ASCA student standards: Mindsets and behaviors for student success.* https://www.schoolcounselor.org/getmedia/7428a787-a452-4abb-afec-d78ec77870cd/mindsets-behaviors.pdf

Association for Career and Technical Education. (2021, December). *Career and technical education's role in career guidance* [Issue Brief]. https://www.acteonline.org/wp-content/uploads/2018/03/Guidance_issuebrief.pdf

Asia Society. (2021). *What is global competence?* https://asiasociety.org/education/what-global-competence

Battelle for Kids. (2020). *P21 partnership for 21st century learning.* https://www.battelleforkids.org/networks/p21/frameworks-resources

Common Core State Standards Initiative. (2021). *Preparing America's students for success.* http://www.corestandards.org/

Imperatore, C. & Hyslop, A. (2018, October). *2018 quality program of study framework.* https://www.acteonline.org/wp-content/uploads/2019/01/HighQualityCTEFramework2018.pdf

Kansas State Department of Education. (2008). *21st century skills.* https://community.ksde.org/Default.aspx?tabid=3203

Kansas State Department of Education. (2019, June). *Kansas work-based learning: Personalized learning plan.* https://www.ksde.org/Portals/0/CSAS/CSAS%20Home/CTE%20Home/Kansas%20Work-Based%20Learning_Personalized%20Learning%20Plan.pdf

Kansas State Department of Education. (2008). *Profile of the 21st century learner and profile of the 21st century learning environment.* https://community.ksde.org/Portals/25/Profile%20Bullets%2011-3-2008%20markup%20v5.pdf

Loup, C., Kornegay, J., & Morgan, J. (2017, January). Career exploration and soft skills: Preparing students for success. Techniques Magazine, p. 14–17. https://www.acteonline.org/wp-content/uploads/2018/05/Techniques-January2017-CareerExplorationSoftSkills.pdf

Mansilla, J. B., & Jackson, A. (2011). *Educating for global competence: Preparing our youth to engage the world.* Asia Society. https://asiasociety.org/files/book-globalcompetence.pdf

Missouri Department of Elementary & Secondary Education. (2021, September). *Essential careers employability scoring guide.* https://dese.mo.gov/media/pdf/memo-sts-9th-and-10gh-grade-curriculum-guidance

National Association of Colleges and Employers. (2021). *Career readiness defined.* https://www.naceweb.org/career-readiness/competencies/career-readiness-defined/

Perkins Collaborative Resource Network. (2021). *Employability skills.* https://cte.ed.gov/initiatives/employability-skills-framework

Perkins Collaborative Resource Network. (n.d.). *Employability skills framework.* https://s3.amazonaws.com/PCRN/docs/Employability_Skills_Framework_OnePager_20180212.pdf

Tennessee Department of Education. (2016). Work-based learning employability skills checklist. In *Work-Based Learning Implementation Guide.* https://documentcloud.adobe.com/link/review?uri=urn:aaid:scds:US:6b3bec4e-054a-41e9-8d93-897f40ff6931

PART III

■

CTE LEARNERS

 ## CHAPTER 8: FOUNDATIONS OF STUDENT-CENTERED LEARNING

Chapter 8 explores the foundations of student-centered learning and its contexts in CTE. This chapter examines several noteworthy research studies on the topic, which provide insight on the value and impact of student-centered learning as a whole. The authors illustrate how experiential education can be utilized as a research-based best practice to promote student-centered learning and also highlight several approaches, such as CTSOs and technology integration, which facilitate student-centered learning. By utilizing the methods discussed in this chapter, readers will enrich student engagement and enhance learning and occupational skill development.

 ## CHAPTER 9: APPROACHES TO INTEGRATED LEARNING

Chapter 9 explores numerous approaches to integrated learning, which are utilized in CTE, such as project-based learning, work-based learning, cooperative education, service learning through community engagement, and the career academy model. Each of these approaches is discussed in detail, with a special emphasis placed on student-centered learning. The items discussed in this chapter would be particularly valuable to CTE instructors, career and technical educators, school administrators, work-based field experience coordinators, career guidance professionals, and policymakers interested in improving student learning and technical skill development.

 CHAPTER 10: DIVERSITY IN CAREER AND TECHNICAL EDUCATION

Chapter 10 highlights the diversity among CTE students, and representation in educational programming is essential to ensure that all learners have opportunities to fully engage in high-quality CTE programs. This includes curricula that are free of bias, nondiscriminatory, and appropriately differentiated for everyone. Therefore, this chapter emphasizes the importance of differentiated instruction and culturally relevant curriculum. Social justice education is also explored, as well as equity in nontraditional careers and considerations for adult learners. Applying the information provided in this chapter is essential to advancing high-quality CTE programs and promoting access for everyone.

 CHAPTER 11: STUDENTS WITH DISABILITIES IN CTE

Chapter 11 investigates the topic of students with disabilities (SWD) in CTE. The author highlights that studies have revealed that SWDs who participate in CTE have a greater likelihood of success. Therefore, this chapter provides an overview of applicable laws related to SWDs and how these impact CTE programs and transition services to help students achieve their post-school goals. Accommodations and modifications are also explored in context, as well as Universal Design for Learning (UDL), which ensures that all students can participate in high-quality CTE. This chapter is an outstanding resource for CTE professionals who are interested in enhancing the quality of CTE programming for SWDs and beyond.

Chapter 8

■

FOUNDATIONS OF STUDENT-CENTERED LEARNING

Mark D. Threeton—Pennsylvania State University
Kevin S. Elliott—Pittsburg State University

Introduction

Have you ever attended a conference and observed disengaged participants in the session? Likely so. Perhaps, you were the disengaged participant in this instance. How about this? Have you ever been teaching, conducting a training session, or delivering professional development, and somewhere along the way, you lost your audience? Whether you experienced this disengagement as a conference participant, student, or even as a career and technical educator, it is clear that the learning experience was lacking something. Disengagement can manifest itself in many different forms and for a multitude of reasons. Disengaged participants at a conference might just get up and leave because the content of the session was not what they expected, while a disengaged student in a CTE program might fail to interact with others, could appear off task, or perhaps just fall asleep.

Since the beginning of CTE in schools, educators have been concerned about the transfer of learning. Each year, career and technical educators are tasked with providing quality instruction to the next generation of technical professionals. This task appears to be particularly challenging today, given the diverse levels of student ability, age, interest, learning styles and personality types, etc., which simultaneously exist in a single CTE program (Threeton & Walter, 2013). This is particularly important to comprehend, as each student has different learning needs, which must be addressed to promote the transfer of learning. For this reason, a student-centered learning approach holds great promise for students within CTE.

Grounded in the principles of constructivism, student-centered learning is an educational method, which allows each individual student to fully engage in the learning process. It provides a foundation where students build new knowledge, skills, and attitudes based on previous learning experiences. While utilizing this method, the teacher often accepts the role of a facilitator, thus encouraging each student to be actively engaged and responsible for their learning. While student-centered learning can be structured in many different ways, a common element among all approaches is that students are actively engaged in the educational process. This engagement involves a combination of doing, feeling, watching, and thinking activities while constructing new meaning and application from the learning experience.

In an effort to provide further insight on this important topic, this chapter will provide an overview of student-centered learning by examining noteworthy research on this topic, as well as exploring the integration of CTSOs and technology, which facilitate student-centered learning. It is the hope of the authors that the content within this chapter will highlight the foundation of student-centered learning while promoting advancements for the future of CTE.

A Foundation for Student-Centered Learning

Over the years there have been several noteworthy studies conducted, which provide insight into the value of student-centered learning as a whole. One such example was published by the Stanford Center for Opportunity Policy in Education (2014). This study utilized a cross-case analysis of four urban high schools, which employed a student-centered learning approach. This investigation revealed that students at all four institutions outperformed a majority of their counterparts' level of student achievement, graduation rates, college prep course completion, and college persistence, in comparison to students at more traditional schools within their representative communities with similar populations. These findings were particularly evident in students of color, low socioeconomic backgrounds, and English language learners (Friedlaender et al., 2014).

Another noteworthy study was published by the UMass Donahue Institute and the Nellie Mae Foundation (2016) and found that a majority of the participating high schools that utilized a student-centered learning approach embracing personalized learning; competency-based learning; anytime, anywhere learning; and a framework of student ownership of their learning reported higher levels of student engagement and better retention of student knowledge from the curriculum as compared to traditional education settings. However, obstacles encountered by educators and administrators in participating institutions did hinder implementation of the anytime, anywhere learning framework, which was highlighted in this study (Shultz et al., 2016).

A study conducted by the RAND Corporation (Pane et al., 2015) investigated approximately 11,000 students at 62 institutions, which utilized personalized learning methods and mainly served learners from low socioeconomic backgrounds. The research also analyzed approximately 30 study schools that employed student-centered strategies, which included learner profiles, learning pathways, competency-based progression, flexible learning environments, and an emphasis on college and career readiness. The results of the study revealed that students made significant improvements in English language arts and mathematics as compared to their counterparts at similar institutions.

Similarly, in 2017 the RAND Corporation (Pane et al., 2017) conducted another investigation and found that students active in schools that promote personalized learning strategies had modest improvements in mathematics and reading as compared to their peers at similar institutions. Furthermore, the study revealed that the more an institution employed personalized learning strategies, the more positive the impact on student achievement.

These findings are significant when considering the value and impact of student-centered learning approaches. Specifically, the related literature on this subject has revealed several key takeaways, which are invaluable to consider while implementing student-centered learning strategies in CTE. First, student-centered learning more often than not involves the educator transitioning to the role of a facilitator. Second, students are more likely to be successful when the educational experience is personalized to align with their interests, ambitions, and learning needs. Third, students are given a voice at the table (i.e., ownership in the learning experience).

Fourth, when students are actively engaged in the learning experience, they tend to gain higher levels of student achievement.

Thankfully, CTE provides a multitude of opportunities to implement student-centered learning methods, which promote the educational benefits noted within the related literature. While comprehending the value and positive impact of student-centered learning is critical, some CTE educators may struggle to actually implement this framework appropriately in their program. This is certainly understandable, given the complexities associated with teaching a wide-ranging program of study, as well as the assessment accountability demands of the day.

Experiential Learning Theory

David Kolb's Experiential Learning Theory (ELT) (1984) provides a strong foundation from which student-centered learning can be structured within any CTE program.

Kolb's ELT is built on six principles (Kolb & Kolb, 2005) that include:

1. Learning is best conceived as a process, not in terms of outcomes. To improve learning, the primary focus should be on engaging students in a process that best enhances their learning, a process that includes feedback on the effectiveness of their learning efforts.
2. All learning is relearning. Learning is best facilitated by a process that draws out the students' beliefs and ideas about a topic so that they can be examined, tested, and integrated with new, more refined ideas.
3. Learning requires the resolution of conflicts between dialectically opposed modes of adaptation to the world. Conflict, differences, and disagreement are what drive the learning process. In the process of learning, one is called upon to move back and forth between opposing modes of reflection and action and feeling and thinking.
4. Learning is a holistic process of adaptation to the world. Not just the result of cognition, learning involves the integrated functioning of the total person thinking, feeling, perceiving, and behaving.
5. Learning results from synergetic transactions between the person and the environment.
6. Learning is the process of creating knowledge. (p. 194)

Kolb's ELT (1984) contains a cycle of four modes of grasping and transforming experience, which help to promote active engagement and transfer of learning. The four modes of Kolb's ELT are:

1. Concrete Experience (CE), where the student actively engages in the learning experience;
2. Reflective Observation (RO), where the student observes and reflects on the learning experience;
3. Abstract Conceptualization (AC), where the student draws conclusions/establishes generalizations from the learning experience; and
4. Active Experimentation (AE), where the student applies the learning experience in a new experiment or activity.

While designing student-centered learning strategies, career and technical educators may wish to integrate these elements in a particular order; however, education literature has revealed that the learning process can begin at any one of the four modes (Smith, 2001; Kolb & Fry, 1975). The import-ant item to comprehend is that the experiential learning process should be structured as a continuous cycle. As subject matter experts, all career and technical educators must utilize their best professional judgment on how to cycle through the four modes of experiential learning based on the structure of the occupational concept being taught. By utilizing this student-centered learning model as a tool, educators will enhance the quality of the educational experience for the learner (see Figure 8.1).

Figure 8.1 Kolb's Experiential Learning Cycle

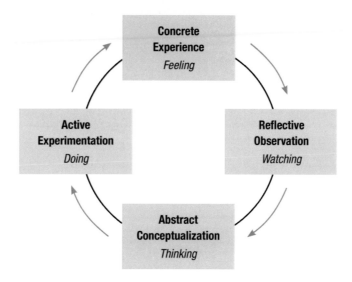

Based on the ELT, David Kolb (1984) identified four learning styles, which align with the four modes of experiential learning. Kolb's learning styles include:

1. Converging, in which AC and AE are the predominant learning preferences;
2. Diverging, in which CE and RO are the predominant learning preferences;
3. Assimilating, in which AC and RO are the predominant learning preferences; and
4. Accommodating, in which CE and AE are the predominant learning preferences.

Kolb's ETL utilizes a Learning Style Inventory (LSI) to assess predominant learning preferences in individuals. The LSI provides an interesting analysis of each individual's approaches to learning, along with a discussion section, which offers valuable information to promote enhanced learning. Using the LSI as a tool, career and technical educators can personalize their student-centered learning activities for each pupil within a formal or nonformal educational setting. It is important to note that the results of the LSI identify the strength of learning preference, not the degree of learning style used.

Over the last few years the concept of learning styles has received some criticism, given that it is impossible to pinpoint one preference or "style" of learning for each individual. Furthermore, if educators customize pedagogy to align with each individual's style, they will be hindering the learning process for students by not exposing them to different types of learning experiences. These are valid arguments; thus, it is important to note that there are no right or wrong classifications or styles of learning. Everyone uses each learning preference or style to some degree. By utilizing a student-centered learning approach based on the revolving four modes of grasping and transforming experience found in the experiential learning cycle (i.e., Figure 1), a career and technical educator promotes enhanced learning and occupational skill development for all students.

Given that experiential learning provides a structure for the learning by doing philosophy of CTE, it is critical to examine specific instances where it is commonly used in our field. As an example, project-based learning, work-based learning, service learning, and community engagement strategies all embrace experiential learning as a foundation from which to facilitate occupational skill development. Additionally, CTSOs and technology integration support the implementation of student-centered learning. CTSO integration and technology integration will be the focus of the remainder of this chapter, and chapter 9 will focus on providing a context for the application of several instructional strategies in CTE, as well as voices from career and technical educators on what is working well for them in their programs.

Career and Technical Student Organization Integration

As a new CTE teacher, you may be provided the opportunity to implement another student-centered learning concept by advising a CTSO as an intra-curricular part of your CTE program. In fact, in many states, having a CTSO is a required component of state-approved CTE programs. Advising has many challenges. However, when the CTE teacher develops a CTSO that supports student learning while promoting college and career-readiness skills, it can be beneficial to the students, the advisor, the institution, and even the community.

An "effective" CTSO may look very different from one institution to another. Community expectations, support from industry partners, and student involvement can all vary significantly. As a new advisor, it is imperative to do your homework. Learn the culture of the community, as well as the expectations and protocols of the institution.

Thompson et al. (2003) provided a model (Figure 8.2 below) that can help a new teacher visualize how CTSOs are a part of an effective CTE program. One key takeaway from the model is how the three components overlap.

Figure 8.2 Relationship Between CTE and CTSOs: Integral Part of CTE Programs (Thompson et al., 2003; Vaughn, 1999)

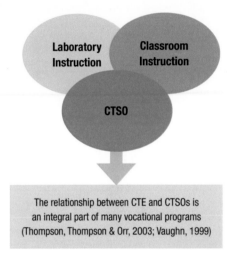

This graphic represents how any one concept does not have to be presented to students independently. Creating content, which allows all three components to support one another, can provide opportunities for more relevant learning in CTE. The CTE teacher creates relevance by integrating the classroom theory in the lab and CTSO, the CTSO components in the lab and classroom, and the lab content with the classroom and CTSO. When a CTE teacher utilizes this model, students are provided exposure to concepts in multiple methods, which can greatly enhance learning and retention.

Several distinct organizations are available to provide meaningful CTSO experiences for CTE students and programs. These CTSOs have stated foci in different areas of CTE. In some cases, teachers may choose to affiliate their programs with one CTSO over another based on such factors as cost and fit with their students and curriculum. The following is a list of CTSOs recognized by the National Coordinating Council for Career and Technical Student Organizations (2021):

- **BPA—Business Professionals of America**
  BPA focuses on students who are "pursuing careers in business management, office administration, information technology and other related career fields" (CTSOs, 2021a, para. 1)

- **DECA**
  DECA is focused on preparing "emerging leaders and entrepreneurs in marketing, finance, hospitality and management" (CTSOs, 2021b, para. 1).

- **FCCLA—Family, Career, and Community Leaders of America**
  FCCLA focuses on "addressing important personal, work, and societal issues through Family and Consumer Sciences education" (CTSOs, 2021c, para. 1).

- **FBLA—PBL—Future Business Leaders of America—Phi Beta Lambda**
  FBLA is focused on "preparing for careers in business and business-related fields" (CTSOs, 2021d, para. 1).

- **HOSA—Health Occupations Student Association**
  The focus of HOSA is "to promote career opportunities in the healthcare industry and to enhance the delivery of quality health care to all people" (CTSOs, 2021e, para. 1).

- **National FFA Organization**
  The National FFA organization (formerly Future Farmers of America) "envisions a future in which all agricultural education students will discover their passions and build on that insight to chart a course for their education, careers and personal futures" (CTSOs, 2021f, para. 1)

- **SkillsUSA**
  SkillsUSA "is a partnership of students, teachers and industry working together to ensure America has a skilled workforce" (CTSOs, 2021g, para. 1).

- **TSA—Technology Student Association**
  The Technology Student Association is "devoted exclusively to the needs of students interested in science, technology, engineering, and mathematics (STEM)" (CTSOs, 2021h, para. 1).

CTE instructors who understand the differences in CTSOs and the best match for their individual situation can begin the process of choosing the level of participation in the organization related to available curriculum, time, and resources.

If you are in the position to select a CTSO for your students, questions to consider include:

- How many other CTSOs are there in your institution?
- How was your CTSO operating prior to you becoming the advisor?
  - Was it active?
  - Was it focused on the objectives determined by the state and national advisors?
- Is there money available to participate in travel and competitions associated with your respective CTSO?
- What is the current perception of fundraising in your school and community?
- How will your leaders be selected?
- Are there other chapters of your CTSO in the area or district?
  - What obligations are there for participation at the local and district/area level?
  - Are there local and district/area level leadership and competitive events?
- Is there a required outfit or official dress for students to wear at events?
  - Who pays for it?
  - How many do you need?
- How much are dues?
  - Local
  - State
  - National

The prompts listed above should provide opportunities for the CTE instructor to make decisions regarding his or her role and level of engagement as a CTSO advisor the first year or two in the classroom. It is recommended to prioritize that engagement based on teaching responsibilities and other duties. Duties outside the classroom can be a large contributing factor for burnout early in one's teaching career, so take care if starting a CTSO as a new teacher (Dainty, 2012).

A final consideration for your level of engagement in CTSOs is how the content of the organization will be integrated into the curriculum. CTSOs are designed to be an integral part of the CTE curriculum, not as a separate add-on. For example, will students be encouraged to excel in competitions during class time? Will all students be exposed to the majority of the content and supplement their learning of the material with the multitude of opportunities CTSOs provide? There are many different perspectives on these questions. It is recommended each CTE teacher explore details of advising a CTSO and mesh it with the curriculum and the school culture and community in an effort to benefit the most students.

VOICES FROM THE FIELD

Rachael Mann—Keynote Speaker, Author, Consultant Phoenix, AZ

CTSOs are the most crucial aspect of the education journey for many students. I have been involved with CTSOs since high school as a chapter officer, advisor, state director, judge, and CTSO trainer and coach. I have witnessed the many testimonials of former students who have experienced the truly life-changing trajectory of belonging to a student organization. Incorporating your CTSO into the curriculum is not only a great way to introduce students to the CTSO, but it also increases student engagement. In turn, it will ensure that recruitment and retainment are high.

Another benefit of an intra-curricular program is that competitive events are used as part of lesson and unit plans to address the standards while getting kids excited about what they are doing! Additional components of an effective CTSO, such as community service, leadership, and event planning, can all be aligned to meet the course content and the CTSO Program of Work simultaneously. Students quickly forget that they are learning as they are so engaged in what is happening. Many students will refer to their CTE class as the name of their CTSO.

If you are new to your role as a CTE teacher, take small steps to integrate your CTSO into the curriculum. Focus on adding only one aspect at a time. Each semester, you will build on the previous work. CTSOs are designed to be student-led, with the adviser/teacher as the guiding light. Remember to allow members to take an active role in leading the CTSO activities, whether within the school day, during lunch, or after school. Ultimately, the CTSO experience will make your role as a teacher and adviser easier, rather than adding to your workload.

When preparing your learning space, make sure that the CTSO is visible in your bulletin boards, posters, and other spaces in the room. When students can visibly see the announcements, peer recognition, and other aspects of the CTSO, they will be excited to get involved and join as members.

Technology Integration

Industry Technology

Technology has always been a part of the CTE classroom. Many of the CTE areas focus on teaching students the newest and most innovative technologies in order to produce or maintain products across many industries. The aircraft and medical industries are two great examples of areas with fast-changing technology designed to provide better service to the public. As new technologies arise, so does the need for qualified technicians. It is critical for CTE programs to provide the necessary skills to students in order to allow them to fill these positions competently.

The theories associated with many technical tasks, such as mechanical and electrical tasks, are critical to know but often taught from a text. The application of the theory is frequently provided through training students to use equipment, which utilizes the most current technology. When this is not possible, technology can be used to simulate application through the use of a virtual environment. Even so, reliance on technology for training can be a challenge for some schools from a financial perspective. Up-to-date pieces of equipment or simulation software may exceed the entire budget allocated to programs, and then they might not provide sufficient access based on the number of students in a class or program. For many CTE instructors, it is critical to engage in partnerships, grants, or other agreements to offset costs and keep resources current.

In addition to purchasing technology, it is critical that CTE instructors stay current, both in their knowledge of industry changes in training and in the use of existing and emerging technology. Taking time to attend conferences and workshops, which teach new tips or tricks to share with students, is vital. If you are able to obtain updated or new technology, be sure to include training as a part of that acquisition. Having a piece of highly technical equipment is nice, but being able to utilize it in your program and having students use it effectively is the key to preparing them to transition to industry.

Online Learning

While these are some of the challenges associated with keeping current technology in the hands of students, the COVID-19 pandemic put technology and online learning at the top of many educators' lists of challenges. Navigating new software, accessing reliable internet service, and developing engaging lessons using technology were items that fell into the laps of teachers almost overnight. Worrying about the quality or relevance of equipment in shops and labs became a secondary concern for teachers and students. The focus suddenly shifted from trying to manage equipment in the regular facility to trying to teach with students and equipment in different locations.

During the pandemic, it was not at all feasible for most students to continue using the technology that had been at their fingertips only a few weeks earlier. For example, welding instructors could not teach welding skills because most students did not have welders at home or in another accessible location. Automotive instructors were tasked with trying to teach skills online without mock-ups or demonstrations normally used to allow students the opportunity to touch and manipulate car components. It was the same for culinary and carpentry instructors. The barriers introduced by distance learning were difficult, and sometimes impossible, to overcome.

Throughout the challenges the pandemic presented, CTE teachers continued to do the best they could to teach their technical content. Technology played a huge role in facilitating instruction for many technical skills. Programs like Zoom and Microsoft Teams provided a virtual classroom where students and teachers could convene and work, but not risk illness. Videos and simulations were more commonly utilized to help students understand the concepts they could no longer touch. Lessons and reviews were covered with programs like Kahoot or Quizlet in an effort to make the content engaging. Overall, teachers and students did their best to make the most of a difficult situation, but in some cases, students were not able to receive the hands-on training so critical to completing technical programs.

Regardless of the circumstances, technology plays an increasingly significant role in CTE. If the focus of a CTE program is to prepare students on industry-standard, highly technical equipment, then students need access to these technologies. It is imperative that the teacher look for innovative ways to provide students with hands-on, relevant experiences, which will increase their employability. Working with industry partners and utilizing advisory boards can positively impact the opportunities CTE teachers can provide students in their programs.

Students often excel with technology and are able to pick up new concepts quickly. Many have never been without a phone or a tablet, and it is a very normal part of their world. Students often know if there is technology associated with the CTE curriculum, and when they are not able to use relevant technology due to cost, availability, or the lack of teacher expertise, a CTE program could be placed at a disadvantage. If students see the instructor as not being current with the technology used in an industry, it can affect enrollment, classroom management, and threaten the viability of a program.

As an instructor in a CTE program, do your best to provide opportunities for students and stay current in your training. Maybe the most important thing to do with technology is to embrace it and find ways to utilize emerging technologies and online learning tools in your classroom.

VOICES FROM THE FIELD

Karen Pitts—Interactive Creative Educational Videos (iCEV) Curriculum Consultant, Clarksville, TN

Some students simply do not fit well into a traditional classroom setting. Online learning allows students the flexibility to create their own classroom and manage their own learning. This is a little scary for some teachers, as they were trained to stand and deliver, but with student access to computers and all the internet has to offer, it is important students navigate the online world effectively, learning how to determine what are credible sources and how to avoid cyber dangers. This is our world today, and it is extremely important that educators become comfortable in the digital age so they can help students learn in all settings.

Summary

Career and technical educators are charged with the task of providing quality instruction to the next generation of technical professionals. Needless to say, this is a challenging task to accomplish. The purpose of this chapter was to provide an overview of student-centered learning methods in CTE by exploring several student-centered instructional approaches and providing a context for the application of these instructional strategies in CTE. By utilizing the methods discussed in this chapter appropriately, career and technical educators will enrich student engagement and promote enhanced learning and occupational skill development.

ACTE's Quality CTE Program of Study Framework Connection

The concepts in this chapter related to the following elements of the *Quality CTE Program of Study Framework* developed by the Association for Career and Technical Education (read more about the framework in chapter 2, Imperatore & Hyslop, 2018):

- **Element 5: Engaging Instruction**

  This element addresses instructional strategies that will support student attainment of relevant knowledge and skills. Instruction should be delivered in a student-centered learning environment to support students in gaining relevant knowledge and skills. Relevant equipment and technology can also be utilized to support student-centered learning.

- **Element 7: Facilities, Equipment, Technology, and Materials**

  This element addresses the alignment, appropriateness, and safety of the physical and material components of a CTE program. Facilities, equipment, technology, and materials should align to curriculum and reflect current workplace practices and requirements, and technology can be used to enhance student-centered learning.

- **Element 10: Career and Technical Student Organizations**

  This element addresses CTSOs and the activities they should engage in as an integral part of the instructional program. CTSOs are an integral part of CTE programs of study curriculum. Organization activities can reinforce relevant technical, academic, and employability knowledge and skills and provide opportunities for students to participate in community and school service activities.

References

Career and Technical Student Organizations (CTSOs). (2021). *About CTSOs.* https://www.ctsos.org

Career and Technical Student Organizations (CTSOs). (2021a). *Business professionals of America.* https://www.ctsos.org/ctsos-2/business-professionals-of-america/

Career and Technical Student Organizations (CTSOs). (2021b). *DECA.* https://www.ctsos.org/ctsos-2/deca/

Career and Technical Student Organizations (CTSOs). (2021c). *Family, careers and community leaders of America.* https://www.ctsos.org/ctsos-2/fccla/

Career and Technical Student Organizations (CTSOs). (2021d). *Future business leaders of America-phi beta lambda.* https://www.ctsos.org/ctsos-2/fbla/

Career and Technical Student Organizations (CTSOs). (2021e). *HOSA—future health professionals.* https://www.ctsos.org/ctsos-2/hosa/

Career and Technical Student Organizations (CTSOs). (2021f). *National FFA organization.* https://www.ctsos.org/ctsos-2/ffa/

Career and Technical Student Organizations (CTSOs). (2021g). *SkillsUSA.* https://www.ctsos.org/ctsos-2/skillsusa/

Career and Technical Student Organizations (CTSOs). (2021h). *Technology student association.* https://www.ctsos.org/ctsos-2/tsa/

Dainty, J. D. (2012). *Predicting influential factors of secondary career and technical education teachers' intent to stay in the profession.* [Doctoral dissertation, University of Arkansas]. ScholarWorks@UARK. https://scholarworks.uark.edu/etd/290

Friedlaender, D., Burns, D., Lewis-Charp, H., Cook-Harvey, C. M., & Darling-Hammond, L. (2014). *Student-centered schools: Closing the opportunity gap* (Research Brief). Stanford Center for Opportunity Policy in Education. http://edpolicy.stanford.edu/projects/633

Imperatore, C. & Hyslop, A. (2018, October). *2018 ACTE quality program of study framework.* Association for Career and Technical Education. https://www.acteonline.org/wp-content/uploads/2019/01/HighQualityCTEFramework2018.pdf

Kolb, A. Y., & Kolb, D. A. (2005). Learning style and learning spaces: Enhancing experiential learning in higher education. *Academy of Management Learning & Education, 4*(2), 192–212. https://doi.org/10.5465/AMLE.2005.17268566

Kolb, D. A., & Fry, R. (1975). Toward an applied theory of experiential learning (C. Cooper Ed.). *Theories of group process.* John Wiley.

Kolb, D. A. (1984). *Experiential learning: Experience as the source of learning and development.* Prentice Hall.

Pane, J. F., Elizabeth D., Steiner, M. D., Hamilton, B., & Hamilton, L. S. (2015). *Continued progress: Promising evidence on personalized learning.* RAND Corporation. https://www.rand.org/pubs/research_reports/RR1365.html

Pane, J. F., Steiner, E., Baird, M., Hamilton, L., & Pane, J. D. (2017). *Informing progress: Insights on personalized learning implementation and effects.* RAND Corporation. https://www.rand.org/pubs/research_reports/RR2042.html

Smith, M. K. (2001). David A. Kolb on experiential learning. E*ncyclopedia of Informal Education, 1–15.* http://www.infed.org/b-explrn.htm.

Thompson, C., Thompson, D. E., & Orr, B. (2003). A factor analysis of variables affecting CTSO advisor's satisfaction. *Journal of Family and Consumer Sciences Education, 21*(2), 1–9.

Threeton, M. D., & Walter, R. A. (2013). *Managing technical programs and facilities.* Whittier Publications.

Vaughn, P. R. (1999). *Handbook for advisors of vocational student organizations* (4th ed.). The American Association for Vocational Instructional Materials.

Chapter 9

■

APPROACHES TO INTEGRATED LEARNING

Mark D. Threeton—Pennsylvania State University
Kevin S. Elliott—Pittsburg State University
Edward C. Fletcher Jr.—The Ohio State University

Introduction

With an understanding of the foundations of student-centered learning, the next question is, "How do I do that?" At the core of student-centered learning is the common element that students are actively engaged in the educational process. This is an integrated approach, which involves a combination of doing, feeling, watching, and thinking activities while constructing new meaning and application from the learning experience. With the instructor often acting as a guide or facilitator, students construct their own understanding as they build new knowledge, skills, and attitudes based on previous learning experiences.

Chapter 9 will focus on the exploration of key applications of the student-centered learning framework, such as within project-based learning, work-based learning, cooperative education, service learning through community engagement, and the career academy model. Regardless of the approach or approaches a teacher chooses to implement in the curriculum, the benefits realized in student learning can be substantial. These approaches are valuable to CTE instructors, CTSO advisors, career and technical teacher educators, school administrators, work-based field experience coordinators, career guidance professionals, and policymakers interested in improving student learning and occupational skill development.

Project-based Learning

Project-based learning is a structured educational experience in which students apply knowledge, skills, and attitudes to develop and refine competence by creating occupationally related products (Threeton & Walter, 2013). Some examples of projects within CTE would include building a house within a construction trades program, designing an advertising campaign in a commercial and advertising arts program, baking a four-tier cake in a baking and pastry arts program, and creating an eco-wind generator in an emerging energy and infrastructure program. While the value of project-based learning is well understood in CTE, there is often confusion about what constitutes a well-structured project. Therefore, selecting and assigning high-quality projects is a major responsibility of career and technical educators.

According to Mergendoller (2021), high-quality project-based learning (HQPBL) involves six essential criteria, which include:

1. *Intellectual challenge and accomplishment:* This includes students learning how to think critically and strive for excellence.
2. *Authenticity:* Students' culture, lives, and future are connected to projects in meaningful and relevant ways.
3. *Public Product:* Work that students accomplish is publicly displayed, discussed, and critiqued.
4. Collaboration: Students work together collaboratively on projects, as well as receive guidance from mentors and experts.
5. *Project Management:* Projects are managed through a structure that enables them to effectively work from initiation to completion.
6. *Reflection:* Students reflect based on their work and learning throughout the project experience.

It is critical for career and technical educators to comprehend that the better the implementation of these six criteria, the higher quality the project will be for the student (Mergendoller, 2021). While projects are a very effective experiential learning method, a wise career and technical educator works collaboratively with their occupational advisory committee in determining when and where projects are appropriate.

VOICES FROM THE FIELD

Benjamin Leskovansky—Insight Pennsylvania Cyber Charter School, Exton, PA

In my game design course, we applied project-based learning (PBL) throughout the entirety of the course. One project in particular involved designing a video game that mimicked the card game 31 (Scat). Students were assigned to build the video game from scratch and, if not familiar with the original card game, had to learn the rules that would be programmed into the video game. Certain assets (i.e., images) for the video game were provided for the students to use, but they also had the freedom to create their own.

In this particular class, we had only a few students on the roster, so we approached each project as a group with the expectation that each student would create their own project. Ideally, if you have the numbers, you can split the students into individual groups, but PBL still works with a small class as well. I found that PBL, especially with a video game design project, allowed for great creativity and innovation. It encouraged students to ask questions, conduct their own research, and brainstorm ways to make their projects (games) unique.

Within our small group, we would have group discussions, share ideas, and help each other trouble-shoot when needed. This sort of collaboration led to great teachable moments, some of which would not have been realized without the PBL approach. Specific to this project, we would even watch and play the game 31 (Scat) together in order to get an idea of how to play and discuss what rules were involved and how we would program them within the video game. Again, this fostered great communication and collaboration within our PBL group.

I truly believe an experience like PBL replicates industry in many ways and can give students a chance to improve their employability skills, especially within CTE.

Mindi Tobias—Central Pennsylvania Institute of Science and Technology, Pleasant Gap, PA

I use a project-based learning activity that I titled "Fabrication of a Provisional Crown" at the end of the year with my junior class. It is an extremely difficult task to master, and it is only covered in one paragraph in the students' textbook. I feel this is not enough information to completely understand the process, so I use the project to supplement the textbook. I break this project into six weeks. The first two weeks include some instruction with both summative and formative assessments, and the final weeks involve the students mostly working on their own to practice, experiment, create a presentation, and submit the final provisional for the tooth in question.

To intrigue the students, I start the project by having a local dentist come in to talk about his need for quality provisionals and about how perfecting this task can lead to a higher salary. I then provide each student a journal to do the work in and give general information about the project, including the project's driving question: As the dental assistant, can you fabricate a temporary crown for tooth #30 for a 62-year-old male patient? This will lead into a discussion of the project description: You will need to complete all steps of preparation, design, and completing a temporary crown insert for tooth #30 for a 62-year-old male patient.

The students are given the opportunity to ask any questions they may have before starting. Notes are given during direct instruction for the students to put in their journals for reference when working on their own. I provide the students with the essential vocabulary terms that they will have to define and write the meanings for in their journal and later correctly use them in their final presentation. In addition, students complete two teamwork activities to strengthen their communication, listening, and critical thinking skills.

This is a fun way to introduce collaborative skills, which students will utilize while working together to create a complete action plan that begins with the patient entering the office and ends with the patient leaving with a completed provisional two hours later. During the process, students will also complete a history lesson on provisional usage and materials over time and a math lesson on percentages, fractions, and estimates. I also incorporate a science-based research activity on provisional material properties. The students will then utilize all of the knowledge and skills learned through the above lessons to determine whether medications are safe to use on the patient, do material mixing calculations, and figure out which provisional material they will use to fabricate their final crown.

After the action plan is created with their partner, the students then move to the clinic area to practice making provisionals on their own with the materials that they had previously researched. The students will have different experiences with the materials that they try, thus leading to different opinions and personal preferences. After trying each one and deciding which one they will use for their final provisional, they start to practice the entire action plan they had previously created. This part of the project usually takes about two weeks.

During week five, I grade the action plans. As a class, we have a discussion on what worked, what didn't, and review presentation techniques. The students then begin to work on their presentations and present them to each other for practice. In week six, each student makes a preliminary presentation to an experienced dental assistant (who provides feedback for improvement). They are then able to reflect and make any changes if they wish. We end the project with each student doing a final presentation for the dentist that came in at the beginning of the project.

This project enables the students to learn the history, industry terms, strengthen their soft skills, build industry relationships, and of course, learn by doing (which includes making mistakes). The students learn so much more than just reading about it in a single paragraph in a textbook.

Work-based Learning

Work-based learning (WBL) is an educational method consisting of sustained and meaningful interactions with industry or community professionals, which foster in-depth engagement and tasks required in a given career field (Imperatore & Hyslop, 2018). There are many different forms of work-based learning that have been integrated within CTE, such as cooperative education, job shadowing, field trips, etc. WBL opportunities should align with standards; reinforce technical, academic, and employability knowledge and skills; and assist students in gaining relevant learning experiences for their career goals (Imperatore & Hyslop, 2018). The following subsections briefly explore various WBL strategies common in CTE programs.

Internships

Internships are intensive WBL experiences where a student works for an extended period with a specific company, workplace, or professional group. Students are able to build and apply skills through the internship, which can be paid or unpaid. Supervision, coaching, and mentoring occur while the student is on the job. Internships allow students to gain deeper insight into the career field and improve their résumés through this type of work experience (Missouri [MO] Department of Elementary & Secondary Education, 2021a).

Apprenticeships

Apprenticeships are "an industry-driven, high-quality career pathway where employers can develop and prepare their future workforce, and individuals can obtain paid work experience, classroom instruction, and a portable, nationally-recognized credential" (U.S. Department of Labor, 2021). There are five core components for starting an apprenticeship (U.S. Department of Labor):

1. *Explore:* Learn about apprenticeship benefits and how employers and sponsors are creating programs across industries and locations.
2. *Build:* Understand options and steps involved to build an apprenticeship program and the tools available to help you get started.
3. *Partner:* Collaborate with apprenticeship representatives, workforce organizations, and educators to build your program.
4. *Register:* Take advantage of the benefits of registering your program, including funding opportunities, tax credits, and no-cost technical assistance.
5. *Launch:* Recruit prospective apprentices, monitor the program, and share program success!

Some states have also started registered youth apprenticeship programs through CTE programs. These programs allow secondary students an opportunity for school-based and work-based learning. Students remain in academic classes to meet high school graduation requirements while also partnering with local businesses or industries for hands-on learning experiences (MO Department of Elementary & Secondary Education, 2021b).

Cooperative Education

Cooperative education is an instructional method, which integrates classroom-based learning and practical work experiences in a field related to the students' academic or career goals (Cooperative Education Internship Association [CEIA], 2021). Often referred to as co-op, this work-based learning method links the educational institution with employers in a collaborative effort to advance student learning through part-time on-the-job experiences (Threeton & Walter, 2013). Although the structure of co-op can vary from one institution to the next, a strong relationship between the school and employer is critical to the success of this student-centered learning experience.

Cooperative education experiences are often supervised by co-op coordinators; however, many career and technical educators facilitate setup and oversight for their student placements. This latter structure is particularly common in locations where a cooperative education coordinator certification is not mandatory.

For this reason, it is important to comprehend the components of quality cooperative education programs (Pennsylvania Department of Education [PDE], 2021), which include:

1. Job placements where students perform work related to acquired skills, with the opportunity to develop additional competencies and contribute to the productivity of the business organization.
2. Certified cooperative education teacher coordinators, with appropriate occupational experience to provide planned, supervised instruction.
3. Worksite training supervisors who can share occupational expertise with students.
4. Accurate and realistic descriptions of the jobs to be performed by students, as well as realistic employer expectations of the skills the students bring to the job.
5. Individualized, written training plans that are correlated to the students' school-based instruction and work-based on-the-job training.
6. Evaluations, which are formal and informal assessments of the students' progress on the job, including feedback and follow-up to assist students in improving performance.
7. Parents/guardians who have a full understanding of their responsibilities in the program.
8. Assistance with job placement in full-time positions or referrals for additional education for graduates.
9. Follow-up studies of graduates that are conducted in a systematic manner.
10. Instruction in all aspects of the industry the students are preparing to enter, which provides a broad base of knowledge of all facets of the business operation, including management, finances, and health and safety.
11. Strong commitment by school administration for the program (p. 1).

Simulated Workplace

Simulated Workplace allows students to transform classrooms into businesses for an authentic workplace environment. Students in the program become the employees. They pass an interview for entry into the class, fill assigned roles within the company, participate in random drug tests, write a company handbook, and pass a safety training (Advance CTE, 2021). West Virginia's [WV] Department of Education (2015) has developed an operational manual, including 12 protocols (See Figure 9.1) and an industry-evaluation rubric. Integrating authentic business practices gives "student access to the necessary skill sets, certifications and academics needed to be successful citizens" (WV Department of Education, 2021).

Figure 9.1 West Virginia's Simulated Workplace Protocols (WV Department of Education, 2015)

1. Student-led companies	7. Workplace teams
2. Application/interview structure	8. Project-based learning/student engagement
3. Formal attendance system	9. Company name and handbook
4. Drug-free work zones	10. Company meetings
5. 5S environment	11. Onsite business review
6. Safe work areas	12. Accountability.

Clinical Work Experience

In health-care programs, clinical work experience is a longer-term, active opportunity where students are able to shadow and provide service to a clinical setting (hospital, long-term care facility, etc.). Students are able to interact with the health-care team (nurses, CNAs, techs, physicians, etc.) to learn more about the culture of the health-care environment and gain a greater understanding of the field (Princeton University, 2021).

Supervised Agricultural Experience

A supervised agricultural experience (SAE) is one of the three components of a school-based agricultural education program (The National Council for Agricultural Education, 2021). SAE is a "student-led, instructor supervised, work-based learning experience that results in measurable outcomes within a predefined, agreed-upon set of Agriculture, Food and Natural Resources (AFNR) Technical Standards and Career Ready Practices aligned to a career plan of study" (The National Council for Agricultural Education, 2017, p. 2). Through involvement in an SAE program, students can learn about expected workplace behaviors and consider multiple agricultural careers (The National Council for Agricultural Education, 2015).

School-Based Enterprises

School-based enterprises (SBE) are entrepreneurial endeavors in a school setting that allow students to provide goods or services (DECA, 2021). "SBEs are managed and operated by students as hands-on learning laboratories" that integrate program standards (DECA, para. 1). Students may choose to sell spirit wear, food or beverages, school supplies, or other items or to provide services to the community, such as through onsite veterinary clinics or automotive repair shops. For some students, SBEs offer a first work experience, while for others, these provide an opportunity to build leadership skills (DECA).

Job Shadowing and Field Trips

Job shadowing is another method of work-based learning in which students engage in career exploration activities through structured workplace observations within business and industry that are specifically related to their career interests. This method is particularly beneficial for young people when they are undecided about their career aspirations and want to explore professional workplaces in action or refine their working knowledge of the occupational environment. Job shadowing can help students narrow down their career interests and also help them select an appropriate CTE program into which they can enroll.

Field trips are another method to promote structured workplace observations. Field trips move students beyond the classroom walls into an immersive experience within business and industry related to the subjects taught in the CTE program. Field trips are a helpful technique for career and technical educators who want to introduce their students to an area of their field that they cannot replicate in the CTE program, such as the production floor of an automaker for automotive technology students.

Field trips and job shadowing alike are typically structured as in-person activities but can also be conducted virtually via video conference platforms. During the COVID-19 pandemic, a multitude of in-person activities were canceled due to health and safety concerns. Many career and technical educators conducted these types of activities virtually out of necessity, and the opportunity to access more distant or restricted workplaces in a virtual fashion has become a more accepted approach for introducing students to certain workplaces.

Service Learning/Community & Family Engagement

Another example of practical, student-centered learning is service learning. According to the South Dakota Department of Education (SDDE, 2012), service learning is "a flexible method of teaching and learning that applies academic and real-world skills to youth-led experiences with community partnerships" (p. 5). This section intends to provide some context of what service learning is, how to plan for an effective service-learning project, and why service learning can be beneficial to students and communities. Some key attributes of effective service-learning models, according to SDDE (2012), include:

- Providing an opportunity for schools and communities to work together
- Focusing on academic learning and civic responsibility
- Addressing a community need while expanding on concepts taught in the classroom.

According to SDDE (2012), service learning is *not* the following:

- Purely volunteering
- Community service hours
- Fulfillment of some type of punishment
- An activity where only one side benefits.

It is evident that to create a true service-learning model, school and community partners must develop a plan and identify goals that address the needs of both groups. CTE teachers could begin by looking for projects and determining how these might enhance an academic concept. For instance, students in a culinary arts program could work with the kitchen staff at a retirement home to develop some new menu items that consider dietary restrictions commonly associated with an elderly population. Rather than just learn about gluten intolerance, it would be more engaging to have students research and create main course options, which could be added to the menu.

The following questions should be asked:

- Is developing a service-learning project worth the investment of time and resources?
- What are the benefits to students?
- Does the community really benefit as well?

According to a study conducted through the City University of New York's Queensborough Community College, many positive results impacted at-risk students upon completion of comprehensive service-learning projects (Ellerton et al., 2015). These included:

- Improved engagement in academics
- More confidence in academics
- More confidence in workplace skills
- Increased interest in civic engagement
- Increased student retention.

Based on these results, it bears considering how impactful service learning is on the majority of students. CTE students should be able to engage in their communities while developing greater interest in academics and workplace skills. Curricular projects should align with student and community needs to make a difference. Rather than starting from scratch, consider using resources from the SDDE, as well as guidelines provided by the National Youth Leadership Council (NYLC). This council has developed standards for service learning and has many online resources (https://www.nylc.org/page/slice).

Another facet of effective student-centered learning is the involvement of families in CTE programs. As you think about student-centered learning, consider the following:

- How much impact does family member support have on student success in technical programs?
- What types of support are beneficial? What might be the concerns?
- How can a CTE teacher involve parents to strengthen academic success for students?
- Multiple studies have been conducted, which focus on family engagement/parental involvement in student education. Research by Camarero-Figuerola et al. (2020) concluded academic performance can be positively influenced by parental involvement. They also determined an effective school-parent relationship can create appropriate relationships where both groups support one another to enhance the students' academic experience.

As CTE teachers work to bolster program effectiveness, it is recommended to think about ways of involving families to enhance engagement and success of students. In the simplest form, family involvement includes good communication. Send home positive notes to students who are doing well. Allow students to organize an open house to showcase the CTE program and invite parents and others in the community.

If parents are invited to participate in a volunteer capacity to your program, remember to set boundaries. Overly enthusiastic parents may unwittingly take over the classroom, and this will lead to confusion for all students. Ask parents to attend events to assist with a project or provide supervision, but include a wide range of parents. Rotating volunteers will send a message that everyone (within reason) is welcome to participate in the program and help build a community to support student success.

Also, CTE teachers should be aware of who is asked to volunteer. The instructor is ultimately responsible for those individuals who are invited into the classroom or extracurricular environments. These volunteers need to be vetted to avoid any distractions or legal issues. Many districts and institutions have volunteer policies and procedures; make sure to identify these policies before inviting volunteers to participate. CTE instructors will benefit from developing a plan for family volunteers, which is approved by the administration.

The Career Academy Model

Stone and Lewis (2012) provide a definition of college and career readiness, which is also aligned with the Perkins V legislation, and offer main objectives for career academies. First, academic knowledge in and of itself is not sufficient; high school graduates need to be able to apply what they learn through the occupational expression of academic knowledge. To that end, "graduates should know how to use mathematics or science to solve real workplace problems" (Stone & Lewis, p. 15) Second, employability skills, such as responsibility, collaboration, and critical thinking/problem solving, are key. Third, technical skills are competencies needed for specific occupational areas.

There have been efforts to inform career academy implementation with the development of standards of practice by school networks, such as NAF (formerly known as the National Academy Foundation). NAF is the largest network of high school career academies. NAF evaluates and continuously monitors its academies based on academy data and follow-up site visits and interviews. Career academies intentionally build students' knowledge to help them understand the postsecondary system and culture and encourage dual enrollment participation where available. The NAF model features four elements:

1. Academy development and structure: Focuses on small learning communities using student cohorts, career-themed and sequenced coursework, common teacher planning, career-themed guidance, and ongoing professional development.
2. Integrated curriculum and instruction: Promotes career and academic learning around a relevant theme (e.g., Business and Finance, Engineering, Health Sciences, Hospitality and Tourism,

Information Technology [IT]) through project-based activities involving core academic content, work-based learning experiences, and internships. Career academies attempt to integrate career-themed curricula with college preparatory coursework. The purpose is for students to learn core academic subjects in an applied, career-oriented fashion.

3. Advisory board: Includes members representing community stakeholder groups to ensure that academies are locally relevant and supported. The advisory board should include members representing community stakeholder groups (e.g., business and industry, teachers, community members, postsecondary partners, and students) to ensure that academies are locally relevant and supported (with equipment, supplies, scholarships, assistance with mock interviews between students and industry professionals, time with industry guest speakers, and mentoring for teachers to ensure up-to-date technology curricula).

4. Work-based learning activities: Career academy students engage in successively progressive work-based learning experiences from ninth through 12th grades that are developmentally and age-appropriate. Work-based learning includes career awareness and exploration activities in ninth (e.g., field trips) and 10th (e.g., job shadowing) grades and experiential opportunities (e.g., industry certifications, paid internships) in 11th and 12th grades.

The career academy model builds upon the premise of contextual teaching and learning to make student learning more meaningful by facilitating connections to real-life applications (Gordon & Schultz, 2020; Hernández-Gantes & Brendefur, 2003). Occupational context serves as the source of relevant learning tasks and applications involving authentic representations of what employees do in the world of work (Hernández-Gantes & Brendefur). Thus, it is expected that, based on the quality of such learning experiences, college and career readiness will be enhanced around a related career context.

The purposeful integration of academic and technical education is a signature feature of successful programs, bringing meaning and relevance to curriculum and instruction (Castellano et al., 2012). The term "curriculum integration" is referred to in a variety of ways—as a method or process to connect skills, themes, concepts, and topics across disciplines and between academic and technical education (Pierce & Hernández-Gantes, 2015). Teachers integrate curriculum and connect multiple content areas to break down overarching theories, concepts, and big ideas that help students and enhance learning from one subject to another (Klein, 2006). Curriculum integration may be implemented around an occupational theme such as IT or may involve concept connections within single subjects, such as arithmetic, algebra, geometry, or across two or more subjects, such as mathematics and CTE (Pierce & Hernández-Gantes).

Work-based learning experiences help students acquire both the employability and technical skills needed to be college and career ready (Hernández-Gantes, 2016; Stone & Lewis, 2012). Work-based learning experiences can include apprenticeships, guest speakers, job shadowing, mock interviews, paid or unpaid internships, and student-run enterprises (Cahill, 2016). In the US, internships are the most common strategy to provide high school students with work-based learning experiences.

Work-based learning may be construed as high-impact practices and are used to adequately prepare students for the world of work (Gamboa et al., 2013). Although the term high-impact practices is usually referred to at the postsecondary levels, it can also be true of work-based learning in secondary settings. Kuh (2015) argued that the results of high-impact practices are that students "invest substantial time and energy to educationally purposeful tasks, interact frequently with their teachers and peers, get feedback often, and apply what they are learning" (p. xi). That is, work-based learning enables students to apply what they know in real-world settings, while building exposure to, preparation for, and experience in their interested career paths (Papadimitriou, 2014).

Summary

Career and technical educators are charged with the task of providing quality instruction to the next generation of technical professionals. Using strategies such as project-based learning, service learning, or the career academies model, allows learning to be integrated for student engagement. Key to each of these strategies is the application of technical, academic, and employability knowledge and skills. Incorporating the methods discussed in this chapter appropriately, career and technical educators will enrich student engagement and promote enhanced learning and occupational skill development.

ACTE's Quality CTE Program of Study Framework Connection

The concepts in this chapter related to the following elements of the *Quality CTE Program of Study Framework* developed by the Association for Career and Technical Education (read more about the framework in chapter 2, Imperatore & Hyslop, 2018):

- **Element 5: Engaging Instruction**
  This element addresses instructional strategies that will support student attainment of relevant knowledge and skills. Instructional approaches, such as project-based learning, are integrated into the program of study. Cross-disciplinary collaboration emphasizes the connection between academic and technical knowledge and skills. Instruction is personalized to meet the needs of a diverse student population.

- **Element 8: Business and Community Partnerships**
  This element addresses business and community partnership recruitment, partnership structure, and the activities partners should be engaged in. Partners ensure extended learning activities, such as work-based learning and CTSO activities. Outreach activities ensure the program of study is informed by employer and community needs.

- **Element 11: Work-based Learning**
  This element addresses the delivery of a continuum of work-based learning activities involving sustained, meaningful interactions with industry or community professionals that foster in-depth, firsthand engagement with the tasks required in a given career field. A full continuum of work-based learning experiences is accessible to students; reinforces relevant technical, academic, and employability knowledge and skills throughout the program of study; and maximizes meaningful interactions with business professionals.

References

Advance CTE. (2021). *Learning that works resource center: West Virginia: Simulated workplace.* https://careertech. org/resource/west-virginia-simulated-workplace

Cahill, C. (2016). *Making work-based learning work. Jobs for the future.* https://jfforg-prod-new.s3.amazonaws.com/ media/documents/WBL_Principles_Paper_062416.pdf

Camarero-Figuerola, Dueñas, & Renta-Davids, (2020). The relationship between family involvement and academic variables: A systematic review. *Research in Social Sciences and Technology, 5*(2). https://doi.org/10.46303/ressat.05.02.4

Castellano, M., Sundell, K., Overman, L. T., & Aliaga, O. A. (2012). Do career and technical education programs of study improve student achievement? Preliminary analyses from a rigorous longitudinal study. *International Journal of Educational Reform, 21*, 98–118. https://doi.org/10.1177/105678791202100202

Cooperative Education Internship Association (CEIA). (2021). *History of cooperative education and internships.* https://www.ceiainc.org/about/history

DECA. (2021). *School-based enterprise.* https://www.deca.org/high-school-programs/school-based-enterprises/

Ellerton, S., Di Meo, C., Pantaleo, J., Kemmerer, A., Bandziukas, M.,& Bradley, M. (2015). Academic Service-Learning Benefits Diverse, Urban Community College Students. *Journal for Civic Commitment, 22.* https://academicworks.cuny.edu/cgi/viewcontent.cgi?article=1035&context=qb_pubs

Gordon, H., & Schultz, D. (2020). *The history and growth of career and technical education in America* (5th ed.). Waveland Press.

Hernández-Gantes, V. M., & Brendefur, J. (2003). Developing authentic, integrated, standards based mathematics curriculum: [More than just] an interdisciplinary collaborative approach. *Journal of Vocational Education Research, 28*(3), 259–284.

Hernández-Gantes, V. M. (2016). College and career readiness for all: The role of career and technical education in the US. In D. Wyse, L. Hayward, & J. Pandya (Eds.), *SAGE handbook of curriculum, pedagogy and assessment* (Vol. 2, pp. 674–689). SAGE Publishing.

Imperatore, C. & Hyslop, A. (2018, October). *2018 ACTE quality program of study framework.* Association for Career and Technical Education. https://www.acteonline.org/wp-content/uploads/2019/01/ HighQualityCTEFramework2018.pdf

Klein, J. T. (2006). Platform for a shared discourse of interdisciplinary education. *Journal of Social Science Education, 6*(2), 10–18. https://doi.org/10.4119/jsse-344

Kuh, G. D. (2015). Foreword. In S. J. Quaye & S. R. Harper (Eds.), *Student engagement in higher education* (pp. ix–xiii). Routledge.

Mergendoller, J. R. (2021). *Defining high quality PBL: A look at the research.* https://hqpbl.org/ wp-content/uploads/2018/04/Defining-High-Quality-PBL-A-Look-at-the-Research-.pdf

Missouri Department of Elementary & Secondary Education. (2021a). *CTE certificate work-based learning experiences definitions.* https://dese.mo.gov/media/pdf/cte-certificate-workbased-learning-experiences-definitions

Missouri Department of Elementary & Secondary Education. (2021b). Registered youth apprenticeships. https:// dese.mo.gov/college-career-readiness/career-education/registered-youth-apprenticeships-school-administrators

Papadimitriou, M. (2014). High school students' perceptions of their internship experiences and related impact on career choices and changes. *Online Journal for Workforce Education & Development, 7*(1), 1–27.

Pennsylvania Department of Education (PDE). (2021). *Cooperative education guidelines for administration: How to comply with federal and state laws and regulations.* https://www.education.pa.gov/Documents/K-12/Career%20 and%20Technical%20Education/Teacher%20Resources/Cooperative%20Education/Cooperative%20 Education%20Guidelines%20for%20Administration.pdf

Pierce, K., & Hernández-Gantes, V. M. (2015). Do mathematics and reading competencies integrated into career and technical education courses improve high school student scores? *Career and Technical Education Research, 39*(3), 213–229. https://doi.org/10.5328/cter39.3.213

Princeton University. (2021). *Health professions advising.* https://hpa.princeton.edu/faqs/activities-faq/ clinical-experience-faq

South Dakota Department of Education [SDDE]. (2012). *Service learning: A practical framework for implementation in South Dakota schools.* https://doe.sd.gov/cte/servicelearning.aspx

Stone, J. R. III., & Lewis, M. V. (2012). *College and career ready in the 21st century: Making high school matter.* Teachers College Press.

The National Council for Agricultural Education. (2015). *Philosophy and guiding principles for execution of the supervised agricultural experience component of the total school based agricultural education program.* https://ffa.app.box.com/s/i8ntesw8zsajaxxdnj5cle6zaf0a6za3

The National Council for Agricultural Education. (2017). *Work-based learning through supervised agricultural experience: Real learning for a real future.* https://ffa.app.box.com/s/exollg1x7q2lntun3su2mdufw07wiklf

The National Council for Agricultural Education. (2021). *SAE for all.* https://saeforall.org/

Threeton, M. D., & Walter, R. A. (2013). *Managing technical programs and facilities.* Whittier.

U.S. Department of Labor. (2021). Jump start your career through apprenticeship. https://www.apprenticeship. gov/career-seekers

West Virginia Department of Education. (2015). *West Virginia simulated workplace operational manual.* https://wvde.state.wv.us/simulated-workplace/files/2015-simulated-workplace-manual.pdf

West Virginia Department of Education. (2021). *Simulated workplace vision.* https://sway.office.com/ ZjlThAIWt3dSZskN?ref=Link

Chapter 10

■

DIVERSITY IN CAREER AND TECHNICAL EDUCATION

Edward C. Fletcher, Jr.—The Ohio State University
Michelle L. Conrad—University of Central Missouri

Introduction

CTE attracts a diverse range of student types and backgrounds. Eighty-eight percent of graduates from secondary education in the United States in 2013 had earned at least one credit in CTE. Twenty percent of 2013 graduates earned at least three credits in CTE and were designated as concentrators. In terms of programming, the secondary education component of CTE programs is highly diverse, with 98 percent of public school districts offering at least one CTE course. Historically, with respect to student demographics, male students have earned more CTE credits compared to females. Black and White graduates earned more credits compared to Asian/Pacific Islander graduates. Students with special needs earned more CTE credits compared to students without special needs. Students who come from lower socioeconomic families earned more CTE credits than their higher socioeconomic counterparts (Liu & Burns, 2020).

Given all the diversity found in students and represented in programming, CTE educators need to ensure that all students have opportunities to engage in high-quality CTE programs of study. This includes curricula that are free of bias, non-discriminatory, and appropriately differentiated for students. This chapter begins with a review of the importance of differentiated instruction and culturally relevant curriculum. Social justice education is explored, as well as equity in nontraditional careers and considerations for adult learners.

Differentiated Instruction

Similar to academic teachers, CTE teachers must endeavor to prepare students from all sorts of backgrounds, including individuals who have psychological, social, emotional, and physical disabilities, as well as academic or economic disadvantages (Rayfield et al., 2011). Gifted and general education students, too, need individualized instruction. To meet the needs of such varying learners, CTE instructors need to differentiate their instruction. The concept of differentiated instruction posits that instructional strategies should vary and be adapted based on the individual and diverse needs of students to maximize students' opportunities for success (Hall et al., 2011). According to Hall et al. (2011), "to differentiate instruction is to recognize students' varying background knowledge, readiness, language, preferences in learning and interests; and to react responsively" (p. 3). Further, teachers must engage in informed decision making by selecting appropriate instructional approaches and resources based on lesson objectives and aligned assessment.

Teachers must consider what content to teach, how best to teach it, and how to appropriately and accurately assess student proficiency of the content learned while also paying close attention to their learners' readiness, interests, and learning preferences (Moon, 2005). While the teaching profession remains largely white (79 percent) and female (77 percent), the K-12 student population in urban schools is increasingly diversified (Goings & Bianco, 2016). For example, even though Black male students comprise 16 percent of the total K-12 U.S. student population, Black male teachers comprise only 2 percent of all teachers (Goings & Bianco, 2016; Kena et al., 2015).

Unfortunately, too many ethnically and racially diverse students are not provided the opportunity for schooling experiences that offer meaningful, diverse student-teacher relationships, as in Goings & Bianco's study (2016) of Black male role models in the classroom. This example and numerous other examples of the lack of diversity in schools demonstrate that there is a need for instructors to utilize culturally responsive pedagogies in the classroom to engage all learners.

VOICES FROM THE FIELD

Vincent Villella—M.Ed, Northwest Area Health Education Center Director, Nome, AK

To understand diversity in CTE, it is critical to understand and build relationships with your students, their families, and the community. I was once teaching in the Yupik village of Quinhagak in Southwest Alaska. As I was teaching, I continued to ask a young lady if she understood what I was saying, and she sat silent in front of me. I asked her why she wasn't saying anything, and she did not respond. I asked again and was met with the same response. The third time I asked, I was angry. I believed she was toying with me. This caused this young lady to begin to cry and leave my room. Only later did I realize that every time I asked this question, she was raising her eyebrows; among the Yupik people, this translates into "Yes."

I share this story with you for two reasons, 1) to let you know that when dealing with diverse populations, you will make mistakes, and that is okay as long as you learn from them, and 2) understanding the diverse population you work with will be key to being a successful educator and giving your students the education they need.

Culturally Relevant Curriculum

Ladson-Billings (1995) posited that the theory of culturally responsive pedagogy is founded on three elements: (a) the need for all students to experience academic success, (b) the need for teachers to be culturally competent, and (c) the need for teachers to build their own cultural consciousness by confronting the status quo in society and schools. First, to capitalize on the strengths of students in the classroom, teachers must assess the knowledge and beliefs students encompass, understand how their students learn, and construct learning experiences to support their achievement. Further, teachers must harness a sociocultural consciousness.

This type of teacher attitude entails: (a) respect for their learners and their ways of knowing, (b) adaptive instructional practices based on the needs of their students, and (c) a dedication to the learning of students. Moreover, instructors with a sociocultural consciousness understand that their upbringing and experiences are not universal but are shaped by their own unique experiences and demographics (e.g., culture, race, ethnicity, gender, language, geographic region, sexual orientation, socioeconomic status, among others).

Gonzalez et al. (2005) expanded the notion of sociocultural consciousness with the concept of "funds of knowledge," which acknowledges that all students are competent based on their unique lived experiences. Their premise is that teachers need to go beyond the classroom and establish experiences and relationships with their students' families to successfully document this competence and knowledge. With this knowledge and understanding, educators may then begin to integrate aspects of their students' home and community cultures into the classroom for instructional purposes.

Ladson-Billings (1995) described the issue of Black students not being permitted to be themselves in the classroom. To address this issue, teachers need to be culturally competent and use culture as a motivation for learning. Instructors can use students' cultural interests as a bridge for learning academic concepts. In addition, teachers need to be reflective practitioners who examine their own cultural assumptions and how it shapes their instructional decision making. And, culturally responsive instructors oftentimes "form and maintain connections with their students within their social contexts" (Banks et al., 2005, p. 245). The outcomes of culturally relevant teaching are classrooms that foster academically challenging environments and curricula that are equitable and responsive to diverse learners.

Instructors must also be cognizant of how race in the United States continues to be a factor in determining school inequities, as we still live in a racialized society (Ladson-Billings & Tate, 1995). Despite the ideological advancements made, particularly between whites and Blacks, Blacks remain disadvantaged based on their race. These socio-historical issues, along with institutional and structural racism, are major factors in understanding why white students consistently outperform Black students—even middle-class Black students—on a variety of student achievement measures. However, multicultural education is likely to lead to an equalizing effect on diverse racial, ethnic, and social groups within schools.

Social Justice in Education

Social justice means looking at how inequality and oppression are socially constructed in every level of society. This can be reflected in an individual's attitudes and behaviors, through policies and practices of institutions, or through societal messages of what is deemed "correct."

CTE curriculum that engages all students in learning needs to connect with the backgrounds and life experiences of the learners. Social justice education allows students to recognize others' perspectives, which is a needed skill for today's diverse workplace. Creating opportunities to recognize the unique perspective each student brings to the culture of the classroom establishes an equitable learning environment (Asia Society, 2021). Recognizing and incorporating social justice concepts into CTE curriculum prepares students for critically examining equitable systems throughout their careers and in the workforce.

If we examine the histories of our laws, policies, and practices, we can question and change inequitable systems to ensure that some are not advantaged while others are disadvantaged (Asia Society, 2021). This includes reviewing curriculum to elicit more emancipatory and participatory instructional strategies, and the co-construction of knowledge between teachers and their students (Freire, 2000).

Using problem-based educational practices that allow students to critically contest inequities, curriculum can identify social challenges and create positive social change. The goal is to empower students to create socially just policies that have the ability to transform our society from its historical and present-day discriminatory and oppressive practices (Bell, 2018; Freire, 2000; Hooks, 1994). These pervasive problems are embedded in local communities and have a negative impact on the livelihood and the trajectories of our students, their families, and members of the community (Gay, 2000; Ladson-Billings, 1995; Merry, 2017). To address these issues, instructors with their students can examine the inequities and power dynamics within society, how inequities and power dynamics operate within our society, the ways that inequitable practices are institutionalized, the oppressors and the oppressed, who devised the rules, and how these practices are exacerbated (Kumashiro, 2012; Sleeter & McLaren, 1995).

The end goal of social justice education is to transform students from mere consumers of knowledge and transmitters of inequities to critically conscious thinkers who will develop positive change and help disrupt oppression in their local communities and within our broader society (Freire, 2000; Hooks, 1994, 2003). CTE curriculum should be designed to engage all students in learning experiences that are respectful of students' backgrounds and life experiences, as well as provide equitable opportunities for participation (Asia Society, 2021). Creating curriculum with an eye for social justice ensures students can recognize the perspectives of others and are prepared for the diverse workforce.

VOICES FROM THE FIELD

Kirstin Bullington—Next Energy Engineering Instructor, Richland Two Institute of Innovation, Columbia, SC

One of the best aspects of teaching engineering in a district learning center is that my students get to collaborate with others from different schools and neighborhoods (my classes consist of students from each of the five district high schools). As my classes are completely project-based, my students learn to appreciate how diversity of backgrounds, ideas, and experiences leads to a more robust engineering solution.

Since most STEM professions require interactions with diverse audiences, I have made a concerted effort to recruit students from all high schools and ensure that our competitive teams reflect the diversity of the district. Our student teams have twice been named national finalists in the Samsung Solve for Tomorrow competition, received a 2019 Lemelson-MIT InvenTeam grant, and were recognized by John Kerry, Special Climate Envoy, for their ongoing solar collaboration with a school in Senegal.

Because I have seen the value of diversity in my student groups, I try to ensure that our outreach programs to younger grades reach the entire community, particularly those that are traditionally underrepresented in STEM. In both classes and in outreach programs, I try to help the students select energy issues that are important to them, and that will highlight the unique talents that each member of the group brings to the table. For instance, several students asked to make their solar instructional videos in Spanish to share with their families in other countries. Making bilingual videos actually helped the entire class learn more of the technical vocabulary needed in that project. As South Carolina becomes more diverse, so too must our instruction and inclusion of all students in CTE classes in order to make each student more competitive in their future careers.

Equity and Nontraditional Careers

What is clear in the educational literature is the need for all students (particularly ethnically and racially diverse learners) to have access to a high-quality, highly rigorous, and highly engaging curriculum with teachers who exhibit care while still holding high expectations (Gordon, 2014). The field of CTE has seen a renewed interest within the new educational paradigm when one views college and career readiness to include employability and technical skill development in addition to core academic (e.g., English, mathematics, and science) knowledge attainment (Stone & Lewis, 2012). This is in stark contrast to the perceptions of CTE as a mechanism to track students based on a host of factors and the funneling of ethnically and racially diverse (particularly African Americans), low-income, and marginalized students into vocational tracks (Oakes & Guiton, 1995).

The current legislation governing CTE programs is the Carl D. Perkins Career and Technical Education Act, last updated in 2018 as Perkins V. The provisions of the legislation focus on preparing CTE students to be both college and career ready, as well as the development of programs of study that lead students from high school into postsecondary education (both two-year and four-year colleges and universities) as well as into the workforce (Castellano et al., 2017).

Although many people believe that, as a nation, the United States has moved beyond racism, classism, and other discriminatory practices, the attitudes and beliefs of some regarding the intellectual and academic abilities of ethnically and racially diverse students continue to impede these students' access and opportunity to full participation in accelerated learning options. These options include advanced placement, concurrent/dual enrollment, gifted, honors, international baccalaureate, as well as STEM courses.

Additionally, many contemporary scholars of gifted and talented education have challenged definitions and theories of giftedness and questioned unfair tests, checklists, policies, procedures, and practices that contribute to persistent underrepresentation of ethnically and racially diverse (e.g., Black and Latinx) students in accelerated learning options. For example, current definitions of giftedness place major emphasis on standardized intelligence tests reflective of white middle-class values, effectively discriminating against students who do not necessarily embrace such values, especially students of color; this results in untapped potential (Ford, 2013; Wright et al., 2017).

Furthermore, cultural and economic class differences cause gifted and talented behaviors to manifest differently across racial-ethnic groups. Processes for identifying gifted and talented students, as well as barriers to accelerated learning options created by narrow standards that reflect, represent, and enforce the languages, literacies, and cultural practices of the status quo, are bound to marginalize much of what ethnically and racially diverse students learn in their homes and communities. Labeling their cultures, learnings, and experiences as irrelevant, substandard, and inferior for school further disconnects ethnically and racially diverse students' outside-of-school lives from the world they are expected to adapt to inside school.

This practice of ranking and sorting students based on their skills to think, speak, and act in ways that represent white students undermines the cultural strengths and assets of ethnically and racially diverse students. Adding socioeconomic status to the injustice equation compounds the problem of underrepresentation. When financial resources are lacking, children may not have access to cognitively stimulating toys, materials, and culturally relevant books and literature. This is not that families with more limited financial resources do not recognize the importance of having their children engaged in a variety of experiences, such as trips to the local museum, libraries, etc., but it is a matter of financial limitations and availability in some neighborhoods.

It is important to debunk the myth that ethnically and racially diverse families do not place a high value and priority on education. The education of students of color is often compromised and placed in jeopardy by these types of structural and environmental biases and limitations, giving these students little opportunity for their gifts and talents to be recognized and cultivated at school.

Too few teachers are formally prepared to work with and understand the experiences and needs of high-performing ethnically and racially diverse learners, and even fewer are trained to recruit and retain culturally different students in accelerated, as well as STEM courses/programs (Ford, 2013). These challenges are a part of a larger issue of racial achievement/opportunity gaps fed by low expectations and cultural competence gaps. Data from the National Center for Educational Statics, Early Childhood Longitudinal Study (2002) found that African American/Black students were 54 percent less likely than White students to be recommended for gifted and talented education programs, even after adjusting for factors such as students' standardized test scores. Notably, African American/Black students were three times more likely to be referred for gifted and talented education programs if their teachers were African American/Black (Grissom & Redding 2016).

These findings suggest that when teachers' implicit biases, stereotypes, and racism are in operation, it makes them less likely to advocate for the inclusion of ethnically and racially diverse students in accelerated courses/programs and potentially less effective when teaching these students. Nonetheless, it is expected that *all* students are prepared to be college and career ready—given the need for them to transition into postsecondary education (e.g., two- or four-year colleges and universities), as well as into the workforce. All students should be encouraged to participate in rigorous curricula and activities. This sentiment is especially important for ethnically and racially diverse students coming from low-income families. Students from low-income backgrounds, particularly, need to know that their zip code is not necessarily their destiny.

CTE curriculum needs to be free of bias, inclusive, and nondiscriminatory. Strategies to ensure that all students are achieving success include:

- Actively recruit students from a variety of backgrounds and abilities
- Differentiate instruction and provide options for all students to be successful
- Examine and disaggregate data such as test scores for bias
- Adapt the curriculum for learner culture and needs

- Ensure opportunities for extended learning, such as CTSO participation and work-based learning experiences, are provided for all students
- Encourage supportive services, such as tutoring or transportation assistance for full participation in the program of study.

Achieving equity in the program of study means that instructors must reflect on their practice and personal biases to ensure all students have the opportunity for access and equity in their career preparation.

Adult Learners

Lifelong learning has become a necessity for many, whether to gain new skills in the same field, change career fields, or for personal interest. CTE programs provide opportunities for adults to stay competitive in the workforce by providing students with access to certificates and IRCs, as well as postsecondary degree programs (Advance CTE, 2011). Older students entering CTE programs also need educators who are aware that there are differences between working with adolescents compared to adults, and the curriculum should take these learner differences into account.

While pedagogy takes into account an instructor's knowledge of how children and adolescents learn and the role of instruction in fostering learning (Collins & O'Brien, 2011), andragogy is defined as "the activities of learners and teachers in planning, realizing, evaluating and correcting adult learning" (Zmeyov, 1998, p. 106). It is based on four assumptions about the characteristics of adult learners, which differ from the assumptions about young learners. These include (Knowles, 1980):

1. *Concept of the learner:* Adults generally have a need to be self-directing.
2. *Role of learners' experience:* Adults have rich life experiences to learn from.
3. *Readiness to learn:* Adults are ready to learn in order to cope with real-life tasks or problems.
4. *Orientation to learning:* Adults see education as a way to increase competence, knowledge, and skills.

For curriculum developers, this means considering how to organize individualized learning opportunities, the learning technologies utilized, the creation of cooperative learning experiences, and contextualizing learning in the students' experience (Zmeyov, 1998). Adults need to understand the reasons for learning specific skills, how to solve problems using their knowledge and skills, and have opportunities to self-assess their progress (Teaching Excellence in Adult Literacy [TEAL], 2011). Through the curriculum, connections should be made between the learning objectives and the learners' needs, interests, and skills. Learning resources (books, videos/media, etc.) and methods (research, electronic discussions, lectures, etc.) should be matched to the learning goals. Self-evaluation of work should provide opportunities for increasing decision-making strategies and reflection on learning (TEAL).

Summary

Whether gender, race, ethnicity, ability level, or age, improving access and equity throughout the CTE curriculum is imperative for all educators and our future workforce. Ensuring curriculum is free of bias, nondiscriminatory, and appropriately differentiated for students should be a regular part of curricular reviews. Continued conversations with industry partners should eliminate barriers to extended learning opportunities and provide all students with opportunities to achieve success.

ACTE's Quality CTE Program of Study Framework Connection

The concepts in this chapter related to the following elements of the *Quality CTE Program of Study Framework* developed by the Association for Career and Technical Education (read more about the framework in chapter 2, Imperatore & Hyslop, 2018):

- **Element 5: Engaging Instruction**
  This element addresses instructional strategies that will support student attainment of relevant knowledge and skills. Instruction should be flexible, differentiated, and personalized to meet the needs of a diverse student population.

- **Element 6: Access and Equity**
  This element addresses CTE program promotion, student recruitment, and supports to ensure access and equity for all student populations. Curriculum, instruction, materials, and assessments should be free from bias, inclusive, and nondiscriminatory. Supportive services should be provided to ensure all students can achieve success in the program of study.

References

Advance CTE. (2011, December). *Career technical education: Keeping adult learners competitive for high-demand jobs.* [Issue Brief]. https://cte.careertech.org/sites/default/files/AdultLearnersCompetitive-Dec2011.pdf

Asia Society. (2021). *Global social justice education framework.* https://asiasociety.org/sites/default/files/inline-files/Global_Social_Justice_Framework.pdf

Banks, J., Cochran-Smith, M., Moll, L., Richert, A., Zeichner, K., LePage, P., Darling-Hammond, L., Duffy, H., & McDonald, M. (2005). Teaching diverse learners. In L. Darling-Hammond & J. Bransford (Eds.), *Preparing teachers for a changing world* (pp. 232–274). Jossey-Bass.

Bell, L. (2018). Theoretical foundations for social justice education. In M. Adams, W. Blumenfeld, C. Castaneda, H. Hackman, M. Peters, & X. Zuniga (Eds.), *Readings for diversity and social justice* (4th ed., pp. 34–40). Routledge.

Castellano, M., Richardson, G., Sundell, K., & Stone, J. (2017). Preparing students for college and career in the United States: The effects of career-themed programs of study on high school performance. *Vocations and Learning, 10*(1), 47–70. https://doi.org/10.1007/s12186-016-9162-7

Collins, J. W., & O'Brien, N. P. (2011). *The greenwood dictionary of education* (2nd ed.). Greenwood.

Ford, D.Y. (2013). *Recruiting and retaining culturally different students in gifted education.* Prufrock Press.

Freire, P. (2000). *Pedagogy of the oppressed.* Continuum.

Gay, G. (2000). *Culturally responsive teaching: Theory, research, and practice.* Teachers College Press.

Goings, R., & Bianco, M. (2016). It's hard to be who you don't see: An exploration of Black male high school students' perspectives on becoming teachers. *The Urban Review, 48*, 628–646. https://doi.org/10.1007/s11256-016-0371-z

Gonzalez, N., Moll, L., & Amanti, C. (2005). *Funds of knowledge: Theorizing practices in households, communities, and classrooms.* Lawrence Erlbaum.

Grissom, J., & Redding, C. (2016). Discretion and disproportionality: Explaining the underrepresentation of high-achieving students of color in gifted programs. *AERA Open.* https://doi.org/10.1177/2332858415622175

Hall, T., Strangman, N., & Meyer, A. (2011). *Differentiated instruction and implications for UDL implementation. (Cooperative Agreement No. H324H990004).* National Center on Accessing the General Curriculum.

Hooks, B. (1994). *Teaching to transgress: Education as the practice of freedom.* Routledge.

Hooks, B. (2003). *Teaching community: A pedagogy of hope.* Routledge.

Imperatore, C. & Hyslop, A. (2018, October). *2018 ACTE quality program of study framework.* Association for Career and Technical Education. https://www.acteonline.org/wp-content/uploads/2019/01/HighQualityCTEFramework2018.pdf

Kena, G., Musu-Gillette, L., Robinson, J., Wang, X., Rathbun, A., Zhang, J. Wilkinson-Flicker, S., Barmer, A., & Dunlop Velez, E. (2015). *The condition of education 2015* (NCES 2015–144). U.S. Department of Education, National Center for Education Statistics. https://nces.ed.gov/pubs2015/2015144.pdf

Knowles, M. S. (1980). *The modern practice of adult education: From pedagogy to andragogy.* Cambridge. http://www.colllearning.info/wp-content/uploads/2019/03/The-Modern-Practice-of-Adult-Education.pdf

Kumashiro, K. (2012). *Bad teacher! How blaming teachers distorts the bigger picture.* Teachers College Press.

Ladson-Billings, G. (1995). Toward a theory of culturally relevant pedagogy. *American Educational Research Journal, 32*(3), 465–491.

Ladson-Billings, G., & Tate, W. (1995). Toward a critical race theory of education. *Teachers College Record, 97*(1), 47–68.

Liu, A., & Burns, L. (2020). *Public high school students' career and technical education coursetaking: 1992 to 2013.* National Center for Education Statistics.

Merry, J. (2017). *Revolutionary teaching and learning: Teacher and student activists and the co-construction of social justice pedagogy for change* [Doctoral dissertation, The Ohio State University]. https://etd.ohiolink.edu/pg_10?0::NO:10:P10_ACCESSION_NUM:osu1512047502495518

Moon, T. (2005). The role of assessment in differentiation. *Theory Into Practice, 44*(3), 226–233.

Oakes, J., & Guiton, G. (1995). Matchmaking: The dynamics of high school tracking decisions. *American Educational Research Journal, 32*(1), https://doi.org/10.3102/00028312032001003

Rayfield, J., Croom, B., Stair, K., & Murray, K. (2011). Differentiating instruction in high school agricultural education courses: A baseline study. *Career and Technical Education Research, 36*(3), 171–185.

Sleeter, C., & McLaren, P. (1995). *Multicultural education, critical pedagogy, and the politics of difference.* State University of New York Press.

Stone, J. R., III, & Lewis, M.V. (2012). *College and career ready in the 21st century: Making high school matter.* Teachers College Press.

Teaching Excellence in Adult Literacy (TEAL). (2011). *Adult learning theories* [Fact Sheet]. American Institutes for Research. https://lincs.ed.gov/sites/default/files/11_%20TEAL_Adult_Learning_Theory.pdf

Wright, B.L., Ford, D.Y. & Young, J.L. (2017). Ignorance or indifference? Seeking equity and excellent for under-represented students of color in gifted education. *Global Education Review, 4*(1), 45–60.

Zmeyov, S. I. (1998). Andragogy: Origins, developments and trends. *International Review of Education, 44*(1), 103–108.

Chapter 11

■

STUDENTS WITH DISABILITIES IN CTE

Michelle L. Conrad—University of Central Missouri

Introduction

Studies have shown that students with disabilities (SWD) who participate in CTE programs have a greater likelihood of success, including graduating within four years (Hehir et al., 2013) and obtaining postsecondary employment (Harvey, 2002; Lee et al., 2016; Theobald et al., 2017; Wagner et al., 2015). CTE allows students to enhance academic learning by providing opportunities to apply knowledge, connect to real-world situations, and explore a variety of careers (Brand et al., 2013). Students' disabilities, however, can vary in type and severity, which can impact their interests, strengths, educational plans, and career goals (Brand et al.; Hehir et al.; Lee et al.).

CTE has been identified as a best practice for SWD transition planning (Harvey et al., 2020; Schmalzried & Harvey, 2014; Test et al., 2006), but students need the assistance of CTE teachers to meet the rigorous curriculum and assessment expectations (Brand et al., 2013). Too often, parents, teachers, administrators, and counselors have low expectations for SWDs, which may lead to students having low career aspirations. When teachers can incorporate multiple types of knowledge and skills into their curriculum and instruction, all students, including those with disabilities, can be more successful (Brand et al.).

This chapter will begin with an overview of relevant laws related to SWDs and how these impact CTE programs. Understanding the laws and impact on CTE programs helps us to discuss transition services. The impact on curriculum will then be explored, specifically through accommodations and modifications in CTE programs. Finally, a review of Universal Design for Learning (UDL), which can ensure all students can participate in high-quality CTE, is presented.

Laws and Legal Implications

The Strengthening Career & Technical Education for the 21st Century Act (Perkins V)

As CTE programs are greatly influenced by Perkins, it should be noted that one focus of Perkins V is to increase the employment possibilities for those who are chronically unemployed or underemployed, a definition that includes individuals with disabilities. Individuals with disabilities are also included in the definition of "special populations" under this law, which triggers specific service and data reporting and disaggregation requirements. For example, data on each of the Perkins accountability indicators, including CTE student academic performance, graduation, and transition, as well as the state's chosen program quality indicator, must be reported specifically for students with disabilities. Disaggregated enrollment data must also be reported, and gaps in participation and performance between students with disabilities and other students must be analyzed and addressed in regular needs assessments and, if necessary, in program improvement plans (Hyslop, 2018).

Section 504 of the Rehabilitation Act of 1973

Section 504 is a civil rights statute, not a programmatic statute. Section 504 requires schools to not discriminate based on a disability if they receive federal financial assistance for educational purposes. Schools must provide students with reasonable accommodations compared to their peers (deBettencourt, 2002). Subpart D applies to K-12 schools, and subpart E applies to postsecondary institutions.

In order to obtain services under Section 504, students must have an identified physical or mental condition that limits a major life activity, such as walking, caring for oneself, hearing, seeing, breathing, learning, or working. The institution or school district determines what "substantially limits" a major life activity—and the condition does not have to impact education (Council for Exceptional Children, 2021). For example, a student in a wheelchair may need physical accommodations or modifications (the use of ramps, elevators, extra time, custom furniture, etc.) to successfully navigate the educational environment but may not actually need any special education services.

Under this statute, for secondary school environments, "appropriate education" means one that is comparable to students without disabilities. There are no specific requirements for parental involvement or the frequency of reviewing plans in this law, unlike IDEA, which is described below (deBettencourt, 2002). At the postsecondary level, Section 504 states that students must have an opportunity to compete with their non-disabled peers. Section 504 requires educational services to be provided in the least restrictive environment, which is alongside students without disabilities to the extent possible (deBettencourt).

Section 508 of the Rehabilitation Act Amendments of 1998

In 1998, Section 508 of the Rehabilitation Act of 1973 was amended to require federal agencies to make electronic and information technology accessible to people with disabilities. This applies to all federally funded programs and services as long as it does not pose an "undue burden." Under this amendment, electronic and information technology must be accessible to those with physical, sensory, and cognitive disabilities. This applies to computer hardware and software, websites, and multimedia when developed, procured, maintained or used. These requirements can become important when considering programs of study and any curriculum-learning websites (U.S. General Services Administration, 2020).

Americans with Disabilities Act of 1990 (ADA)

The Americans with Disabilities Act (ADA) became law in 1990. It is a civil rights law prohibiting discrimination against individuals with disabilities in all areas of life, including jobs, schools, transportation, and general public spaces. It is divided into five sections related to different areas of public life and ensures "reasonable accommodations" are made without causing "undue hardship" (difficulty or expense) (ADA National Network, 2017). In CTE, ADA should be kept in mind for both the school environment but also work-based learning environments.

Americans with Disabilities Act Amendment Act of 2008 (ADAAA)

The Americans with Disabilities Act Amendments Act (ADAAA) went into effect on January 1, 2009, and made major changes to the terms within the definition of disability that had existed in law previously. The definition itself did not change, defining a disability as a physical or mental impairment that substantially limits one or more major life activities; a record of such an impairment; or being regarded as having an impairment (Job Accommodation Network, 2021).

A major change was how the ADAAA expanded the definition of "major life activities." Major life activities, which previously included caring for oneself, performing manual tasks, seeing, hearing, eating, sleeping, walking, standing, etc., now also include the operation of major bodily functions (immune system, cell growth, digestive system, respiratory system, etc.). There was no formal definition of "substantially limits," but the ADAAA set rules for determining whether a person is substantially limited by a disability. These changes applied and continue to apply to the ADA and the Rehabilitation Act. The ADAAA amendments described here may require CTE programs at secondary or postsecondary levels to make new accommodations for students with disabilities in the program of study (Job Accommodation Network, 2021).

Individuals with Disabilities Education Act (IDEA)

Thirteen Categories of Disabilities under IDEA:

1. Autism
2. Specific Learning Disability
3. Speech or Language Impairment
4. Emotional Disturbance
5. Traumatic Brain Injury
6. Visual Impairment
7. Hearing Impairment
8. Deafness
9. Mental Retardation
10. Deaf-blindness
11. Multiple Disabilities
12. Orthopedic Impairment
13. Other Health Impairment*

* Attention Deficit/Hyperactivity Disorder (ADD/ADHD) may be served under IDEA if it causes a learning or emotional disability or if the student meets the criteria for Other Health Impairment (varies by state).

The Individuals with Disabilities Education Act (IDEA) is a federal law that governs special education services in the United States. Under IDEA, school districts are required to identify and evaluate children who may have a disability. Once a child is evaluated and meets the eligibility of one or more of the 13 categories of disabilities, the district is then required to provide a free and appropriate public education (FAPE) (deBettencourt, 2002).

How the district provides a student with a free and appropriate public education is documented in an Individualized Education Plan (IEP). IEPs ensure students are successful in the K-12 system. An IEP requires cooperative planning with a team composed of parents, at least one regular education teacher, at least one special education teacher, a representative of the district who is qualified to provide or supervise the instruction to meet the needs of the learner with disabilities, an individual to interpret any evaluation results, others with special expertise related to the learner (if appropriate), and the learner (when appropriate) (Sarkees-Wircenski & Scott, 2003).

IEP meetings must be initiated and conducted periodically, but at least once every 12 months, to review the annual goals and to revise the IEP as appropriate (deBettencourt, 2002). Although this is only required once each year, parents have the right to request an IEP meeting at any time if they feel a student is not progressing appropriately. Like Section 504, IDEA requires that services for SWDs are provided within the least restrictive environment (deBettencourt).

VOICES FROM THE FIELD

Jeff Green—Assistant Director, Northland Career Center, Platte County, MO

In my time as an automotive instructor, accommodating students with disabilities (SWD) is something that was planned for often. It wasn't always easy, but it was important to me that all my students had an equitable opportunity to be successful in my classroom and shop.

In my second or third year of teaching, I found out a few days before school started that I would have a hearing impaired student, whom we will call Matt. Matt could read lips and benefited from wireless hearing aids. If I was willing to wear a microphone, he could hear me pretty well. Otherwise, I had to be looking at him directly. This was a no brainer in the classroom, but in the shop, it was more of a struggle. The microphone was still useful, but in most circumstances, wearing something around your neck was a safety hazard. Our solution was to have class leaders (another student) repeat directly to Matt so he could read the student's lips. In another situation, we had a deaf interpreter attend class as well.

Transition Services

IDEA requires that SWDs in high school have transition plans developed, including activities needed to help students achieve their post-school goals, including postsecondary education and employment (Brand et al., 2013; Wagner et al., 2015). Transition services are defined as coordinated activities for a student with a disability that are results-oriented and meet academic and functional needs (Harvey et al., 2020). Transition IEPs should include goals and objectives based on the student's interests, nature of severity of the student's disability, skills, and abilities. The IEP team then determines the school activities that are needed for the student to acquire the relevant work-related skills and behaviors (Sarkees-Wircenski & Scott, 2003).

It is important that SWDs have access to specific CTE programs where instruction, adaptive support services, and accommodations are available (Brand et al., 2013; Harvey et al., 2020). Various postsecondary options, accommodations, or special programs should also be included in transition planning so that students can make more informed decisions (Brand et al.). Transition services are meant to prepare SWDs for adult life. Postsecondary education, career goals, work options, and linkages with adult service providers should all be components of a transition IEP to help the student move from school to adult life (U.S. Department of Education, 2000).

CTE instructors know the labor market and have specialized expertise in preparing students for future employment. Therefore, CTE and special educators need to collaborate to support SWDs and ensure CTE programs provide the most effective experience for SWDs. The Association for Career and Technical Education Quality CTE Program of Study Framework specifically includes "Access & Equity" as one of 12 elements of a high-quality CTE program. CTE programs should be inclusive of SWDs in facilities, curriculum, instruction, assessments, work-based learning experiences, and CTSO participation (Imperatore & Hyslop, 2018).

Research has shown, however, that career and technical educators often have limited training on how to adapt instruction, lack consistent communication with special educators, and are often not included in IEP meetings. In area career centers, sometimes CTE teachers are not even aware of SWDs in their program until late in the year (Brand et al., 2013; Schmalzried & Harvey, 2014). With increased accountability through Perkins V for all students, CTE administrators and instructors need to continue to improve the communication with special educators and take greater accountability for improving the CTE model for SWDs (Harvey et al., 2020).

Accommodations & Modifications

CTE allows SWDs to demonstrate their knowledge and skills in a real-world setting that is connected to their career interests, which can increase self-esteem, motivation, confidence, and engagement (Brand et al., 2013). IEPs will detail particular accommodations and modifications for SWDs, but CTE instructors should understand the differences between the two concepts and the impact of both on curriculum. Harvey et al. (2020) recommend starting with the "industry-aligned curriculum and IRCs to support the continuum of available careers" (p. 72). CTE teachers should keep this as the foundation when considering how to accommodate and/or modify the curriculum.

An "accommodation" does not alter what is being taught. SWDs can participate in the same course of study as students without disabilities and use the same grading scale, but there is an adjustment, such as in the environment, curriculum format, or equipment used (Sarkees-Wircenski & Scott, 2003; University of Washington, 2021). For example, SWDs may be given extra time on assignments, an oral rather than written exam, small group instruction, an extra study guide or graphic organizer, or immediate feedback.

A "modification" does alter or change a process or object for SWDs who may not be able to comprehend all of the content an instructor is teaching (Sarkees-Wircenski & Scott, 2003; University of Washington, 2021). A change may be needed to the equipment or facility, or assignments might be reduced in number or modified significantly. For example, an instructor may need to select only the foundational learning objectives for the student to master, or alter some learning objectives to be taught at a different level; assignments may be shortened; or alternate curriculum may be used. This requires careful balance when there are state or federal accountability requirements in play related to student attainment of industry certifications or other similar goals.

CTE instructors should seek out assistance from special educators to collaborate and cooperate to make the best decisions for SWDs and ensure that a student's transition plans aren't personalized for his or her career goals (Brand et al., 2013; Schmalzried & Harvey, 2014). Goals for students should be measurable and observable and help students reach their potential. No matter the level of CTE instruction, understanding students' rights under the law, where to seek out assistance for meeting students' needs, and helping students achieve goals can ensure all students are employable as they leave CTE programs.

VOICES FROM THE FIELD

Jeff Green—Assistant Director, Northland Career Center, Platte County, MO

Later in my CTE career, I had the opportunity to serve as a student support and transition coordinator for a career center. My job was to help all SWDs transition into the career center and support them and the teachers. There were three important parts to this role:

1. Having a process to acquire the information from the sending schools (ex. IEPs, 504s, case manager info, etc.);
2. Sharing the information prior to the student attending with the teacher;
3. Being an active participant in IEP and 504 meetings, including getting teacher feedback prior to those meetings (participation could be virtual, in-person, or via phone).

The teachers didn't attend frequently unless it was very necessary for the success of the student. Oftentimes, it was my job to attend as the teacher.

We have been successful as a school in helping our SWD population, which comprises 22–25 percent of the total population at the career center. It takes creativity and dedication, but that is why teachers are here, to help all students learn.

Universal Design for Learning (UDL)

UDL as a curriculum design framework was previously described (see chapter 3); however, its relevance to students with disabilities should be noted. UDL provides for flexible alternatives to be built into instructional design for learners with different abilities and backgrounds (Sarkees-Wircenski & Scott, 2003). While educators have typically adapted the textbook or exams through accommodations and modifications, adapting the curricular design allows flexible options for all students (Posey, 2021; Sarkees-Wircenski & Scott). "In a UDL learning environment, differences in experience, knowledge, and ability are expected" (Posey, para. 4). UDL provides an opportunity for all students to work at their own pace, determine support and resources needed as they work toward goals, and provide opportunities to demonstrate learning in a variety of ways (CAST, 2018; Sarkees-Wircenski & Scott; Posey).

VOICES FROM THE FIELD

Amanda Bastoni—Former Photo/Video Teacher ConVal Regional High School, Former CTE Director Nashua Technology Center, CAST Research Scientist, Peterborough, NH

Instead of going through traditional teacher preparation programs, most CTE educators come directly from industry, often without the same pedagogical training as their peers. On top of this, many CTE teachers are singletons—meaning they are the only automotive, welding, or culinary teachers in their school or district.

Coupled together, these factors can leave CTE educators feeling isolated and siloed as they try to develop teaching strategies to support students with disabilities—especially as many CTE teachers are working in dangerous lab environments, where students could get injured.

UDL provides CTE teachers with a common language they can use to discuss concerns across programs, and it provides tangible strategies they can start using right away as they proactively design learning experiences for the wide range of learners that walk into their classrooms every day.

Summary

Having a basic understanding of legal implications of students with disabilities can assist CTE teachers and instructors in the development of curricular plans with the flexibility to meet the needs of all students. Creating a curriculum that is free from bias and inclusive allows all students to have the opportunity to be successful in their career plans. SWDs have a greater likelihood of success through the career and transition plans that CTE can provide. Having the ability to make appropriate accommodations and modifications provides the additional support students with disabilities need to access the curriculum and achieve their career goals.

ACTE's Quality CTE Program of Study Framework Connection

The concepts in this chapter related to the following elements of the *Quality CTE Program of Study Framework* developed by the Association for Career and Technical Education (read more about the framework in chapter 2, Imperatore & Hyslop, 2018):

- **Element 6: Access and Equity**
  This element addresses CTE program promotion, student recruitment, and supports to ensure access and equity for all student populations. Curriculum, instruction, materials, and assessments should be free from bias, inclusive, and offered in a way to ensure that all students can achieve success in the program of study, including through accommodations as appropriate. Supportive services should also be offered as appropriate, and there should be actions taken to eliminate barriers for students with disabilities to extended learning experiences.

References

ADA National Network. (2017). *An overview of the Americans with disabilities act.* https://adata.org/sites/adata.org/files/files/ADA_Overview_final2017.pdf

Brand, B., Valent, A., & Danielson, L. (2013, March). *Improving college and career readiness for students with disabilities.* American Institutes for Research. https://ccrscenter.org/sites/default/files/Improving%20College%20and%20Career%20Readiness%20for%20Students%20with%20Disabilities.pdf

CAST. (2018). *Universal design for learning guidelines version 2.2* [graphic organizer]. CAST, Inc. https://udlguidelines.cast.org/binaries/content/assets/udlguidelines/udlg-v2-2/udlg_graphicorganizer_v2-2_numbers-no.pdf

Council for Exceptional Children. (2021). *Understanding the differences between IDEA and Section 504.* WETA. http://www.ldonline.org/article/6086/

deBettencourt, L. U. (2002). Understanding the differences between IDEA and Section 504. *Teaching Exceptional Children, 34*(3), 16–23.

Harvey, M. W. (2002). Comparison of postsecondary transitional outcomes between students with and without disabilities by secondary vocational education participation: Findings from the National Education Longitudinal Study. *Career Development and Transition for Exceptional Individuals, 25*(2), 99-122. https://doi.org/10.1177/088572880202500202

Harvey, M. W., Rowe, D. A., Test, D. W., Imperatore, C., Lombardi, A., Conrad, M., Szymanski, A., & Barnett, K. (2020). Partnering to improve career and technical education for students with disabilities: A position paper of the division on career development and transition. *Career Development and Transition for Exceptional Individuals, 43*(2), 67–77. https://doi.org/10.1177/2165143419887839

Hehir, T., Dougherty, S., & Grindal, T. (2013). *Students with disabilities in Massachusetts career and technical education programs.* Massachusetts Department of Elementary and Secondary Education. https://www.researchgate.net/publication/316479359_Students_with_Disabilities_in_Massachusetts_Career_and_Technical_Education_Programs

Imperatore, C., & Hyslop, A. (2018). *2018 ACTE quality CTE program of study framework.* ACTE. https://www.acteonline.org/wp-content/uploads/2019/01/HighQualityCTEFramework2018.pdf

Job Accommodation Network. (2021). *Americans with disabilities act amendments act.* https://askjan.org/topics/Americans-with-Disabilities-Act-Amendments-Act.cfm

Lee, H., Rojewski, J. W., & Gregg, N. (2016). Causal effects of career-technical education on postsecondary work outcomes of individuals with high-incidence disabilities. *Exceptionality, 24*(2), 79–92. https://doi.org/10.1080/09362835.2014.986608

Posey, A. (2021). *Lesson planning with universal design for learning.* CAST, Inc. https://www.understood.org/en/school-learning/for-educators/universal-design-for-learning/lesson-planning-with-universal-design-for-learning-udl

Sarkees-Wircenski, M., & Scott, J. L. (2003). *Special populations in career and technical education.* American Technical Publishers, Inc.

Schmalzried, J. E., & Harvey, M. W. (2014). Perceptions of special education and career and technical education collaboration and communication. *Career Development and Transition for Exceptional Individuals, 37*(2), 84–96. https://doi.org/10.1177/2165143412467666

Test, D. W., Aspel, N. P., & Everson, J. M. (2006). *Transition methods for youth with disabilities.* Pearson Education.

Theobald, T., Goldhaber, D., Gratz, T., & Holden, K. L. (2017). *Career and technical education, inclusion, and postsecondary outcomes for students with disabilities* (CEDR working paper 2017). University of Washington. https://caldercenter.org/publications/career-and-technical-education-inclusion-and-postsecondary-outcomes-students

U.S. Department of Education. (2000). *A guide to the individualized education program.* https://www2.ed.gov/parents/needs/speced/iepguide/iepguide.pdf

U.S. General Services Administration. (2020). *Section508.gov: IT accessibility laws and policies.* http://section508.gov/manage/laws-and-policies

University of Washington. (2021). *What is the difference between accommodation and modification for a student with a disability?* https://www.washington.edu/doit/what-difference-between-accommodation-and-modification-student-disability

Wagner, M. M., Newman, L. A., & Javitz, H. S. (2015). The benefits of high school career and technical education (CTE) for youth with learning disabilities. *Journal of Learning Disabilities,* 1–13.

PART IV

■

CURRICULUM
CONSTRUCTION AND REVIEW

 CHAPTER 12: CURRICULUM STANDARDS, GOALS, AND OBJECTIVES

Chapter 12 explores the importance of curricular standards, goals, levels of learning, and objectives within CTE curriculum and instruction. The chapter compares teaching with well-constructed objectives to a map a driver would use on a long trip. Both are essential to successfully reaching your destination. The same is true for the other elements contained within this chapter. Therefore, standards, curricular goals, objectives versus outcomes, levels of learning, and planning assessments are thoroughly examined with the aim of establishing and maintaining high-quality CTE programs that reach their intended target.

 CHAPTER 13: CURRICULUM PLANNING

Chapter 13 continues with examining curriculum planning within CTE. The chapter continues with the illustration that curriculum planning is similar to planning a road trip across the country. Both require a multitude of forethought and organization. If the advanced planning isn't completed thoroughly, you won't reach the intended destination. Therefore, this chapter provides specific details about the curriculum planning process, including scope, sequence, and curriculum mapping, as well as unit and lesson planning. Using this chapter as a resource, readers will be well equipped to successfully navigate the curriculum planning journey.

 CHAPTER 14: CURRICULUM REVIEW & REVISION

Chapter 14 explains that with the ever-changing nature of business and industry, CTE curriculum must continuously evolve or it will quickly become out of date. Therefore, this chapter provides an overview of program evaluation, accreditation reviews, and the Perkins Comprehensive Local Needs Assessment (CLNA). A continuous curriculum improvement process is also illustrated in context to ensure CTE curriculum remains current with industry expectations.

Chapter 12

■

CURRICULUM STANDARDS, GOALS, & OBJECTIVES

Kevin S. Elliott—Pittsburg State University
Howard R. D. Gordon—University of Nevada, Las Vegas, National Institute for Automotive Service Excellence

Introduction

Have you ever purchased something that required directions to assemble, but decided to put it together without reading the directions? How did that go for you? Or have you ever taken a long trip to a specific destination without a map or directions only to end up lost or frustrated and asking for help? The first one is fairly common, and the second one would be a waste of time and resources. Both examples show how an endeavor undertaken without a plan can end up being a lost cause.

The same is true for teaching. Developing a well-written objective provides those "directions" for successful completion of the task. Without these, you can become lost and might even give up before you finish what you started. This is the same with teaching a lesson. Consider the objective as the primary component, which allows you and your students to know what is expected, when it needs to be completed, and to what level or standard. Basically, an objective is one of your most critical elements when teaching.

Curriculum goals and objectives are crucial components of teacher planning. Effective development of these elements directly impacts student learning. Goals and standards help define instruction and the connection to other learning or industry expectations, or sometimes, both. Learning objectives are commonly associated with the unit or lesson and help shape how information will be shared, assessed, and/or applied. This chapter will address the importance of goals, levels of learning, objectives, assessment, and alignment.

Standards

The process of developing learning goals and objectives begins with knowing the specific standards, benchmarks, and supporting knowledge students in your state, school district, or institution are required to learn. A standard is defined as an established reference. "Specifically, standards define the work to be performed, how well the work must be done, and the level of knowledge and skills required" (Aragon et al., 2004, p. 1). Standards help ensure quality, indicate goals, and promote change. Also, standards are more likely to enable communication, protection, harmonization, simplification, and valuation (Hill et al., 1992). (See Part 2 of this text for additional information about CTE technical, academic, and employability skill standards).

VOICES FROM THE FIELD

Melissa Scott—former Assistant Director of Career and Technical Education, Nevada Department of Education

I facilitated many writing teams to develop state standards for CTE programs of study, and at each session I started out by explaining the difference between standards and curriculum and who is responsible for each. In my case, the state is responsible for standards—what students should know upon completion of the program. These apply to every program in the state. The local district or teacher is responsible for how it is taught or the curriculum. The trick is to be sure the curriculum is aligned to standards. We have an instructional materials approval process in place, directed at the state level, to ensure this happens.

Standards should be specific enough to include measurable performance indicators and be relevant to current industry needs. Likewise, curriculum should include unit learning objectives. Both performance indicators and learning objectives should be transparent to students and other stakeholders.

Curricular Goals

Curricular goals are broad statements written from an instructor or institution's perspective that give the general content and direction of a learning experience and lead to long-term educational outcomes (DePaul University, 2021). Goals should incorporate a description of knowledge and skills to be learned and the concepts to be understood. Bottoms et al. (1997) reported that when designing challenging career and technical education courses, course goals should include the major concepts or processes that students need to learn; topics, concepts, and procedures from academic fields that students need to apply; and the qualities of a successful worker. The following may be examples of curricular goals from a variety of CTE courses:

- *Animal Science*: Introduce students to animal husbandry methods for domestic cattle.
- *Accounting*: Students will have a working knowledge of GAAP (Generally Accepted Accounting Principles).
- *Graphic Design*: Apply software skills to solve introductory visual design problems typically found in the field.
- *Health Science*: Demonstrate cultural competence related to quality patient care.

Objectives vs. Outcomes

In this text, we are using "learning objective" to mean "the desired outcome of an educational activity" (Collins & O'Brien, 2011, p. 266). While this text is using the term "learning objective," sometimes the term "learning outcome" is used. Education, like every other occupation, has its own jargon. As new CTE teachers can attest, this jargon is often overwhelming. A learning objective should specify what a learner should know or be able to do as a result of instruction. Some institutions or schools may call these outcomes, while others may use the terms "learning targets" or "learning goals." Depending on local preferences, you may need to clarify how terminology is being used. We describe learning goals as those broader statements as described earlier and use the term learning objectives as statements of desired outcomes. To be specific in those desired outcomes, the verbs selected need to be carefully considered through "levels of learning" to create measurable learning objectives.

Levels of Learning

Levels of learning address the importance of teaching at various "levels" for understanding. Objectives need to be aligned with industry standards. As curriculum developers, however, we need to determine at what level we expect students to learn. Some objectives only require a surface familiarity of concepts, while other objectives may require a full understanding, ability to apply knowledge, or solve critical problems based on the content. Two models that are used in many schools, districts, and institutions will be reviewed here: Bloom's Taxonomy and Webb's Depth of Knowledge.

Bloom's Taxonomy

In the 1950s, educational researcher Benjamin Bloom, with help from other researchers, developed the basis for writing educational objectives in the cognitive, psychomotor, and affective domains (Bloom et al., 1956). His work, called "Bloom's Taxonomy," has been modified over time but is used in education as a framework for categorizing the level of educational objectives from low to high, which is also thought of as simple to complex or concrete to abstract. Bloom did not develop the affective and psychomotor domains to the degree that the cognitive domain was developed, but others used his foundation to create a usable organizational structure (Hoque, 2016; Nilson, 2016). The following discusses each of the domains and how these apply to objective writing.

Cognitive Domain Objectives

Cognitive objectives focus on knowledge and critical thinking skills. Bloom uses terms like "define" and "describe" at the basic levels of learning in the cognitive domain. Conversely, "synthesize," "discriminate," and "justify" are verbs, which indicate a higher level of comprehension. Objectives should also be reflective of the level of mastery you want students to achieve. Keep in mind, higher levels of mastery build on lower levels, and your objectives should progress as your students learn and knowledge becomes more complex.

Cognitive Domain

Verbs for Learning Objectives

(Nilson, 2016)

1. Knowledge/ Remembering	2. Comprehension/ Understanding	3. Application/ Applying	4. Analysis/ Analyzing	5. Evaluation/ Evaluating	6. Synthesis/ Creating
Identify	Describe	Apply	Analyze	Assess	Adapt
Define	Explain	Compute	Calculate	Convince	Build
List	Locate	Demonstrate	Classify	DefendRank	Integrate
Match	Paraphrase	Determine	Differentiate	Recommend	Design
Recall	Summarize	Illustrate	Distinguish	Critique	Formulate
Select	Report	Operate	Investigate		Manage
		Manipulate	Compare		Produce
			Contrast		

Psychomotor Domain Objectives

Psychomotor objectives focus on actions and behaviors. These are what we expect students to be able to do. This is at the heart of CTE! Words like "find" and "sort" are at the lowest level of the taxonomy. As you move from simple to complex or concrete to abstract psychomotor objectives, students may be expected to create, regulate, and manipulate (Bixler, 2007).

Psychomotor Domain

Verbs for Learning Objectives

(Saint Paul College, 2021)

1. Imitation	2. Manipulation	3. Precision	4. Articulation	5. Naturalization
Follow	Build	Demonstrate	Construct	Invent
Repeat	Perform	Show	Combine	Design
Copy	Execute	Control	Coordinate	Manage
Match	Operate	Complete	Adapt	
Identify			Integrate	

Affective Domain Objectives

Krathwohl et al. (1964) developed the affective taxonomy, which is intended to measure thoughts and feelings toward a subject or activity. This domain is typically difficult to evaluate and works well with a rubric containing descriptors, which allow the students to have a goal for effective completion or development of a product or process. Lower-level affective verbs include "listen," "look," and "discern." Higher-level verbs include "relate," "regulate," and "judge" (Clark, 2015; The Peak Performance Center, 2021).

Affective Domain

Verbs for Learning Objectives

(The Second Principle, 2021)

1. Receiving	2. Responding	3. Valuing	4. Organizing	5. Internalizing
Capture	Contribute	Believe	Examine	Review
Experience	Satisfy	Justify	Create	Conclude
Pursue	Conform	Respect	Integrate	Resolve
Attend	Cooperate	Persuade	Clarify	Judge
Perceive	Allow	Search	Systematize	Internalize

Webb's Depth of Knowledge (DOK)

In 1997, Norman Webb developed a Depth of Knowledge (DOK) model to analyze cognitive expectations in standards, learning activities, and assessments (Mississippi State University, 2009). The model includes four levels (Aungst, 2014):

- *Level 1*: Recall and Reproduction: Recall of facts or rote memorization and application of simple procedures. Includes defining, copying, computing, recognizing.
- *Level 2*: Skills and Concepts: Decision making about approaches to ideas. Tasks include more than one step. Includes comparing, organizing, summarizing.
- *Level 3*: Strategic Thinking: Planning and evidence are needed. Thinking is more abstract. Tasks include multiple possible responses. Includes problem solving, designing experiments, analyzing characteristics.

- *Level 4*: Extended Thinking: Complex cognitive effort needed. Synthesizing information from multiple sources over extended periods of time or transferring knowledge between environments. Includes designing a survey and interpreting results, extracting themes from texts, original writing.

The focus of Webb's DOK is on the cognitive domain. In CTE this could be seen as a drawback, as performance and employability objectives may not be best represented. While a newer and widely utilized model is used in schools for curriculum, we often see the older Bloom's Taxonomy in use in CTE, as it tends to still better represent the integration of multiple types of skills that career and technical educators expect students to develop. Whether your institution, school, or district uses Bloom's Taxonomy or Webb's DOK, the idea is to build a curriculum that moves from foundational skills to more complex and specific skills in the content area. These models provide a basis to form learning objectives to align the curriculum with the assessments.

VOICES FROM THEORY AND RESEARCH

How students learn is not defined by one specific set of terms, nor is there a handbook of "best ways for students to learn." Instead, CTE instructors must find strategies to connect with students, which help them understand the concepts and hands-on skills in the most effective way possible. In many cases, this can look very different for each student. Educational theorists have studied learning styles and methodology for many years without identifying one practice that works for every student. Therefore, it is imperative CTE instructors continue to be flexible and include many strategies in their instruction. In order to meet the unique needs of students and the variety of learning styles they possess, teachers must rely on the work of researchers and clinicians who have studied learning.

In this section, we will share some thoughts from one expert who developed theories or practices focused on increasing student learning. John Stevenson (2001) addressed the challenge of specifying knowledge and placing it into identifiable categories within CTE. His work focused on the difficulty of applying concepts associated with CTE into recognizable standards, outcomes, and competencies, which allowed students to clearly understand the connection between the concept and practical application. Stevenson's research resulted in the following recommendations:

- "a focus on plural types and qualities of knowledge;"
- "opportunities for plural types of learning experiences for accessing, acquiring and communicating vocational knowledge in plural, but connected ways;"

- "situated learning where there are rich artefacts, authentic culture, obvious purposes and explicit feedback;"
- "explicit valuing of non-expressible knowledge, such as automatic procedures and encapsulated concepts;"
- "explicit attempts to create, present and depict knowledge in ways that are functionally useful as opposed to, or in addition to being discipline based;"
- "opportunities for individuals to connect meanings that they construct on experiences in various life pursuits" (Stevenson, 2001, p. 659)

In the recommendations above, Stevenson is encouraging CTE teachers to apply both the knowledge and practical application components of the content. One without the other likely will result in students who lack a deep understanding of the concepts. However, a rich, effective CTE lesson, according to Stevenson (2001), provides more worthwhile learning opportunities for a wider variety of students. Be sure you have good models, diagrams, or mock-ups. Help students make the connections between the theory (book) and application. Give them a chance to get immersed in the hands-on components to allow them to connect the theory and the task.

Learning Objectives

A well-written objective has three well-designed components. These are the condition, the performance, and the criterion. Each of these helps the instructor develop a logical and measurable objective. Whether you are new or a veteran to writing objectives, reviewing these concepts will help create meaningful and clear objectives with the potential to drastically improve student understanding.

Before looking at the components, let's look at an objective that can be found in a culinary arts lesson: "Students will learn to measure ingredients for a cake." Looking at this objective, there are some issues. What are we giving the students to succeed? How do we really know if they "learned"? How are we going to measure the accuracy of properly making a cake? It can be a bad cake and still be a cake. Let's further explore the three components in order to create a more accurate learning objective.

The condition defines the circumstances under which the student will be assessed (Nilson, 2016). Is there a time constraint? Is there a predetermined location? What supplies will be provided? Adding "Using the resources and materials supplied" to the beginning of our culinary arts objective would provide some guidance, which should improve student success in achieving this objective. The original objective did not give any indication of what to use. Some students will know what to use or know to find a recipe. Others will try without any of these resources. These students may struggle to succeed. Providing the condition allows each student, or group of students, a chance to be successful and increases the chance all cakes will start in the same way.

The performance informs what learners will be able to do specifically at the end of instruction (Weber State University, 2021). It focuses on a clear and specific action verb based on the level of knowledge expected—for example, "define," "classify," "compute," "analyze." Changing the verb in the original objective from "learn" to "measure" describes what the teacher wants each student group to complete. In this case, it is "measure all ingredients." This is simply stated, but in combination with the condition and criterion, it doesn't have to be complex.

The criterion determines how an instructor will evaluate and ultimately grade performance (Nilson, 2016; Weber, 2021). How many references are needed? How long should a presentation be? What's the tolerance range on a machined part? These are the details often found on a scoring guide or rubric. In the objective, there is no mention of a benchmark of any kind. Adding "as specified in a recipe" to the end of the objective provides a more detailed benchmark for students. The instructor can physically see if the measurements are correct before students proceed to the next step. If students just put ingredients in a bowl and mix these up, it would be difficult to ensure each student understood the concept.

Our new culinary arts objective would then be:

"Using the resources and materials supplied, students will measure all ingredients for a cake
          condition   *performance*

as specified in the recipe."
        criterion

Assessing Student Learning

Rigorous curricula standards demand high-quality assessments of student learning to ensure that students have mastered both academic and technical content. Therefore, "when we say we are 'assessing a student's competency,' we mean we are collecting information to help us decide the degree to which the student has achieved the learning targets" (Nitko, 1996, p. 4).

According to Bottoms et al. (1997, p. 68), the four major purposes of assessing student learning are to:

1. Motivate students to meet high performance standards and to become independent learners.
2. Determine if students have learned the essential course content so instructors can address any gaps that may exist.
3. Help teachers see whether the instructional plan worked and how they can augment it in the future.
4. Determine a student's course grade.

While assessment is not the focus of this text, it must be addressed in the context of quality CTE curriculum. Multiple forms of assessment should be built into the curriculum and aligned to the learning objectives and ultimately the standards (Imperatore & Hyslop, 2018). In order to utilize assessment for student learning and understand its role in the curriculum, there must be a general understanding of formative and summative assessment, as well as what it means to "align" assessments.

Formative and Summative Assessments

Formative assessments are defined as planned assessments that are primarily concerned with gathering information about learning, as well as provide guidance for both teacher and student. Specifically, formative assessments are more likely to be *informal* and include the following sources: classroom questions, clicker questions, homework exercises, observations of students, one-minute reflection, weekly quizzes, writing assignments (Anderson & Krathwohl, 2001; Banks, 2005).

Banks (2005) defined summative assessments as "a type of <u>formal</u> assessment used to measure students' outcomes at the end of the instructional program or course. They may be used to determine if the student achieved mastery of an instructional segment or an academic program" (p. 30). Some examples of summative assessments are presentations, projects, research papers, and standardized tests. Anderson and Krathwohl (2001, p. 246) suggested that both formative and summative assessments are generally intertwined in the classroom.

Assessment Alignment

As instructors, we decide what assessments to use and how to assess these, but we need to make sure that our learning objectives *align* with our assessments. Let's return to our cake-baking objective: "Using the resources and materials supplied, students will measure all ingredients for a cake as specified in the recipe." This objective says "will measure ingredients for a cake." So, we would expect students to actually perform (psychomotor domain) measuring the ingredients in order to demonstrate their competence.

If the teacher gives a word problem on a test that has the students reading a recipe and calculating measurements, does that fulfill this objective? It does not assess if the student can actually *measure* the ingredients, but rather it measures if the student knows how (cognitive domain) to *calculate* measurements for a recipe. Some might say students need to know how to do the calculations before they are given supplies. True, but aligning assessments means that the summative assessment task is actually what students are expected to achieve and is communicated in the learning objective.

It is important the parts of the lesson align with other elements of the content. Curriculum designers need to take care with the verbs used in learning objectives to ensure these align with what students are expected to know or be able to do. Those verbs, as described earlier, need to be consistent with the level of performance that the instructor actually expects of students. If students need to be able to repair a flat tire, but they never get to practice on a tire, and the assessment has the students explaining how to fix a flat tire, the curriculum and assessment are not completely aligned. It may be a formative assessment component to first be able to observe and explain prior to the summative, but it is not actually repairing the flat tire.

Aligning the learning objectives, the instructional activities, and the assessments ensures continuity. Objectives should not stand alone but must support the entire process. As students work up to the more difficult levels of your content, the objectives should also reflect increased complexity or higher levels of thinking and performance, such as described in Bloom's Taxonomy or Webb's Depth of Knowledge.

Summary

The science of teaching involves using standards as the foundation. When you take the standards and create objectives, that process can be regarded as the art of teaching. CTE standards are articulated expectations of what students should be able to know and do at the completion of a course or program and set goals for student learning. A taxonomy can be considered as a framework for curriculum decisions and help to categorize objectives as cognitive, affective, or psychomotor. A typical objective statement includes three components: condition, performance, and criterion.

CTE standards must include opportunities for students to acquire the knowledge and skills that are essential for today's workplace. High-quality CTE programs should engage students in a coherent and aligned program with assessments that determine how much a student has learned and whether he or she has performed to a level of proficiency.

ACTE's Quality CTE Program of Study Framework Connection

The concepts in this chapter related to the following elements of the *Quality CTE Program of Study Framework* developed by the Association for Career and Technical Education (read more about the framework in chapter 2, Imperatore & Hyslop, 2018):

- **Element 3: Student Assessment**
  This element addresses knowledge and skills that should be assessed through CTE programs and the types and quality of assessments used. Assessments should be aligned to standards and appropriate to students' current level of knowledge and skills. Both formative and summative assessments should be integrated throughout the program of study, be valid and reliable, and validate student learning.

- **Element 5: Engaging Instruction**
  This element addresses instructional strategies that will support student attainment of relevant knowledge and skills. Programs of study instruction should be driven by relevant content area standards, and clear learning objectives to ensure learning activity yields desired student outcomes.

References

Anderson L.W., & Krathwohl, D. R. (2001). *A taxonomy for learning, teaching and assessing: A revision of Bloom's taxonomy of educational objectives*. Addison Wesley Longman, Inc.

Aragon, A., Woo, H-J., and Marvel, M. R. (2004). Analysis of the integration of skill standards into community college curriculum. *National research center for career and technical education, 44*(2). University of Minnesota. https://files.eric.ed.gov/fulltext/ED492350.pdf

Aungst, G. (2014). Using Webb's depth of knowledge to increase rigor. *Edutopia*. https://www.edutopia.org/blog/webbs-depth-knowledge-increase-rigor-gerald-aungst

Banks, S. R. (2005). *Classroom assessment issues and practices*. Pearson Education, Inc.

Bixler, B. (2007). *Psychomotor Domain*. http://users.rowan.edu/~cone/curriculum/psychomotor.htm

Bloom, B.S., Engelhart, M.D., Furst, E.J., Hill, W.H., & Krathwohl, D.R. (1956). *Taxonomy of educational objectives, handbook I: The cognitive domain.* David McKay Co., Inc.

Bottoms, G., Pucel, D. J., & Phillips, I. (1997). *A guide to preparing a syllabus: Designing challenging vocational courses.* Southern Regional Education Board.

Clark, D. (2015). *Bloom's taxonomy: The affective domain.* http://knowledgejump.com/hrd/Bloom/affective_domain.html

Collins, J. W., & O'Brien, N. P. (2011). *The Greenwood dictionary of education* (2nd ed.). Greenwood.

DePaul University. (2021). *Course objectives and learning outcomes.* https://resources.depaul.edu/teaching-commons/teaching-guides/course-design/Pages/course-objectives-learning-outcomes.aspx

Hill, P. T., Harvey, J., & Praskac, A. (1992). *Pandora's box: Accountability and performance standards in vocational education.* https://eric.ed.gov/?id=ED353408

Hoque, M. E. (2016, September). Three domains of learning: Cognitive, affective and psychomotor. T*he Journal of EFL Education and Research 2*(2), 45–52. https://www.researchgate.net/profile/Md-Hoque-44/publication/330811334_Three_Domains_of_Learning_Cognitive_Affective_and_Psychomotor/links/5c54a5e9458515a4c7502bd5/Three-Domains-of-Learning-Cognitive-Affective-and-Psychomotor.pdf

Imperatore, C. & Hyslop, A. (2018). *2018 ACTE quality CTE program of study framework.* Association for Career & Technical Education. https://www.acteonline.org/wp-content/uploads/2019/01/HighQualityCTEFramework2018.pdf

Krathwohl, D.R., Bloom, B.S., & Masia, B.B. (1964). *Taxonomy of educational objectives, the classification of educational goals: Handbook II: Affective domain.* David McKay Company, Inc.

Mississippi State University. (2009). *Webb's depth of knowledge guide: Career and technical education definitions.* https://www.aps.edu/sapr/documents/resources/Webbs_DOK_Guide.pdf

Nilson, L. B. (2016). *Teaching at its best: A research-based resource for college instructors.* Jossey-Bass.

Nitko, A. J. (1996). *Educational assessment of students* (2nd edition). Prentice-Hall, Inc.

Saint Paul College. (2021). *Writing learning outcomes.* https://www.saintpaul.edu/aei/learning-outcomes

Stevenson, J. (2001). Vocational knowledge and its specification. *Journal of Vocational Education & Training, 53*(4), 647–662, https://doi.org/10.1080/13636820100200182

The Peak Performance Center. (2021). *Affective domain of learning.* https://thepeakperformancecenter.com/educational-learning/learning/process/domains-of-learning/affective-domain/

The Second Principle. (2021). *Three domains of learning: Cognitive, affective, psychomotor.* https://thesecondprinciple.com/instructional-design/threedomainsoflearning/

Weber State University. (2021). Learning objective vs. learning activity. https://weber.instructure.com/courses/307280/pages/learning-objective-vs-learning-activity

Chapter 13

■

CURRICULUM PLANNING

Michelle L. Conrad—University of Central Missouri

Introduction

For a moment, let's think about driving across the country. Where are you leaving from? What highways will you take? How long will it take? How far can you travel each day? Where will you stop to take breaks? Who else is traveling with you that might want to approve of your plans?

Planning a trip is similar to planning a curriculum. Just as you would use a map and create a plan for your cross-country trip, you want to create the same type of plan for teaching. Depending on the program or course, you'll need to determine your starting point for a particular program or class, how you will sequence your content, how much content will be included in each section of the course, how much time you'll spend on each section, and when you will plan assessments. Curricular plans include all the details of how to sequence and organize materials for teaching.

Curricular plans, however, also provide the framework for being adaptable. Oftentimes students may or may not learn the material within the time frame you were hoping for, sometimes learning more quickly and other times not understanding the material at all. Unpredictable situations, such as field trips, sick days, snow days, CTSO events, assemblies, and other unexpected events, will come up and make it difficult to accomplish everything that you initially plan to do. If the COVID-19 pandemic has taught us anything, it is to be flexible and prepared to teach content in multiple ways.

Being adaptable, however, means we must be prepared. Being prepared starts with our curricular plans. As reviewed in chapter 2, a variety of models exist for designing curriculum. This chapter will provide details for the organizing of content to document a particular program or course. We will start with an overview of sequencing content for learning and then move into developing curriculum maps, as well as unit and lesson plans.

Scope, Sequence, and Curriculum Mapping

As previous chapters have discussed, knowing the standards and developing learning objectives with aligned assessments allows a teacher to ensure that the curriculum will prepare students for the workplace and future learning. Once you have established the standards to be taught and the learning objectives and assessments for your content, then you need to sequence content in ways that make sense for the content and the students, building from one concept to the next. Where do you start? Where do you stop? How "deep" do you go?

The term *scope* refers to the breadth and depth of content and skills included in the curriculum (IBE-UNESCO, 2021). In CTE, this includes the technical, academic, and employability knowledge and skills students need to be successful. Once you, as the instructor, have the material that is to be taught, you can "map" a year's curriculum in "chunks" as it is actually going to be taught or is planned to be taught (Burns, 2001). A calendar or a school planner provides a place to start organizing the chunks of material. The term *sequence* then refers to how these chunks of skills and content will be ordered and presented over time (IBE-UNESCO).

Start by putting your learning objectives into an order that builds from introductory materials to more complex material within the scope of what is to be taught. Students can't apply, analyze, synthesize, or evaluate knowledge if they don't know the terminology or basic facts of the field. They need to master the most basic skills and procedures first (Nilson, 2016).

For a program, determine which objectives belong in each course. For a particular course, determine what learning objectives can be taught or grouped together. If you are planning for an entire program, you may want to work

What is meant by horizontal and vertical alignment?

Horizontal alignment means that teachers work across a grade level to map course content to ensure that curriculum is aligned between classrooms and teachers. Vertical alignment means curriculum builds from foundational skills to more complex skills from one grade level to the next, or in CTE, for example, from secondary to postsecondary to workplace learning.

with other instructors at the same or varying levels, employers, and administrators to determine which learning objectives should be taught in each course in a program of study. Curricular planning in this way ensures alignment between levels and that students are mastering standards in a sequence that builds from one level to another.

Curriculum mapping, then, is a process to sequence the content and skills being taught. These may also be known as curriculum guides, scope and sequences, or pacing guides. Different curriculum maps can be used at different levels of program planning and include different information. Once you have your learning objectives organized to build skills from foundational to more complex, you can create a curriculum map for an entire CTE program or for particular courses. Let's explore these levels a little further.

Program Curriculum Map

A curriculum map for a CTE program may not include the level of detail that is contained in a course curriculum map. The program will want to note where each learning objective is addressed in particular courses in the program. For example, a graphic design program developed the following program curriculum map (Figure 13.1).

Figure 13.1 Graphic Design Program Curriculum Map

Program Name: Graphic Design		Introduction to Computer Graphics	Drawing I	Graphic Design History, Theory, & Practice	Graphic Design I	Graphic Design II
1	Recognize how graphic design is a form of communication and art.			History of Album Design Project	Service Activity: Cultural Event Poster Project	
2	Utilize design processes and principles to create visual product to convey a message to a targeted audience.	Newsletter Project	Sketchbook Term Project			Portfolio Review— Marketing Ads Component
3	Solve problems across a wide range of media.	Product Marketing Ads Project		History of Album Design Project		Portfolio Review— Marketing Ads Component
4	Apply software and hardware skills in the creation, reproduction, and distribution of visual messages.	Newsletter Project			Service Activity: Cultural Event Poster Project	Portfolio Review— Marketing Ads Component
5	Explore career paths within the graphics industry.	Job Shadow Journal		Graphic Designers Research Project		Portfolio Review— Personal Choices Component

Notice in this example that there are five program learning outcomes, and particular assignments are assessed in five courses throughout the program. Program faculty should work together to determine where content is introduced, reinforced, and summatively assessed. This normally means including one or two formative assessments and a summative assessment (See chapter 12 for additional information on formative and summative assessments). For example, in this program, program learning goal number 3, "Solve problems across a wide range of media," is introduced with concepts in the introduction to computer graphics course, where it is formatively assessed through a product marketing ads project. In the graphic design history, theory, and practice course, a history of album design project reinforces these concepts and again, formatively assesses students. In the final marketing ads component of the portfolio, students are summatively assessed on this program learning outcome.

WBL opportunities should also be integrated into a program curriculum map. As discussed in chapter 9, WBL experiences provide students an opportunity to receive training and learn skills through authentic workplace tasks (U.S. Department of Education, 2017). In this graphic design program example, we see a job shadow journal assignment. Other WBL experiences could be integrated into a program as well. Also note in this example that a service activity project is used as a program assessment. Although not included in this example, instructors may also want to integrate CTSO activities as major program assessments.

Utilizing a program curriculum map allows a visual way to show the sequence of where the program's content and skills are taught and assessed throughout the curriculum to meet learning outcomes. Through curriculum mapping, a program can demonstrate that courses are appropriately sequenced. It is not merely bundling credits in a field but rather documents how student learning progresses in a field of study and grows critical skills (Veltri et al., 2011).

Course Curriculum Map

A course curriculum map then provides an overview of the topics, learning objectives, standards alignment, assessments, instructional strategies, etc., that are included in a particular course. Again, once the learning objectives have been sequenced in a way that builds from introductory concepts to more complex material, you can divide the content into the "big ideas" or units of instruction. While this text is focused on the curriculum development process, course curriculum maps are also related to implementing instruction and should be considered in the planning process (Lattuca & Stark, 2009). Time should be planned for teaching, demonstrations, practice, lab activities, assessments, and review activities (Leshin et al., 1992).

The example in Figure 13.2 is from the first page of a personal finance course curriculum map and only shows one "big idea" or unit, but we see a duration/dates column, the big idea, the concepts within this idea, the learning objectives, alignment to standards, major instructional activities, and assessment. This is not the only way to set up curriculum maps; there are a variety of curriculum mapping templates available through a variety of organizations. Some break down the learning objectives into technical, academic, and employability skills, while others focus on knowledge and skills. Others do not include standards alignment because the standards are included on the unit templates. Some districts or colleges will require a particular template, while others allow instructors to determine what works best for their instructional style.

Although not present in this initial unit from this personal finance curriculum map, CTSOs should also be reflected in course curriculum maps for CTE courses. CTSOs are an integral part of a CTE program of study and enhance student learning "through contextual instruction, leadership and personal development, applied learning and real world application" (Hyslop, 2018; NCC-CTSO, 2021). Noting where CTSO learning opportunities are integrated into the course through the curriculum map allows all stakeholders an opportunity to understand the co-curricular engagement with these organizations.

Figure 13.2 Personal Finance Course Curriculum Map

Program Area: HS Business
Course: Personal Finance
Duration: 16 Weeks

Duration / Dates	Big Idea # (Unit Title)	Concepts - Competencies / Skills	SLOs	Alignment (Technical, Academic, & Employability Skills)	Major Instructional Activities	Assessment
Two weeks	I. Financial Decision Making: Choice is the central principle of financial decision making for individuals, businesses and government. People make many choices every day in markets where buyers and sellers interact. This interaction determines market prices and allocates scarce goods and services based on supply and demand. Every decision incurs an opportunity cost. Opportunity cost is the next-best alternative when a decision is made; it is what is given up.	1: Unlimited Wants & Resources	A. Evaluate the role of choice in decision making	MLS PF.I.1.A	1. Your Values & Money - Student activity packet. Read article linked in #2 aloud together.	1. PACED Model - buying a house, individual project to fill out PACED model template with options, criteria to base decision on, final decision rationale
			B. Apply a rational decision making process to satisfy wants.	MLS PF.I.1.B	2. PACED Model practice - buying a car with table partner presentation and worksheet 3. Play "The Bean Game"	
	2: Choice & Decision Making		A. Explain how today's choices have future consequences.	MLS PF.I.2.A	1. TEDTalk. Battle Between Present & Future Self w/ reflection	2. Ultimatum Game - takeaway reflection questions
			B. Explain the causal relationship between choice and opportunity cost.	MLS PF.I.2.B	2. Play the Ultimatum Game w/ reflection & discussion and PBS Video-Economic Decision	3. PBS Economists EdPuzzle embedded quiz on decision making
					OR ANALYZE The influence of advertisements	
			C. Analyze how choices can result in unintended consequences.	MLS PF.I.2.C	3. ANALYZE Activity - Change a Bad Financial Habit	4. Daily bell ringers to check prior day's learning and link to today's learning
						5. Exit ticket quizzes

Used with Permission, Amanda Drew, Business Teacher, Moberly, MO.

Curriculum Mapping Benefits

Students have to achieve foundational skills first and then proceed to higher levels of thinking, combining both knowledge and skills to achieve the later more challenging outcomes (Nilson, 2016). Curriculum mapping at the program or course levels allows teachers, administrators, or other stakeholders to see the big picture of the curriculum, as well as how the subject matter has been broken into smaller concepts, the organization of those concepts, and how the concepts are pulled together based on interrelationships (Van Patten et al., 1986).

VOICES FROM THE FIELD

Dr. David M. Yost—Associate Professor, CTE Teacher Educator, Marshall University, WV

For over 10 years, I have had the opportunity to train and mentor new CTE teachers coming from industry into CTE teaching. Though very motivated to share their expertise and experiences from their profession, most are apprehensive when it comes to understanding instructional tools such as curriculum mapping, unit plans, and lesson plans. My task has been to present these items, so critical to teaching, in a way that is simple and logical. I use the example of going on a trip, using the three as follows:

- First, look at the overall trip from point A to B, which is the overview or *Curriculum Map*. You establish the number of days you have and then begin to plan the details.

- Second, begin planning on the different parts of the trip along the way. The parts might include gas stops, overnight stays, meals, and sights to see. These are grouped together as *Units*.

- Third, there will be specific things that must be accomplished for the trip to be a successful experience, or *Lesson Plans*.

To further new CTE teachers' understanding of curriculum maps, unit plans, and lesson plans, I present them with a handout (Figure 1) of how the three are combined to prepare knowledge and skills lessons used to promote student learning.

Unit & Lesson Planning

A curriculum map provides the big picture of the learning process and demonstrates the sequence of outcomes throughout a course or program but does not necessarily provide the level of detail needed for entering a classroom or lab and teaching the content (Nilson, 2016). This is where unit and lesson planning can assist in creating more meaningful learning experiences (Larbi-Apau & Moseley, 2009). Depending on your teaching environment, you may use one or both of these. Some comprehensive school districts require daily lesson plans, while other environments, like area career centers or community colleges with longer class meeting times, may prefer a daily schedule as part of a unit plan. Some faculty have the latitude to determine for themselves what types of plans they use, while others have to submit their plans (and in a specific format).

Unit Plans

Unit plans are a way to pull out one major concept of the course to provide an in-depth overview of a group of objectives. Major topics or chunks of content that were grouped together on a curriculum map become the units of instruction. Unit plans often include additional detail not included on a curriculum map, such as critical or essential questions, an overview of individual lessons within the unit, a calendar plan, CTSO integration, differentiation strategies, and unit assessments. Figure 13.3 provides an example of a unit on housing styles from a housing and interior design course.

Figure 13.3 Housing Styles Unit Plan, Housing & Interior Design Course

Housing Styles Unit

TITLE: Housing Styles   TEACHER: _____   COURSE: Housing & Interior Design   DURATION: 10 Days, 50 Minute Periods

STANDARDS ADDRESSED		
Career/Technical Knowledge and Skills	**Academic Knowledge and Skills**	**Employability Skills**
11.5 Analyze design and development of architecture, interiors, and furnishings through the ages. 11.5.3 Illustrate the development of architectural styles throughout history. 11.5.4 Compare and contrast historical architectural details to current housing and interior design trends.	**Identify:** students will be able to name various traditional homes based on photos. **Analyze:** students will be able to distinguish various traditional homes based on characteristics. **Apply:** students will build a historically accurate 3D model home.	Creativity Collaboration Innovation skills

PROJECT DEFINITION & GOALS
Students will identify and analyze traditional housing styles and build a 3D model home that is historically accurate.

ESSENTIAL QUESTION
How do traditional housing styles influence new homes that are built today?

ASSESSMENT

FORMATIVE

- ☐ Quizzes/Tests
- ☑ Notes/Graphic Representations
- ☐ Rough Draft
- ☑ Practice Presentation
- ☐ Preliminary Plans/Goals/Checklists of Progress
- ☐ Journal/Learning Log

SUMMATIVE

- ☑ Multiple Choice/Short Answer Test
- ☐ Essay Test
- ☑ Written Product with Rubric
- ☑ Oral Presentation with Rubric
- ☑ Other Product or Performance with Rubric
- ☐ Self-Evaluation or Reflection

MATERIALS AND RESOURCES

Textbook Resources:
Homes & Interiors, Careers in Housing & Interior Design
NATIONAL EDITION
Grade Levels: 10 - 12
Copyright: 2007
MHID: 007874427X I ISBN 13: 9780078744273

SUPPORT, MODIFICATIONS, AND EXTENSIONS

Notes can be shared with students who struggle to take independent notes.
Fill in the blank note taking guides may help students who struggle to take complete/accurate notes.

CALENDAR OF MAJOR LEARNING ACTIVITIES				
Week 1				
Monday	**Tuesday**	**Wednesday**	**Thursday**	**Friday**
Housing styles anticipatory set to introduce unit. Choose 10-20 historical homes to present to class with preferred notes delivery method.	Continue notes presentation until all chosen homes are taught and notes are taken.	Review homes using various review games. One of my favorites for this unit is the Fly Swatter Game.	Introduce "3D Model Home" project, assign groups, and allow students to start planning. Picture Examples	Model Home Work Day
Week 2				
Monday	**Tuesday**	**Wednesday**	**Thursday**	**Friday**
Model Home Work Day	Model Home Work Day	Model Home Work Day	Students will create a yard sign - 1 slide with information about their house for printing. Place yard signs on the model home.	Homes tour with optional housing styles quiz.

Used with permission, Nicole McFadden, Family Consumer Science Teacher, Wentzville, MO.

The essential question provides an overarching idea for students to engage in the topic. For some unit templates that include project-based learning, including a scenario may also help frame the topic and engage students. Planning for how to differentiate within the unit allows the instructor to plan how to keep students who move ahead engaged and how students who need additional time will have that opportunity. The calendar planning is helpful in estimating when each lesson will be taught, as well as in scheduling speakers, field trips, CTSO events, or working around holiday or school activities. Unit assessments are typically summative in nature, making up a portion of a student's grade, and can include tests (which may mimic industry credential exams), products, or presentations.

Lesson Plans

The lesson plans that make up each unit are the daily plans of how to deliver instruction (Leshin et al., 1992). Lesson plans are the intentional planning of how the instructor will engage participants during the time frame of the course period. It is what the teacher does to deliver the lesson. A common lesson structure includes at least four components:

- *Bell Ringer*: A bell ringer or bell work is a short exercise or mini-assessment (three to five minutes) that students complete when they first enter the classroom. It allows the instructor an opportunity to complete administrative tasks such as attendance or answering student questions. Bell ringers can include integrating academic skills, reinforcing technical skills, or building employability skills. Ideas include journaling, reading an article, working on a vocabulary puzzle, creating a flowchart or diagram of a process or procedure, or career readiness activities through CTSOs (Finley, 2013; Mendoza, 2018; SkillsUSA, 2020).

- *Introduction*: The introduction to the lesson should be something that hooks students and gets them excited to learn. This can build on the bell ringer or be separate from it but should focus student attention on the lesson, provide a framework for the students to understand what the lesson entails, clarify the goals of the lesson, and provide an overview of how new content will integrate with previous learning (Peace Corps, 1986).

- *Body*: The body of the lesson is a step-by-step guide that provides the instructor with a series of activities for the learning period. It includes questions to ask, stories to tell, when to take breaks, what activities to begin, etc. This is where instruction is detailed, including lectures, practice, demonstrations, research projects, labs, and discussions. Learning activities should also take into account the diverse backgrounds of the students in the course. Depending on student experience, age, and communication needs, learning activities can be structured to ensure appropriate task levels, challenges, support services, and types of engagement (Larbi-Apau & Moseley, 2009). An instructor should also include resources, materials, and technology to teach the lesson. CTE instructors should consider what they will be doing while students are working or practicing skills. If students are in the lab working with equipment, the instructor should not be sitting behind a desk!

- *Closure*: The last component of a lesson is the ending. Just as the introduction helps to organize information, how a lesson ends can help with student retention and understanding (Peace Corps, 1986). When will students begin to clean up? How much time is needed? If it has been a lab or project day, students may need five to 10 minutes to clean and organize the materials, tools, and equipment that they have been using. A lesson should never just end; make sure to have a recap time for students to process where they are, or give students an exit ticket to summarize main teaching points from the day's work, ending with a preview of what the next day will bring (Peace Corps, 1986).

Failure to plan effective teaching practices will result in a failure of students to learn. Let's consider an example of a lesson plan from an advanced culinary arts course. Figure 13.4 shows a lesson plan for a lesson titled "All About the Choux Dough!" in an introduction to the bakeshop unit. Notice each of the four components in this example. Instructional materials should be designed with clear directions to ensure successful learning (Larbi-Apau & Moseley, 2009).

VOICES FROM THE FIELD

Martin P. Hanley—Director, Pike-Lincoln Technical Center, Eolia, MO

To have an effective curriculum, the instructor needs to have a few components: course skills, related and embedded academic skills, and those essential, employability skills. All of these need to be addressed in a solid curriculum. To help make the curriculum even more effective, the curriculum designer should enlist the aid of community partners in the related field. For example, in a law enforcement curriculum, local police agencies, sheriffs, and security firms should be contacted for input into real-world projects.

Having industry support helps answer the "why are we learning this?" questions from the students. It also provides a framework for the related, embedded academic skills. When teaching a lesson, the instructor will be able to show how the academic skills fit in perfectly with the career skills being taught. Tying it all together are the essential skills, or employability skills. As the students learn more, they discover how to be more effective in their chosen area. They become more employable and develop a greater sense of pride in themselves.

This is not just a hypothetical concept. In developing our law enforcement curriculum, our instructor worked closely with community partners to develop a curriculum plan such that, even in the middle of a global pandemic, students were prepared for work and life after school. In one instance, a substitute teacher did not show up, and the students knew exactly what the lesson plan was for the day and were able to work through the instructional process. They even followed the proper procedures and called in attendance. It would have been helpful if they had also included that there was not a substitute teacher present, but it proved that we truly prepared them for life after the classroom. This particular program has almost 100 percent placement because the students are prepared for their chosen careers and future learning opportunities.

Figure 13.4 All About the Choux Dough! Lesson Plan, Introduction to the Bakeshop Unit

Lesson Plan

TITLE: All About the Choux Dough!   TEACHER: _____   DURATION: 55 minutes
COURSE: Advanced Culinary Arts   UNIT: Introduction to the Bakeshop

STANDARD ALIGNMENT: 8.5.2   "Demonstrate professional skill for a variety of cooking methods including […] baking using professional equipment and current technologies"

8.5.10   "Prepare breads, baked goods and desserts using safe handling and professional preparation techniques"

Learning Outcome(s)
The student will be able to: (1-2 goals, add additional lines if necessary)
LO1:   After watching the Alton Brown video "Choux Shine" students will explain what a high quality choux pastry is, identifying ingredients and steps to producing choux pastry, with a target score of 80%.
LO2:   After watching the Alton Brown video "Choux Shine", students will work with their lab groups to write lab plans with no errors.

Materials, Supplies, Equipment, References, Technology, and other Resources:	
• Video: Choux Shine • Video worksheet	• Lab planning sheets on Google Classroom • Post it notes

Lesson Plan: (This needs to be written so that anyone could interpret exactly what you are planning to do). Don't forget a bell-ringer/intro to the lesson and a closure. *Add more lines as necessary.*	Assessment: (what are you doing to check for understanding?)	Instructional strategy: (what are you doing to teach?)	Learning activity: (what are the students doing?)	LO: (what is the LO this ties to?)
Bellringer: What do you think Choux pastry is? Describe a choux pastry and tell me what it is used for.	bellringer		bellringer	1
Intro: Cold call students to explain what they think choux pastry is and what it is used for. Review questions from yesterday's lecture- What is the chain of command in the kitchen? What can you tell me about ingredients in baked goods? What happens if I increase temperature but decrease cooking time in baked goods?	Q&A	Questioning	Questioning	1
Finish bakeshop lecture (10 minutes)	Q&A	lecture	Note taking	1,2
Show video "Choux Shine" (24 minutes). Give video guide for students to complete. Stop video at critical points to emphasize choux pastry techniques.	Q&A Discussion Worksheet	Video	Worksheet	1
Allow last 20 minutes to plan lab. Lab plans need to be turned in before the bell or submitted by 8:00 PM.	Graded lab plan	Group work Cooperative learning	Lab plan	2
Closure: Remind students that lab is tomorrow. Exit ticket- sticky wall- what are they uncertain about with the lab tomorrow?	Sticky note		Reflective thinking	2

Extension(s):	If groups get done lab planning, they should look up a recipe for custard filling that could be used in their choux pastry.
Technology Integration: (if none, explain why)	Google classroom and Google docs

Used with permission, Dr. Krystle Gremaud, Assistant Professor, University of Central Missouri

Summary

Curriculum planning takes both time and effort but results in a road map for your program and courses, as well as details about the mile markers along the way. Whether in a school district or a postsecondary environment, also consider who approves your curriculum. Oftentimes this can include groups of teachers or faculty, administrators, and board members—individuals who are not knowledgeable about your content.

Curriculum committees may be established to review curriculum and provide recommendations. Although a CTE program may operate in isolation, it is important to remember that others who deal with facilities and budgets will be assessing your curriculum and will be interested to know how well your students are learning.

Industry representatives or advisory committee members will also be evaluating your curriculum. They are interested in students being career ready, with technical skills needed for their companies, but also the employability skills to show up on time, communicate well, and work on a diverse team. Curriculum materials should be transparent enough for anyone to understand. They should provide that road map to communicate a clear direction.

ACTE's Quality CTE Program of Study Framework Connection

The concepts in this chapter related to the following elements of the *Quality CTE Program of Study Framework* developed by the Association for Career and Technical Education (read more about the framework in chapter 2, Imperatore & Hyslop, 2018):

- **Element 1: Standards-aligned and Integrated Curriculum**
  This element of the framework addresses the development, implementation, and revision of a program of study's curriculum, including relevant knowledge and skills. Sequencing curriculum content ensures students prepare to further their education and for emerging careers. Unit and lesson plans build opportunities for authentic student application of knowledge and skills. Ensuring that the curriculum is written in ways that all can understand contributes to making the curriculum accessible, and having the curriculum reviewed by those involved in the curriculum approval process brings in another group of relevant stakeholders.

- **Element 2: Sequencing and Articulation**
  This element addresses course sequencing, knowledge and skill progression, and alignment and coordination across courses in a program, as well as across learner levels, such as from secondary to postsecondary education. The program of study curriculum should sequence courses across multiple levels of education and incorporate learning of technical, academic, and employability skills. Through the use of curriculum maps, CTE educators can ensure foundational knowledge is presented first, content is non-duplicative and vertically aligned between levels, and the sequence leads to recognized credentials at the secondary and/or postsecondary level.

References

Burns, R. C. (2001). *Curriculum handbook*. ASCD.

Finley, T. (2013, September 6). *Bell ringer exercises*. Edutopia. https://www.edutopia.org/blog/bell-ringer-exercises-todd-finley

Hyslop, A. (2018). Perkins V: *The official guide to the strengthening career and technical education for the 21st century act*. ACTE.

IBE-UNESCO. (2021). *International bureau of education*. http://www.ibe.unesco.org/en

Imperatore, C. & Hyslop, A. (2018, October). *2018 ACTE quality program of study framework*. Association for Career and Technical Education. https://www.acteonline.org/wp-content/uploads/2019/01/HighQualityCTEFramework2018.pdf

Larbi-Apau, J. A. & Moseley, J. L. (2009). Communication in performance-based training and instruction: From design to practice. *Performance Improvement*, *48*(9), 7–16. https://doi.org/10.1002/pfi.20103

Lattuca, L. R. & Stark, J. S. (2009). *Shaping the college curriculum: Academic plans in context* (2nd Ed.). Jossey Bass.

Leshin, C. B., Pollock, J., & Reigeluth, C. M. (1992). *Instructional design strategies and tactics*. Educational Technology Publications.

Mendoza, J. (2018, October 18). Bellringers: *What are they and why teachers should use them*. LearnSafe. https://learnsafe.com/bellringers-what-are-they-and-why-should-teachers-use-them/

NCC-CTSO (2021). National Coordinating Council - Career & Technical Student Organizations. https://www.ctsos.org/

Nilson, L. B. (2016). *Teaching at its best: A research-based resource for college instructors* (4th ed.). Jossey Bass.

Peace Corps. (1986). *Teacher training: A reference manual*. Community Development Library. http://www.nzdl.org/cgi-bin/library?e=d-00000-00---off-0cdl--00-0----0-10-0---0---0direct-10---4-------0-1l--11-en-50---20-about---00-0-1-00-0--4----0-0-11-10-0utfZz-8-10&cl=CL2.20&d=HASH011134b2acbbe27c1aae8abe.5.7&gt=1

SkillsUSA Inc. (2020). *Integration activity sheet: Ignite*. SkillsUSA. https://www.skillsusa.org/wp-content/uploads/2020/12/Integ%E2%80%93Activity-Sheets-Batch-2-Ignite-v4.pdf

U.S. Department of Education. (2017). *Work-based learning toolkit*. https://cte.ed.gov/wbltoolkit/index.html

Van Patten, J., Chao, C. & Reigeluth, C. M. (1986). A review of strategies for sequencing and synthesizing instruction. *Review of Educational Research*, *56*(4), 437–471.

Veltri, N. F., Webb, H. W., Matveev, A. G., & Zapatero, E. G. (2011). Curriculum mapping as a tool for continuous improvement of IS curriculum. *Journal of Information Systems Education*, *22*(1), 31–42.

Chapter 14

■

CURRICULUM REVIEW & REVISION

Alisha Hyslop—Association for Career & Technical Education
Michelle L. Conrad—University of Central Missouri

Introduction

Once you have fully developed program and course curriculum maps and fleshed out unit and lesson plans, you may think you are set! However, the feeling may be short-lived. CTE curriculum, perhaps more than any other subject matter, must constantly evolve to reflect the changing nature of work and skills students need to be successful in high-skill, high-wage, and in-demand careers. Formal CTE standards are often updated on a regular basis, requiring regular reviews of curriculum to adapt to new content requirements.

In addition to being aware of changing formal standards, CTE educators should engage in routine curriculum review and revision processes on their own to reflect the needs of their students, communities, and employer partners. For example, there may be new industry certifications introduced to prepare students in a particular field or new employers entering your community with slightly different technical skill requirements. Results on student performance metrics or input from your business advisory board or similar groups may also influence changes in curriculum. Reviewing and evaluating your curriculum should be an ongoing process, one that considers all these types of inputs.

This chapter will begin with an overview of program evaluation and include an overview of accreditation reviews and the Perkins Comprehensive Local Needs Assessment (CLNA). A continuous curriculum improvement process is presented, detailing steps to think about how program evaluation and curriculum revision can be organized to ensure CTE curriculum is always current with industry expectations.

Overview of Program Evaluation

Program evaluation activities provide important opportunities for reviewing and revising curriculum and may be built into your CTE system in a number of ways, both formal and informal. For example, many states require programs to undergo a formal evaluation and re-approval process every three to five years to be eligible for continued funding. In addition to state requirements, certification and accrediting bodies often require different types of evaluation, and program evaluation is required as part of the implementation of the federal Perkins Act (the specifics of that evaluation will be discussed more below).

More informal evaluation processes occur on a regular basis within CTE programs as well, as educators make judgments about student performance, policies, programs, or instruction (Fitzpatrick et al., 2011). While these informal evaluations lack systematic procedures, they can also be useful in curricular revisions.

Generally speaking, evaluation has been defined as "the identification, clarification, and application of defensible criteria to determine an evaluation object's value" (Fitzpatrick et al., 2011, p. 7). Each evaluation process requires a set of standards or "criteria" on which the evaluation will be based. Those criteria may be developed at the local, state, or even national level and can help you see how your program and curriculum measure up.

One set of formal criteria designed specifically to be useful in CTE programs is ACTE's Quality CTE Program of Study Framework, described first in chapter 2. This framework contains 92 criteria across 12 elements that can be used to evaluate CTE programs (Imperatore & Hyslop, 2018). The framework is accompanied by a self-evaluation tool that can guide CTE practitioners through an evaluation of their CTE programs. The tool can be used in whole or broken down into smaller sections to look at single elements and their related criteria (Association for Career and Technical Education [ACTE], 2018).

Accreditation Reviews

CTE programs may also need to align with content-specific or postsecondary accreditation requirements, requiring a specific, structured program evaluation. The entire program of study from secondary through postsecondary can be influenced by these requirements. Accreditation is defined as "a process of external quality review created and used by higher education to scrutinize colleges, universities, and programs for quality assurance and quality improvement" (Eaton, 2009, p. 79).

The United States' accreditation system is a nongovernmental, third-party structure that is decentralized and complex (Eaton, 2009). There are four types of accrediting bodies:

1. *Regional:* Accredit public and private, nonprofit, degree-granting, two- and four-year institutions.
2. *National, Faith-Related:* Accredit religiously affiliated, nonprofit, and degree-granting institutions.
3. *National, Career-Related:* Accredit for-profit, career-based, degree, and non-degree institutions
4. *Programmatic:* Accredit specific programs and free-standing schools, including law, medicine, business, nursing, social work, pharmacy, journalism, etc.

The major roles of accreditation include quality assurance, access to federal and state funds, ensuring private sector confidence, and easing transfer of courses and programs among colleges and universities (Eaton; Gillen et al., 2010).

Accreditation requires a number of steps, the first of which most often includes a self-study where programs or institutions review and document evidence of accomplishments. A site visit by educators from related content areas ensures a peer review primarily by instructors and administrative peers. These visiting teams review the self-study and clarify information with the program(s) and institution. Following the site visit, the accreditation body determines whether to grant new accreditation, affirm ongoing accreditation, or deny accreditation (Eaton, 2009).

As a part of the accreditation review process, CTE programs need to ensure quality assessments that align to student learning outcomes that are reflected in the program's curriculum map (discussed in Chapters 12 & 13). Any program alignment or dual credit agreements also need to reflect these same quality standards and be part of the review process. It is necessary for CTE curriculum developers at any level to investigate and understand the influence of accreditation in the review process, whether for the program or the postsecondary institution.

In addition to accreditation in the higher education context, some CTE programs are accredited at the program level by the industries they prepare students to enter. For example, automotive technology programs are often accredited by the ASE Education Foundation. The ASE accreditation process resembles postsecondary institution accreditation, including site visits and materials review. These accreditation reviews can also be helpful evaluations to inform curriculum.

Perkins Comprehensive Local Needs Assessment

As described in chapter 1, the Carl D. Perkins Career and Technical Education Act is the primary federal investment in CTE, and the policies and requirements it contains greatly shape CTE programs and institutions across the country. Many states also use the Perkins Act to shape state policies and procedures as well, increasing its importance. The law has included data, accountability, evaluation, and continuous improvement requirements for many years, but the most recent version, Perkins V, passed by Congress in 2018, took those requirements a step further. Perkins V requires a CLNA as a form of large-scale formal CTE program evaluation that can be very useful in informing curriculum decisions and revisions.

The CLNA was designed to help better connect the planning, spending, and accountability pieces of the Perkins Act but is really much more than that. Each recipient of Perkins funds (so each school district or consortium at the secondary level) must complete a CLNA approximately every two years, although state requirements vary on exact timing and deadlines. The CLNA has to cover six main areas, although states may also supplement these topics as they operationalize requirements for their local recipients. The six required components of the CLNA are:

1. Performance on federal accountability indicators
2. Alignment to labor market needs
3. Scope, size, and quality of programs offered
4. Progress toward implementing programs and programs of study
5. Recruitment, retention, and training of faculty and staff
6. Progress toward improving access and equity (ACTE, 2019)

At the local level, completing the CLNA requires extensive planning and data collection, including gathering input from a long list of key program stakeholders. Then, local leaders must sift through this data to develop conclusions, identify priority needs, and in some states, set goals for the future. In some cases, the CLNA may be used to drive formal changes that impact curriculum, such as adding courses, programs or significant blocks of content or implementing new supports for lower-performing students. Perhaps more importantly, though, both the data gathering and the goal-setting processes of the CLNA can be instrumental in helping to inform curriculum review and revision.

Consider the following examples of ways that data collected under particular parts of the CLNA can be used related to curriculum decisions:

- Under the first part of the CLNA, data on student performance should be closely examined. If these data show that students in your program are struggling to meet performance targets on the academic assessment indicators under Perkins, it may be necessary to enhance the focus on academic integration within your curriculum.

- Data on your local labor, job openings, employment statistics, and employer skill needs should inform the second part of the CLNA. You may need to update your curriculum to reflect any new skills or skills that employers report are in higher demand.

- The third part of the CLNA relates to program size, scope, and quality. Every state had to create its own definition of this term, and that definition is the focus of this part of the needs assessment. The definitions often focus on program elements like work-based learning, industry certifications, and CTSOs. If one of these areas comes up as lacking as you evaluate your program, it will be important to revisit the curriculum map described in chapter 13 to see how you can better structure content to ensure all learners have access to the full range of quality program elements.

- The fifth section of the CLNA, related to teacher recruitment, retention, and training, may not be as relevant to program curriculum but could surface areas where educators need additional support around both curriculum development and implementation.

- Finally, the last standard section of the CLNA looks to address equitable access for all learners. Data and conclusions from this section of the needs assessment might help you adjust your curriculum to better meet the needs of diverse learners or students with disabilities, such as through implementing strategies like UDL.

Regardless of whether you come out of the CLNA with formal program-specific goals or more informal conclusions, it can be an important component of a continuous program improvement cycle.

VOICES FROM THE FIELD

Melissa Scott—former Assistant Director of Career and Technical Education, Nevada Department of Education

Perkins V requires that eligible agencies align funded programs of study with a high-skill, high-wage, in-demand career pathway identified through a CLNA. State plans must be updated every four years and CLNAs completed every two years. This in itself begs for review and revision of CTE programs.

I facilitated several of the workgroups for our state plan development, and the discussions were rich and promising. While written with good intention, implementation is not an easy task. Legacy faculty and popular programs don't like to change. Review of programs and curriculum identifies areas in need of revision or improvement. Each state and local education agency must examine all programs and funding streams and use the data from the CLNA to make wise choices on CTE programs that work best for their community and students.

Then, there is the question of a quality program. How does one know if the program is a good one and the standards are being taught? Nevada implemented a system to review CTE programs for quality based on ACTE's CTE Quality Program standards. This has provided both the state and district administration a different view of programs and has been a way to recognize outstanding programs.

Continuous Curriculum Improvement

As mentioned at the beginning of the chapter, educators often say curriculum is never "done." Especially in CTE, new technology, new industry processes, or student assessments may trigger the need to review and revise curriculum almost constantly. Aside from the specific required evaluations discussed above, such as accreditation reviews and the CLNA, a focused and sustained process ensures programs of study curriculum are continuously reviewed and prepare students for the workforce (Conrad, 2021).

A sustained process with a variety of data points and an opportunity for stakeholder input allows for review and revision on a regular basis to stay current with the field. Various industries may have improvement processes that can be utilized within CTE programs, such as the Institute for Healthcare Improvement's (2021) "Plan-Do-Study-Act" process. Most schools/districts or colleges have a continuous improvement process for curricular improvement as well. The following describes a simple model, as shown in Figure 14.1, for use in CTE programs (Conrad, 2021).

Figure 14.1 CTE Curriculum Review Process (Conrad, 2021)

1. Collect Evidence

Although a circular process, collecting evidence or data can be considered a first step. Consider the data collected for the CLNA above. How is this data collected, stored, and utilized in the process of evaluating curriculum? Program data, such as the recruitment and retention of students, CTSO participation rates, IRC attainment, graduate placement and satisfaction data, student work artifacts, behavioral data from employers, and other student learning assessment data are all data points to be collected, organized, and reviewed (Conrad, 2021).

2. Analyze Evidence

Analyzing the available evidence then allows CTE programs to determine whether data are reliable and valid, or if anything is missing. What data reveal curricular strengths? What are challenge areas? Are there surprises? In analyzing evidence, are there particular groups of students who should gain attention, such as students with accommodations or English learners? These data points should then be shared with stakeholders (Conrad, 2021).

What does reliable and valid mean? Why are these important?

Reliability is "the consistency or dependability of an assessment tool" (Suskie, 2018, p. 30). Validity refers to "the usefulness of information" or whether it measures what it is intended to measure (Suskie, p. 28). If you go on a diet, and every day you get on a scale, you would expect the scale to be "reliable" (work correctly) and "valid" (accurately reflect your weight). We rely on many tools in CTE to work correctly and give us specific measures accurately.

Consider if you observe students performing a task but don't use a scoring guide or rubric. Would you be consistent in what you were looking for? Would each student's score be consistent? It would not be a reliable measure if you weren't looking for the same criteria for each student. On the other hand, consider if you give a written test, but the students are not familiar with the spelling of vocabulary words. The test might be reliable because it consistently reports low scores, but would it be measuring what you wanted to measure? It would not be valid because your scores are actually based on the vocabulary, not on the concepts you intended to test.

In education, we need to check measures for reliability and validity. Make sure that the evidence you are collecting is consistent and accurately reflects what it should be measuring; otherwise the evidence and data you share with stakeholders could be misleading.

3. Share Results

Sharing the results allows programs to solicit feedback. What changes do stakeholders feel need to be made based on the evidence taken as a whole? Consider if there are additional changes needed based on changes in the subject area, including industry trends or equipment upgrades, policy changes, or accreditation adjustments. Use these stakeholder conversations to determine whether the program is focusing on the "right" standards, how students can gain additional skills to be successful, and overall what others think of the curriculum (Conrad, 2021).

4. Identify Changes

Once data are analyzed and shared with stakeholders, this process should result in identifying needed changes or updates. The conversation on changes may start with the same stakeholders who provided feedback but should continue through instructor reflection. Do teaching practices need to change? Does lab or instructional time on particular concepts need to be altered? Do particular groups of students need additional interventions or support? Are work-based learning opportunities available and connected to curricular goals?

Broader conversations may also be needed within the school or campus at the department level or with supervisors to consider if additional professional development or equipment is needed, which may involve additional planning time or have budget implications (Conrad, 2021).

5. Implement Changes

When changes have been identified, then these can be implemented. A timeline to work toward change should be made. There may be changes that can be made immediately, while others may take a longer period of time. Research, funding, or additional feedback may be needed in order to fully implement the identified changes. However, having an implementation plan that can also be reviewed with stakeholders allows everyone to see how the program is growing and adapting to stay current with industry and community needs (Conrad, 2021).

Using a curricular change model to collect and analyze program evaluation results allows a program to review how well learning objectives are aligned to standards if there are technological updates to be considered, how successful students are in the field, and what data shows students are learning. This type of process allows CTE programs to determine when changes are needed within the curriculum to remain current with industry expectations and practices, as well as consider updates to teaching methodologies and materials.

Checklist for Continuous Improvement

Collect Evidence

☐ Data points are determined.
☐ Data collection process is identified.
☐ Data reporting mechanism is established.

Analyze Evidence

☐ Reliability and validity of data are established.
☐ Data are disaggregated by student populations.
☐ Evidence (data) is examined for strengths and challenges.

Share Results

☐ Evidence results are shared with stakeholders.
☐ Stakeholder meeting(s) are scheduled and conducted to examine data.
☐ Feedback is solicited on trends in the data (electronically, face to face, individually, small group, etc.).

Identify Changes

☐ Feedback/suggestions for updates or changes is solicited.
☐ Industry feedback is solicited on emerging trends in the field.
☐ All feedback is used to reflect on updates/changes.
☐ Feedback is discussed with colleagues and supervisors (and students!).
☐ Additional resources or needed professional development is considered.

Implement Changes

☐ A prioritized list of changes based on resources and constraints is created.
☐ Timeline for implementation is created.
☐ New or modified evidence to collect is determined (returning to Collecting Evidence).
☐ Changes are put into practice.

Stakeholder Involvement

Stakeholder involvement throughout the review and revision process should be planned and intentional. There are many data points that should be considered, but it is also important not to overwhelm advisory committees and other stakeholders. Select a limited number of significant items for meetings or feedback rather than trying to evaluate all aspects of the program at once (New Jersey Department of Education, n.d.). As discussed previously (see chapters 4 and 5), stakeholder engagement should be an organized process from curriculum development through program review and revision (Kerka, 2002).

Consider using the checklist in Figure 14.1 to select the focus of a stakeholder meeting, such as an advisory board meeting. An initial meeting for the year may focus on the changes being implemented from the previous year. A second meeting can focus on the evidence results being shared and discussed, along with how the curriculum is meeting industry needs. And a final meeting could solicit feedback, recommendations, and suggestions for next steps. Effective advisory committees can provide ongoing support and evaluation of the curriculum but should be structured in a way to best use members' time and expertise (Kerka; NJ Department of Education).

Summary

The vast and changing nature of business and industry means CTE curriculum cannot be static. Administrators, curriculum developers, and instructors must consistently review curriculum to determine how well it meets student needs and is responsive to change. Accreditation and policy requirements influence every step of a continuous review process, from the data collected and reviewed to the internal and external stakeholder feedback and changes made. Keeping CTE curriculum dynamic impacts the ultimate quality of the program and its contribution to student growth.

ACTE's Quality CTE Program of Study Framework Connection

The concepts in this chapter related to the following elements of the *Quality CTE Program of Study Framework* developed by the Association for Career and Technical Education (read more about the framework in chapter 2, Imperatore & Hyslop, 2018):

- **Element 1: Standards-aligned and Integrated Curriculum**
  This element of the framework addresses the development, implementation, and revision of a program of study's curriculum, including relevant knowledge and skills. CTE curriculum should be reviewed regularly by all relevant stakeholders and revised to reflect industry demands. The curriculum should be updated to incorporate in-demand and emerging careers, as well as the latest advances in industry, evidenced-based program models, and evaluations of student performance.

- **Element 8: Business and Community Partnerships**
  This element addresses business and community partnership recruitment, partnership structure, and the activities partners should be engaged in. Partners and other stakeholders should participate in the review of curriculum to ensure that the program of study meets current and future workforce demand. Partners can also help to evaluate the effectiveness of the program in preparing students for further education and careers.

- **Element 12: Data and Program Improvement**
  This element addresses access to data and the collection, reporting, and use of data for continuous evaluation and program improvement. Valid and reliable data should be collected and shared in an easy-to-understand format with stakeholders to inform program of study decision-making and support curriculum revision for program improvement.

References

Association for Career and Technical Education. (2018). *2018 ACTE quality CTE program of study framework: Self-evaluation instrument.* https://www.acteonline.org/wp-content/uploads/2019/09/HighQualityCTEFramework2018_WithRubric_LowRes.pdf

Association for Career and Technical Education. (2019). *Maximizing Perkins V's comprehensive local needs assessment & local application to drive CTE program quality and equity.* https://www.acteonline.org/wp-content/uploads/2019/03/Local_Tool_Needs_Assessment_FINAL_3.18.2019.pdf

Conrad, M. L. (2021). *CTE high quality framework: Standards-aligned and integrated curriculum.* [online training course]. ACTE Online Learning Network. https://www.ctelearn.org/certified-courses/high-quality-cte

Eaton, J. S. (2009). Accreditation in the United States. *New Directions for Higher Education, 145,* 79–86. https://doi.org/10.1002/he.337

Fitzpatrick, J. L., Sanders, J. R., & Worthen, B. R. (2011). *Program evaluation: Alternative approaches and practical guidelines.* Upper Saddle River, NJ: Pearson Education, Inc.

Gillen, A., Bennett, D. L., & Vedder, R. (2010, October). The inmates running the asylum? An analysis of higher education accreditation. A policy paper from the Center for College Affordability and Productivity.

Imperatore, C. & Hyslop, A. (2018, October). *2018 ACTE quality program of study framework.* Association for Career and Technical Education. https://www.acteonline.org/wp-content/uploads/2019/01/HighQualityCTEFramework2018.pdf

Institute for Healthcare Improvement. (2021). *Tools: Plan-do-study-act worksheet.* http://www.ihi.org/resources/Pages/Tools/PlanDoStudyActWorksheet.aspx

Kerka, S. (2002). Effective advisory committees. *National Dissemination Center for Career and Technical Education.* https://www.govinfo.gov/content/pkg/ERIC-ED463411/pdf/ERIC-ED463411.pdf

New Jersey Department of Education. (n.d.). CTE program advisory committee handbook. *Office of Career Readiness.* https://www.nj.gov/education/cte/study/approval/CTEProgramAdvisoryCommitteeHandbook.pdf

Suskie, L. (2018). *Assessing student learning: A common sense guide* (3rd ed.). Jossey-Bass.

INDEX